BORDERS AND BRIDGES

BORDERS AND BRIDGES

A History of U.S.– Latin American Relations

Stewart Brewer

Foreword by Michael LaRosa

PRAEGER SECURITY INTERNATIONAL
Westport, Connecticut • London

Library of Congress Cataloging-in-Publication Data

Brewer, Stewart, 1971–
   Borders and bridges : a history of U.S.–Latin American relations / Stewart
   Brewer; foreword by Michael LaRosa.
     p. cm.
   Includes bibliographical references and index.
   ISBN 0–275–98204–1 (alk. paper)
   1. Latin America—Relations—United States.   2. United States—Relations—
   Latin America.   I. Title.
  F1418.B815   2006
  327.8073–dc22   2006008443

British Library Cataloguing in Publication Data is available.

Library of Congress Catalog Card Number: 2006008443
ISBN: 0–275–98204–1

First published in 2006

Praeger Security International, 88 Post Road West, Westport, CT 06881
An imprint of Greenwood Publishing Group, Inc.
www.praeger.com

Printed in the United States of America

The paper used in this book complies with the
Permanent Paper Standard issued by the National
Information Standards Organization (Z39.48–1984).

10 9 8 7 6 5 4 3 2 1

Copyright Acknowledgments

The author and publisher gratefully acknowledge permission for use of the following material:

Excerpt from "Mending Wall" from *The Poetry of Robert Frost* edited by Edward Connery Lathem. Copyright 1930, 1939, 1969 by Henry Holt and Company. Copyright 1958 by Robert Frost, copyright 1967 by Lesley Frost Ballantine. Reprinted by permission of Henry Holt and Company, LLC.

Excerpt from *The Bridge of San Luis Rey* by Thornton Wilder. Copyright © 1928 The Wilder Family LLC and the Barbara Hogenson Agency, Inc. All rights reserved.

Map created by XNR Productions Inc.

Jacket photo by Larry Luxner, www.luxner.com.

For my wife Shannon who has shown me acceptance and love far beyond my own capacities and merits, and for my daughter Brooke who has taught me the joys of fatherhood and the blessings of life.

Contents

Foreword

The field of U.S.–Latin American relations is exceedingly difficult to catego-
rize or organize. Its complexity has generated interdisciplinary scholarship
over the years, from historians, political scientists, economists, journalists,
and literary theorists—representing a variety of approaches and political
positions, from ultraconservative to Marxist.

Several generations ago, the field seemed to be the exclusive purview of
diplomatic historians. Dexter Perkins studied the Monroe Doctrine in his as-
siduously researched 1927 book *The Monroe Doctrine, 1823–1826*. Later,
in 1943, Samuel Flagg Bemis wrote a comprehensive history of U.S. diplomacy toward Latin America titled *The Latin American Policy of the United
States*. This episodic, policy-driven approach was replaced by scholarship
that focused on "structures" and long-term economic policies shaped by the
"dependency" school and the innovative work of Latin American scholars
like Raul Prébisch, Fernando Henrique Cardozo, Enzo Faletto, and Eduardo
Galeano. U.S. historians engaged in an academic dialogue with their Latin
American colleagues; this encouraged broad thinking and creative economic
research on the "macro" questions of "north–south" relations. In 1970,
American scholars Stanley J. and Barbara H. Stein published the ground-
breaking *The Colonial Heritage of Latin America*, and thirteen years later,
Walter LaFeber released *Inevitable Revolutions*, an economic history of
Central America and the Caribbean as related to U.S. history and policies.

The University of Georgia Press has contributed to the expansion of
scholarship on U.S.–Latin American relations more than any other press in

the United States. Historian Lester D. Langley's leadership and vision has allowed for the organization of a remarkable series of books dedicated to individual Latin American countries' political, economic, and diplomatic relations with the United States. Louis A. Pérez Jr., Stephen Randall, Michael Conniff, Lawrence Clayton et al., all have published important works that study individual "cases" and integrate the unique history (and idiosyncrasies) of specific Latin American nations in determining their dealings with the United States. Historian Fredrick Pike, in 1992, challenged us to adopt a more cultural interpretation of "myths and stereotypes." His monumental study influenced a new generation of scholars who prefer to study cultural issues that shape economic and political relationships of the American hemisphere. Work by Catherine C. LeGrand, Ricardo D. Salvatore, and Gilbert M. Joeseph, particularly their 1998 edited collection *Close Encounters of Empire: Writing the Cultural History of U.S.–Latin American Relations*, has moved the field in a direction that focuses on culture while integrating new scholarship on race, gender, identity, and "theory"—both cultural and literary.

Historian Stewart Brewer's work is a broad synthetic approach and contributes to the field by offering a single volume overview of a complex relationship and history. Professor Brewer, in a clearly written, jargon-free book, makes the case that it is important to study the history of political, diplomatic, and economic relations between the United States and Latin America because that relationship grows ever more dependent and complicated with economic integration, and the technological changes that allow for the copious and immediate flow of information among the nations and peoples of the Americas. Brewer is correct to note that Latin America tends to get "pushed aside" by U.S. policymakers whenever a "more significant" worldwide crisis appears. For example, during the 1930s—as the United States rebuilt its economy in the wake of the Great Depression—Latin Americans were left basically to fend for themselves. Thus, during the 1930s, a group of petty, murderous dictators emerged unchallenged (and sometimes supported by the United States) in Central America and the Caribbean at a time when the official U.S. stance toward Latin America was called "The Good Neighbor Policy." Latin America was ignored again at the conclusion of the Second World War—when the priority of the United States was to rebuild the economies of Western Europe and Japan. The Vietnam War and its aftermath derailed Kennedy's Latin American plan—"The Alliance for Progress"—much like the 9-11 and post-9-11 policies of the Bush administration have meant a near-total turning away from Latin America. Current U.S. policy is reactive, as demonstrated in U.S. dealings with Venezuela, Colombia, and Mexico. The U.S. "nonpolicy" with Cuba is, in fact, medieval, and reminds us of the darkest days of the Cold War.

Brewer's work forces the reader to consider and envision more creative, proactive policies for the future of U.S.–Latin American relations. The author explores the ebb and flow of U.S. policy in the region, contextualizing the relationship for readers unfamiliar with the strange, contradictory, and ever-evolving dialogue between the United States and the Latin American region. He writes about Kennedy administration policies, especially the Alliance for Progress that provided billions of dollars for social development in Latin America. Brewer reminds us of recent history, during the 1970s, when the U.S. president challenged Latin American dictators to stop murdering their citizens, and withheld military aid from the worst abusers—the Argentines, Brazilians, Chileans, and Guatemalans. The Carter administration's emphasis on human rights was short-lived, of course, lasting only as long as his administration (1977–1980), but Mr. Carter is fondly remembered in Latin America for his staunch defense of human rights. The former president was awarded the Nobel Peace Prize in 2002.

Of course, U.S.–Latin American relations are much more than a series of doctrines, tensions, or military interventions. These are mere symptoms of the larger problem that has plagued the Latin American region since the earliest days of the colonial period: poverty and inequality. According to statistics produced by the United Nations, there are currently 222 million people classified as poor in Latin America (or 43 percent of the total population), and of those, 96 million live in a state of "extreme" poverty, which means that they fight daily simply to survive. Political upheaval, social violence, and military repression are the inevitable consequences of such widespread poverty and neglect; citizens of the United States—the world's wealthiest society—must reconcile the complex, historic factors that have created and maintained such poverty. People grow weary of living in poverty, and those who earn an average of $5 a day (in Mexico) will naturally gravitate toward the border of a society viewed as the land of endless wealth and opportunity.

Future research and challenges relating to U.S.–Latin American relations should focus on cultural questions, assimilation issues, education, and job creation. The United States is not an "English language only" country—it never has been. Currently, there are about 45 million people living in the United States who speak Spanish as a first language, a number equal to the entire population of the Republic of Colombia. How will the United States absorb—and integrate into its society—Latin American culture, the Spanish and Portuguese languages, and the unique social customs of Latin Americans? These questions are currently being addressed by scholars, journalists, and cultural figures, facilitated by the development of "borderlands" studies that has produced important scholarship across disciplines. Recent work by the journalist Juan Gonzalez, Urban Studies specialist Mike Davis, authors Ana Castillo and Carlos Fuentes, and sociologist Douglas Massey all point toward an exciting future of scholarship, centered at the border and grounded in expanding our understanding of the cultural implications of U.S.–Latin American relations.

A bridge metaphor is appropriate in thinking about U.S.–Latin American relations; too much of the recent rhetoric has been uninformed, unusually cruel (California's 1994 disastrous Proposition 187 comes to mind), and hostile toward our neighbors: The term "illegal alien" is an unfortunate nomenclature that only obfuscates the plight of people who—generally—come to the United States to work and support loved ones here and abroad. Bridges carry us over difficult terrain. Bridges move us, of course, in two directions and open new possibilities and opportunities. Stewart Brewer's *Borders and Bridges* invites us all to take a journey that begins with a thorough historic understanding of the issues and challenges that have shaped U.S.–Latin American relations.

Michael LaRosa
September 2005
Memphis, TN

Preface and Acknowledgments

Borders and Bridges presents some of the complex issues in U.S.–Latin American relations from the time the United States and the nations of Latin America became independent countries in the late 1700s and early 1800s, up through the turn of the twenty-first century. As a narrative history, this book illuminates many of the motivations behind the actions and reactions of political leaders in the United States and the Latin American countries over the more than two hundred years of their coexistence in the western hemisphere.

The diplomatic, military, economic, and social interactions between the countries of Latin America and the United States over this extended time period have bestowed upon the western hemisphere a unique and distinguishing place in the cultural, social, and political history of the world, and *Borders and Bridges* offers a synthesis of much of the literature and ongoing research that exists in this vibrant and exciting area of the history of the hemisphere. Now, as we enter the twenty-first century, and in the wake of the 9-11 terrorist attacks and the ensuing War on Terror, the relationship between the United States and the countries of Latin America is more important than ever in both defining and creating a strong, unified, and cooperative hemisphere that is prepared to face the challenges of a new century.

This book is the result of several years of interest, teaching, and reading in U.S.–Latin American relations. I would like to acknowledge the following people who helped in some way to make this book possible. At Rhodes

College I would like to thank Sarah Addison, Julie Clary, Jenny Dill, Carrie Eaker, Mandy Haggerty, David Haney, Lindsay Hughes, Jack Leslie, Scott Puttick, Andrea Strickland, Page Thead, John Wade Therrell, Sarah Tuttle, and Anne Williams, all of whom helped me clarify my initial thoughts and organize this information in a coherent and meaningful way.

At Dana College I would like to thank Cisco Cole, Jason Lozier, Paul Peterson, John Roan, Maria Roesler, Marcus Taylor, and Chris Williams, who all helped in my final synthesis and setting down of this information. Iain Anderson, Chair of the History Department at Dana College, provided encouragement and support, and Thomas Nielsen, Linda Fleming, and the entire Dana College Library staff were all exceptionally helpful in acquiring source materials for this book.

I am grateful for the assistance and observations of Fredrick B. Pike, Emeritus Professor of History from Notre Dame University, who took the time to read and comment on the manuscript as it was prepared for publication. I would also like to thank Michael LaRosa, Professor of History at Rhodes College, for his interest in this project and his encouragement to the very end. Thomas L. Pearcy, Professor of History at Slippery Rock University, and Eduardo Obregón Pagán, Chair of the Department of Language, Cultures, and History at the Arizona State University West campus, both read portions of the manuscript and offered discerning comments. I likewise am especially grateful for and appreciate the assistance of Michael J. Kryzanek, Professor of Political Science at Bridgewater State College, for his valuable observations and his willingness to comment on the manuscript and suggest constructive improvements.

Additionally, I would like to thank my editor at Praeger Publishers, Hilary D. Claggett, for helping me prepare the book for publication and seeing this project through to completion; Sue and Steve Howe for their encouragement and financial contributions to this project; and Bruce B. Solnick, Emeritus Professor of History from the University at Albany, State University of New York, who read parts of the manuscript, and who tutored me in the infancy of my interest in U.S.–Latin American relations.

Finally, I would like to express the deepest gratitude to my family for the support and encouragement they have all given me as I have written this book. My wife Shannon read parts of the manuscript and made observations on clarity and brevity, and my daughter Brooke was patient with me even when she didn't want to be. Thanks is not enough.

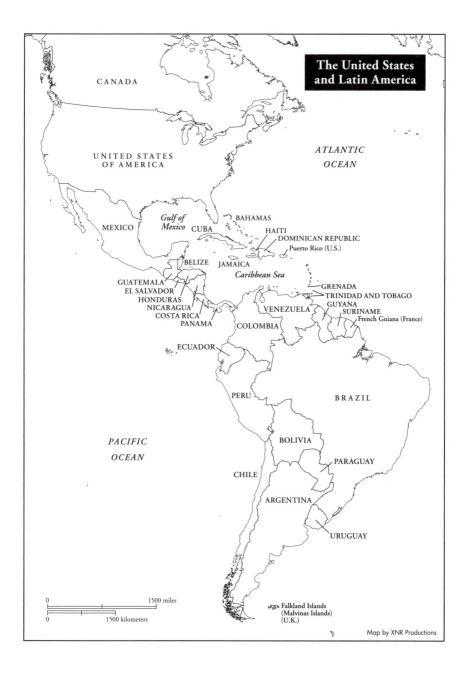

The United States
and Latin America

CANADA

UNITED STATES
OF AMERICA

ATLANTIC
OCEAN

Gulf of
Mexico

MEXICO

BAHAMAS

CUBA

HAITI

DOMINICAN REPUBLIC

Puerto Rico (U.S.)

BELIZE

JAMAICA

Caribbean Sea

GUATEMALA

EL SALVADOR

HONDURAS

NICARAGUA

COSTA RICA

PANAMA

GRENADA

TRINIDAD AND TOBAGO

GUYANA

SURINAME

French Guiana (France)

VENEZUELA

COLOMBIA

ECUADOR

PERU

BRAZIL

PACIFIC
OCEAN

BOLIVIA

PARAGUAY

CHILE

ARGENTINA

URUGUAY

0   1500 miles

0   1500 kilometers

Falkland Islands
(Malvinas Islands)
(U.K.)

Map by XNR Productions

1

Foundations and Perceptions

[The North Americans] are always among us, even when they ignore us or turn their back on us. Their shadow covers the whole hemisphere. It is the shadow of a giant. And the idea we have of that giant is the same that can be found in fairy tales and legends; a great fellow of kind disposition, a bit simple, and innocent who ignores his own strength and who we can fool most of the time, but whose wrath can destroy us.   – Octavio Paz

The United States appears to be destined by Providence to plague America with misery in the name of Liberty.   – Simón Bolívar

What the United States does best is to understand itself. What it does worst is understand others.   – Carlos Fuentes

The year 1959 was an exceptionally significant year in world history, and in U.S.–Latin American relations. In 1959, Alaska and Hawaii became the forty-ninth and the fiftieth U.S. states. Fidel Castro toppled the regime of Fulgencio Batista in Cuba, and declared himself Cuba's leader. U.S. Vice President Richard Nixon and Soviet Premier Nikita S. Khrushchev engaged each other in the "Kitchen Debate." The Dalai Lama fled Chinese-occupied Tibet for safety in India. The St. Lawrence Seaway opened to shipping traffic. The U.S. space program took photos of earth from space, and the Soviet space program achieved a hard landing on the moon. The Barbie doll was introduced to the American public and the Marx brothers made their final live television appearance. In addition, in 1959, the U.S. government began construction on the Bridge of the Americas in Panama.

Another significant year in the history of the world and in U.S.–Latin American relations was 1962. In that year, Fidel Castro was excommunicated by Pope John XXIII, and later that same year the Kennedy administration put into effect a trade embargo against the island of Cuba. John Glenn became the first American to orbit the earth, and Israel executed Adolf Eichmann after a yearlong trial wherein Eichmann was convicted on fifteen counts of crimes against humanity. The Cuban Missile Crisis brought the world to the brink of nuclear war after the Soviet Union placed long-range nuclear missiles in Cuba. Marilyn Monroe died of an apparent overdose, and the Beatles released their first two singles. Finally, the United States completed construction on the Bridge of the Americas, and the structure was officially declared open on October 12, 1962.

In Panama City, arching over the Panama Canal's exit into the Pacific Ocean spans the Bridge of the Americas. This picturesque bridge is over 5,000 feet long and rises over 350 feet into the air. Construction on the bridge began on October 12, 1959. By the time of its completion, the bridge cost the U.S. government around $20 million. The choice to both begin and end construction of the Bridge of the Americas on October 12 was no accident. In the history of the western hemisphere, and of U.S.–Latin American relations, the date October 12 is extremely significant. On October 12, 1492, Christopher Columbus made landfall somewhere in the Bahamas, setting the stage for one of the greatest colonization efforts in world history by the Spanish Empire. On October 12, 1822, Brazilian leader Dom Pedro ended Brazilian colonial status by declaring Brazilian independence from Portugal after over 300 years of economic and political domination. On October 12, 1968, the Summer Olympic Games opened in Mexico City, just days after the Mexican government sanctioned the slaughter of hundreds of protesters in downtown Mexico City. Finally, October 12 is known as Columbus Day in the United States, Hispanic Day in Spain, Discovery Day in the Bahamas, and *Dia de la Raza* (Day of the Race) in Latin America—all holidays designated to commemorate, in one way or another, the presence of Christopher Columbus in the New World, and the subsequent intermingling of societies, governments, economies, and races in the hemisphere.

Construction of the Bridge of the Americas was steeped in chronological symbolism as one of the significant events that occurred in the middle of the twentieth century. But the Bridge of the Americas is also significant for its geographic location. It has the honor of being the only bridge in the world to span two continents. It serves as the juncture that connects the Pan-American Highway between North and South America. The Pan-American Highway is the longest road on earth, stretching more than 29,800 miles from Alaska to Chile. With the exception of a 50-mile "gap" on the border between Panama and Colombia, the entire road is more or less paved.[1]

The Pan-American Highway links the ecological diversity of the hemisphere, passing through mountains, tundra, deserts, jungles, urban sprawl, and vast rural spaces. The highway also links the political, cultural, and racial diversity of the hemisphere, connecting Alaska to Canada and Canada to the United States. The highway traverses through Mexico, Guatemala, El Salvador, Honduras, Nicaragua, Costa Rica, and Panama. In South America the Pan-American Highway passes through Colombia, Ecuador, Peru, Chile, and Argentina. There are also multiple segues that connect the Pan-American Highway with other Latin American countries to the east such as Venezuela, Uruguay, Paraguay, and Brazil.

The Bridge of the Americas is a symbol of both unity and asperity in the Americas. It represents the ability that Americans—North, Central, and South—have to cross cultural and ethnic boundaries as the hemisphere attempts to move toward greater economic and political harmony. The bridge also represents, for some, the proclivity of the United States to cross economic and political borders—sometimes in an effort to build and strengthen, sometimes to compel and regulate through force, but almost always with impunity.

We live in a world of walls and fences, of borders and bridges. We draw lines on maps to distinguish territories from each other. But more importantly, the lines we portray on maps accomplish much more than mere political delineation. Identities and worldviews, perspectives, and attitudes are all built up and sustained inside and outside the lines we construct. In the western hemisphere, these lines on maps distinguish and divide people by language, skin color, economy, and even religion. The walls we build serve to keep ideas, cultures, languages, and perspectives both in and out as we interact with our hemispheric neighbors.

In his collection of poetry entitled *North of Boston*, the prolific American poet and writer Robert Frost penned these words in his poem "Mending Wall":

> Something there is that doesn't love a wall,
> That sends the frozen-ground-swell under it,
> And spills the upper boulders in the sun;
> And makes gaps even two can pass abreast. [...]
> I let my neighbor know beyond the hill;
> And on a day we meet to walk the line
> And set the wall between us once again.
> We keep the wall between us as we go. [...]
> He is all pine and I am apple orchard.
> My apple trees will never get across
> And eat the cones under his pines, I tell him.
> He only says "Good fences make good neighbors"
> Spring is the mischief in me, and I wonder

If I could put a notion in his head:
"*Why* do they make good neighbors? Isn't it
Where there are cows? But here there are no cows.
Before I'd build a wall I'd ask to know
What I was walling in or walling out,
And to whom I was like to give offence.
Something there is that doesn't love a wall,
That wants it down." [...]
He says it again, "Good fences make good neighbors."[2]

Over the course of history in the Americas, those walls and fences have occasionally been allowed to fall into disrepair as they have crumbled under the ambivalence of inactivity. At other times those same walls have been purposely knocked to the ground so that the nations of the hemisphere could interact with each other in much more aggressive ways.

PERCEPTIONS AND PERSPECTIVES

From the very beginning of the relationship between the United States and Latin America, both sides have viewed the other with varying degrees of curiosity and animosity. Perceptions and perspectives are essential when one designs to comprehend another. Unfortunately, Latin Americans and U.S. citizens seem to have misunderstood each other from the very beginning of their tempestuous relationship.

As Michael Kryzanek observed, "The view from the south is...not one of renewed interest but, rather, ongoing aggravation over a neighbor often described in mosterlike terms as the 'Colossus of the North.'"[3] Likewise, Fredrick Pike has argued that the foundations of the relationship between the North and the South in the western hemisphere have focused on such tangible variables as race and skin color, religion, emotion, gender, and the supremacy over nature. In the early history of the United States, the wild and untamed wilderness of the frontier was a challenge to be controlled and dominated. And from the very beginning, the nascent United States viewed Latin America as something akin to feral nature, something to be tamed and controlled. Is it any wonder, then, that early perceptions of the United States from inside Latin America tended to focus on the dominating and authoritarian nature of the *Norteamericanos*.[4]

Pike continues, "To [the North Americans] the Latin American... became a figure fraught with hope. Thanks to the primitive, passionate, emotional, intuitive, heedless, childlike, effeminate Latin American, the civilized, restrained, rational, calculating, mature, masculine Yankee had some fair promise of being able to forge a hermaphrodite hemisphere." In other words, the hemisphere was composed of opposite components that, when merged, formed a whole not unlike the relationship between a male and a female. And the United States became the dominant player in the relationship.[5]

By contrast, at the turn of the twentieth century, Latin American writer José Enrique Rodó argued that citizens of the United States, while possessed of many admirable traits, seemed to have neglected some of the more important aspects of civilization—such as the idea that there is a spiritual and even pious element in the wildness of nature and in the nations of Latin America that cannot be dominated. He observed,

> There is in these North Americans a lively and insatiable curiosity and an avid thirst for enlightenment. Professing their reverence for public education with an obsessiveness that resembles monomania—glorious and productive as it may be—they have made the school the hub of their prosperity, and a child's soul the most valued of all precious commodities. Although their culture is far from being refined or spiritual, it is admirably efficient as long as it is directed to the practical goal of realizing an immediate end.[6]

Americans and Latin Americans have tried to understand each other's culture and behavior from the first contacts they shared. Sometimes they have succeeded. Often they have failed. And although the association between the United States and Latin America has been at times filled with bitterness and anguish, this relationship represents a symbiotic bond, a love–hate connection between the two that has been absolutely essential because both entities are, in many ways, so fundamentally divergent from each other that each provides some of what the other lacks, and thus the relationship has the potential to work to the advantage of both.

Nevertheless, instead of a fraternal relationship, the affinity between Latin America and the United States rapidly became a paternal one. The benevolent paternalism displayed by the United States—in the form of economic aid and political manipulation—never successfully evolved into the amicable hemispheric fraternalism that Latin America so desperately desired. And Latin American nations have resented the United States for it. And at the same time, there is almost a sense of buried yearning or jealousy on the part of the United States which has perhaps longed to be as unencumbered as Latin America seems to be.

HEMISPHERIC RELATIONS

In July of 2005, the United States of America had a population of 295 million people, living in an area of 3.7 million square miles, and with a GDP of $11.75 trillion. By contrast, all of the nations of Latin America—including Mexico, Central America, South America, and the Caribbean islands—had a combined population of 560 million people, living in a total area of 7.9 million square miles, and with an average GDP of $118 billion (ranging from Brazil's $1.4 trillion economy to the tiny island of Montserrat with a GDP of only $29 million).[7]

Throughout the history of relations between the United States and Latin America, several important islands mark the path of progress between these obviously divergent economic and sociopolitical entities. These islands, like landmarks in the tides of history, not only represent the important episodes of interaction between the nations of the Americas, but they also characterize the more noticeable occurrences in the hemisphere over the past 250 years. In 1783 the United States of America won its independence from Britain. Less than fifty years later in the early years of the nineteenth century most of the countries of Latin America were formed as they too achieved freedom from the European colonial powers of Spain and Portugal. In 1823, U.S. President James Monroe proclaimed that the western hemisphere was henceforth off limits to the aggression of European nations; his statement came to be known as the Monroe Doctrine. The United States and Mexico then went to war against each other in 1846, resulting in Mexico's loss of nearly one-half of its northern territory, all in the name of Manifest Destiny. In 1898 the United States encouraged the decrepit Spanish Empire to forfeit its remaining Latin American colonies in Cuba and Puerto Rico.

In 1903, President Theodore Roosevelt "took" Panama from Colombia and proceeded to construct the Panama Canal, sparking several decades of U.S. military intervention in Latin America under the aegis of the New World Policeman. Franklin D. Roosevelt reversed this aggressive posture in the 1930s by proclaiming his Good Neighbor Policy wherein the United States pledged to cease its aggressive domination of the hemisphere through the use of its military. In 1959, Fidel Castro seized power in Cuba, eventually turned it into a Communist state, and accepted long-range Soviet nuclear missiles which ignited the Cuban Missile Crisis. In 1977, President Jimmy Carter proclaimed that Human Rights, not the Cold War, would dictate his Latin American foreign policy. Then throughout the decade of the 1980s Ronald Reagan returned American attention to the Cold War and Central American countries as the last vestiges of the Good Neighbor Policy faded away. By 1994 the North American Free Trade Agreement (NAFTA) went into effect, thus linking Canada, the United States, and Mexico in an economic relationship that prompted other similar ventures throughout the hemisphere and the world. Finally, on December 31, 1999, the United States gave the Panama Canal back to Panama as per the conditions negotiated by President Jimmy Carter in 1977.

Throughout most of these major episodes, the political concept of hegemony recurs over and over. The United States has viewed Latin America as an assortment of nations that must be urbanized, influenced, sheltered, and preserved for the good of the entire hemisphere. By contrast, Latin American countries have viewed the United States as intrusive, harassing, overbearing, and overly enthusiastic to get involved in Latin American affairs for the good of the United States. The United States has called its actions benevolent paternalism. Latin America has called them hegemony.

For the most part, the United States and the countries of Latin America have been political associates, economic collaborators, and military allies. The awkward friendship between the nations of Latin America and the United States can perhaps best be described by the Spanish phrase *dolor agradable*, or pleasant pain. Nevertheless, Latin Americans are left with the dilemma of whether or not it is beneficial to have the United States pay close attention to them. Over the decades and centuries of this enduring relationship, Latin Americans have been left to decide which alternative they prefer, aggressive hegemony or benign neglect. As we cross the threshold of the twenty-first century, we can hope that a new alternative will present itself—one built upon hemispheric fraternity and brotherhood instead of dominion and indifference.

2

The European Enlightenment and the Birth of U.S.–Latin American Relations

Never interrupt your enemy when he is making a mistake.

– Napoleon Bonaparte

Does it not look as if God were not only preparing in our Anglo-Saxon civilization the die with which to stamp the peoples of the earth, but as if he were also massing behind that die the mighty power with which to press it? . . . There can be no reasonable doubt that North America is to be . . . the principal seat of power, the center of life and influence. . . . America is to have the great preponderance of numbers and of wealth, and by the logic of events will follow the scepter of controlling influence.
– Josiah Strong

To some it might seem curious to commence a discussion of U.S.–Latin American relations in eighteenth-century Western Europe. After all, in terms of ethnicity, geography, population, socioeconomic status, and even religion, modern Western Europe, Latin America, and the United States all share more differences than similarities. But most of the nations of the western hemisphere trace their modern political, economic, and national development back to the sixteenth and seventeenth centuries when they existed as European colonies. Therefore, most of the modern nations in the western hemisphere were born of European traditions, customs, languages, religions, and philosophies, which all endured for the first several generations of their existence as independent and autonomous countries.

Many of the texts, monographs, and other books that deal with U.S.–Latin American relations begin with the 1823 Monroe Doctrine, the 1846 Mexican War, or some other early nineteenth-century episode in this complex relationship. But if the chronology of U.S.–Latin American relations is begun in the early years of the nineteenth century, some of the vital foundations of the relationship between the United States and Latin America tend to get ignored. These foundations were laid years before either the United States or the countries of Latin America were fully independent from their mother countries; these foundations were forged while both were still considered colonies of European powers.[1]

This chapter will outline some of the key events in Europe that led directly to the collapse of the Spanish imperial system and the destructive wars for independence that were fought in the western hemisphere during the final decades of the 1700s and the early decades of the 1800s. While Spain wallowed in the tailspin of its own decline, its Latin American colonies entered into economic and commercial relationships with Great Britain and the nascent United States. These early financial relationships existed for the benefit and survival of both the Latin American nations and the United States, and shaped the establishment of later interactions between most of the countries in the western hemisphere.[2]

BEGINNINGS

When Christopher Columbus returned to Spain in 1493 after completing his famous first crossing of the Atlantic Ocean, Western Europe entered an era of empire building unlike anything the world had ever experienced. The western hemisphere was soon carved up among the then prominent European powers, and for the next 400 years, territories in the Americas were traded, purchased, conquered, and occupied repeatedly. The principal players in this New World land-grab were Portugal, Spain, France, England, and the Dutch. Other European nations attempted to break into this sometimes lucrative venture of empire building and exploration—particularly Germany, Russia, and Sweden—but their efforts in the western hemisphere came too late to take advantage of the vast tracks of New World territory. Furthermore, these predominantly landlocked European countries did not share the added benefits of geographic location on the Atlantic Ocean, which gave the Western European nations a significant advantage.

After 1493, Spain began to consolidate its holdings in Europe and in the New World, and very soon became the largest world empire in the history of the world to that point. Indeed, the sun never did set on the Spanish Empire long before the British ventured into North America, Africa, and India.

Other European powers observed with interest as the Spanish unloaded ships laden with silver bullion and exotic tropical products. Soon France, Britain, Portugal, and the Dutch desired their own lands and colonies in the New World in order to reap these same benefits. But religious differences, coupled with economic jealousies, soon led to a series of wars on the European continent which had lasting consequences in the Americas as well. Between roughly 1689 and 1815, European nations engaged in a series of heated conflicts—sometimes called the 100 Years War—which has been accurately described as a period of sustained perpetual warfare sprinkled with intermittent periods of peace.

Some of the major conflicts that devastated Europe and the Americas during these years include the Glorious Revolution (1688), the War of the Grand Alliance (1689–1697), the War of Spanish Succession (1701–1714), the War of Jenkin's Ear (1739–1743), the War of Austrian Succession (1741–1748), the Seven Years' War—which actually began in the western hemisphere as the French and Indian War—(1756–1763), the American Revolution (1775–1783), the French Revolution (1789–1799), and finally the Napoleonic Wars (1803–1815) which culminated in the War of 1812 between Britain and the newly formed United States of America.

But it was also during this period of frequent conflicts and bloodshed that European thinkers began to transform the world intellectually. Between 1753 and 1820, changes and advancements in Europe had stunning effects in the New World that Christopher Columbus had encountered in 1492. The Scientific Revolution, Enlightenment, Industrial Revolution, and the growing secularism of Western Europe all influenced the western hemisphere in meaningful ways. These radical precursors that resulted in the American and French Revolutions, and the chaos that precipitated the subsequent independence movements in Latin America, all began in European palaces and courts. In many ways, the political, economic, and social agendas of Western Europe functioned as the catalyst that led to the wars for independence in the New World, and culminated in the emergence of the United States and the Latin American Republics.

THE ENLIGHTENMENT

The eighteenth-century European Enlightenment was the result of several antecedents that had roots in medieval European history. European society had changed and evolved over centuries through episodes such as the religious crusades to the Levant, the Renaissance, the Age of Exploration and discovery that produced explorers such as Columbus, Magellan, and Díaz, the Protestant Reformation that was promulgated by reformers such as Hus, Luther, Calvin, and Zwingli, and the Scientific Revolution of Copernicus, Galileo, Newton, and others. Changes in art, literature, music, and religion had profound influences upon European minds during these years.

Factors such as human reason, empiricism, materialism, and the secularization of society all enticed portions of the European population to question the relationship between faith and reason, between God and man. Scholars began to seriously probe the relationship between human beings and the physical world around them. Soon, some of the old notions about the geocentric nature of the earth and the biblical account of creation came into doubt and were, to a large degree, supplanted by thoughts centered more on the *here* than the *hereafter*.

And naturally, this kind of thinking and questioning eventually included the nature and role of government and politics in the everyday lives of modest Europeans. The resulting philosophical movement produced writers and thinkers such as Voltaire, Montesquieu, Rousseau, Locke, Smith, and others. Most spoke out against religious fanaticism, and many posited that government restricted man's liberty and equality. The teachings and attitudes of these European philosophers had far-reaching effects on European society, but one of the most immediate results in Europe was revolution and violence. Both the American and French Revolutions resulted from the concepts of liberalism, born of the new enlightened thinking and empirical reasoning of eighteenth-century Europe, while Britain's contemporaneous Industrial Revolution was no less influenced by such thinking.

But while Europe underwent these radical changes in thought and behavior, the Spanish Latin American colonies continued to exist much as they had for the previous 300 years. Because Latin America was so far removed geographically from the events and thoughts of Western Europe, and also because of the way these colonies were governed by Spain and Portugal, most of the Latin American populations remained undereducated and marginally aware of the changing attitudes in European thought.

THE TWILIGHT OF THE SPANISH EMPIRE

Charles III (1716–1788), king of Spain and its Latin American colonies, was aware of the changes sweeping across Europe during the Age of Enlightenment. But he guaranteed that Spain would remain staunchly Catholic in religion, and conservative both politically and economically. Charles III himself was intrigued by some of the innovations that emerged from the Enlightenment, but he was more preoccupied with the notion of keeping the associated revolutionary and liberal thoughts and ideas out of his empire.

One of the methods implemented by the Spanish crown and the Catholic Church for controlling thought and action throughout the Spanish Empire was an index of prohibited books. The index functioned simply as a list of literature that was forbidden throughout the empire. Persons caught reading items from the index could be remanded to the Inquisition for interrogation and punishment. But human nature being what it is, the censor often proved to be the best salesman. A list of prohibited books in the hands of the clergy and the monarchy turned out to be nothing more than an elaborate shopping list in the hands of smugglers, black marketers, and contraband merchants.

Over a period of decades, between the middle of the eighteenth century and the turn of the nineteenth, prohibited literature made its way across the Atlantic Ocean from Europe to the western hemisphere, and as a result some Latin Americans began to question the traditional political and religious authority that they had lived with for so many years. Was monarchy the only means of governing a population? Was the Roman Catholic Church the only viable option for eternal salvation of the soul? These and many more questions caused Latin Americans to begin to rethink some of their past loyalties in light of new Liberalist trends. Ideas such as *liberty* and *equality* sounded hopeful to a Latin American population that was mired in racial, ethnic, cultural, and economic divisions and castes.

But perhaps the most important effect of the European Enlightenment in the Spanish New World Empire was the galvanizing of the liberal, Creole strata of society, against the more conservative Peninsulars. The difference between Creoles and Peninsulars in the Spanish Empire was really nothing more than semantics and definitions. Both Peninsulars and Creoles were persons of Spanish blood by both the paternal and maternal lineages. The distinguishing characteristic was to be found in the fact that Peninsulars were born in Spain, while Creoles were born in the New World. Though miniscule, this distinction was enough to exclude Creoles from participation in certain religious and political responsibilities reserved only for persons born in Spain. These tensions had existed since the first Spanish children were born in the Americas in the sixteenth century. But at the beginning of the nineteenth century, the frustrations of many Creoles had reached the breaking point regarding the system of rights and privileges that were constantly denied to them by virtue of the location of their birth.

Charles III was arguably the best king that the Spanish Bourbon dynasty had produced since they acquired the Spanish throne in 1700. He was aware of these tensions between Creoles and Peninsulars, and he tried to maintain order and prosperity throughout his empire despite these and other stresses. As a result, in 1788 when Charles III died, the Spanish Empire was reasonably prosperous and seemingly strong. But under the veneer of prosperity that Charles III had created and maintained were the seeds of decay and dissolution that would eventually culminate in the complete collapse of the Spanish colonial system.

Charles III was succeeded as king of Spain by his son Charles IV (1748–1819) who was forty years old when he ascended the Spanish throne. Charles IV was simply not up to the standard set by his father. He persisted in partaking of the benefits and luxuries of the office of monarch—such as hunting on a frequent, and sometimes daily basis, collecting clocks, and traveling—while managing at the same time to avoid or evade the responsibilities and obligations that were associated with the office and position of the monarchy.

But the work of governance could not be ignored, and Charles IV discovered a way to dispatch his responsibilities as king and still maintain enough time to indulge in the pleasures that he craved. He ruled through a minister, Manuel de Godoy (1767–1851). In 1792 when he was raised to the office of First Minister, Godoy was young and ambitious. He had been promoted rapidly through the ranks of the Spanish military because of his ambition, determination, and hard work, and also by virtue of the fact that the Queen, Maria Louisa, had taken a fancy to him that extended to both public and private affairs.

So through a combination of ambition and good fortune, Godoy found himself First Minister of the Spanish Empire, second only to the ambivalent Charles IV. And while Charles IV, Maria Louisa, and Godoy saw to the affairs of Spain and its colonies, Great Britain concluded the venture of losing its own colonies in North America in 1783, a circumstance that would have devastating consequences for Spain several years later.

THE AMERICAN REVOLUTION

When the thirteen North American colonies refused any longer to submit to British control in the final years of the eighteenth century, some European nations saw this mercantilistic catastrophe an opportunity to revive age-old antagonisms against Great Britain. The French placed themselves at the vanguard of British opposition, and attempted to provide aid for the floundering North American colonies in their struggle for independence.[3] The French also demanded that Spain join them in their anti-British persuasions. Spain tried to appear circumspect in this awkward situation, by declaring its alliance with France, but not overtly with the thirteen colonies in North America that were in the process of becoming the United States of America. Of course, this alliance with France placed Spain, a colonial power, in the very awkward and inappropriate business of helping another country lose its colonies.[4] Furthermore, the Spanish did not agree with the Liberalist ideas of government that were becoming so popular in the North American colonies. So Spain tried to stay as uninvolved as it could and still uphold the conditions of the alliance that brought it into the conflict at France's side in the first place.[5]

Spain justified its involvement in the American Revolution in several ways. First of all, Spain offered financial aid and support to the rebelling colonies because this would have the effect of weakening Britain's position in the New World, and possibly the balance of power in Europe as well. Spain also contributed financially to the French military which engaged British troops in North America in various locations. Finally, Spain hoped that after the American Revolution was concluded, France would help them recover some land they had lost to Britain over the years, territories such as Florida, Jamaica, and Gibraltar to name only a few.

In the end, Spain managed to resecure and fortify its position in Florida in 1784, but ultimately, Spain lost more than it gained through its alliance with France, and in due course the British refused to forfeit Gibraltar or Jamaica. And unfortunately, Spain's control of Florida was short-lived; by 1814, Spain actually lost control of some of the territory of northern Florida to the fledgling United States when U.S. President Andrew Jackson seized Pensacola during the War of 1812.

And as if these indignities were not enough, Spanish participation in the American Revolutionary War came back to haunt Spain in another more serious way during the early years of the nineteenth century when Creoles in Spain's New World colonies tried to emulate what they had witnessed in North America by waging their own wars for independence.

But perhaps the most important result of the American Revolution in terms of the impetus of U.S.–Latin American relations was the fact that following the American Revolution, Spain and the United States now shared a common border in North America. That border was not well defined in many places; it comprised the Louisiana territory that lay vaguely between Texas and Florida in the Mississippi and Missouri River valleys, and its boundaries shifted and migrated over the next several years.

This border became even more important when the French, Spanish, and the United States tried to decide what to do with the Louisiana territory in the early years of the nineteenth century. Previously in 1682, Louisiana had been claimed for France by the famous French cleric and explorer René Robert Cavelier, Sieur de La Salle. But during the French and Indian War of the next century that ended in 1763, the French were soundly defeated by the British and virtually forced off of the North American continent. The French did not want the British to overrun Louisiana, however, so they negotiated a secret treaty with Spain—the Treaty of Fontainebleau of 1762—wherein the entire Louisiana territory was ceded by France to Spain so that the British could not claim or occupy the land.

Between 1762 and 1800 Spain controlled Louisiana and tried to make it profitable. However, following the American Revolutionary War, Louisiana became the border region between the Spanish North American Empire and the new United States of America. Spain feared losing Louisiana to the aggressive Americans, and therefore negotiated a second, equally furtive and surreptitious treaty—the Treaty of San Ildefonso of 1800—which retroceded the Louisiana territory from Spain back to Napoleonic France. Napoleon desired Louisiana as a base from which to reassert French power over Haiti and the Caribbean. But in 1803, when Haiti proved unconquerable, Napoleon decided to sell all 530 million acres of the Louisiana territory to the United States for the tidy sum of $15 million, thus creating a direct border between the United States and the Spanish Empire in North America for the second time in their shared history.

One final consequence of the American Revolution, and one of the major obstacles that the former British colonies had to come to terms with after the British surrendered their sovereignty over their former North American colonies, was trade and commerce. For obvious reasons, Britain was initially no longer willing to engage in economic exchanges with the United States. So the fledgling United States looked to the nearby Spanish colonies for trade opportunities. Unfortunately, Spanish law prohibited trade outside the empire except on rare and controlled occasions. And because the Spanish colonies of Latin America were under the economic and political control of Spain, they could not legally decide on their own to trade with the United States, which was geographically closer, or with the powerful British Empire, which was more economically stable.

Therefore, the first real commercial contacts between the United States and Latin America came in the form of black market trade and illegal shipping of contraband to and from certain Latin American port cities. If Spain had been as strong economically and politically as it appeared on the outside, perhaps this economic relationship with the United States would not have flourished to the extent that it did. But as the eighteenth century came to a close, Spain began to suffer the dramatic effects born of economic decline and inept leadership, which prevented much growth in the New World for several decades and led to feelings of frustration among the Latin American populations, predominantly the Creoles.

THE SPANISH EMPIRE IN DECLINE

In 1789, the French Revolution sent ripples of excitement and terror across continental Europe. Much of the liberal strata of European society applauded what was happening in France, while most monarchs feared public uprisings in their own lands through emulation by local radicals. But by 1792, the French Revolution began to appear too radical even for the staunchest liberals who feared that regicide was perhaps going too far.[6]

Spain joined much of the European continent in speaking out against some of the radical actions taken by France, which in turn led to a retaliatory French invasion of Spain in 1795. Meanwhile, Spanish First Minister Godoy had become increasingly unpopular with the Spanish population who feared that Godoy meant to somehow supplant the heir to the Spanish throne, Prince Ferdinand (1784–1833), the eldest son of King Charles IV. In 1795, oblivious to public sentiment, Charles IV bestowed on First Minister Godoy the title "Prince of the Peace" for his role in negotiating the Treaty of Basel with France that concluded the hostilities and fighting between France and Spain earlier that year. However, to most Spaniards, this title approached blasphemy because it was too uncomfortably similar to biblical passages that referenced Jesus Christ as the "Prince of Peace."[7]

In 1799 Napoleon Bonaparte became First Consul of France. He later named himself Consul for Life in 1802, and then crowned himself Emperor in 1804. As Napoleon prepared to invade France's old enemy Great Britain, he called yet again upon Spain to support him militarily and politically by virtue of the Family Compact agreement between the two nations—a fairly brave request given the fact that Spain and France had recently just concluded hostilities with each other through the Treaty of Basel a decade earlier. The result was the famous 1805 Battle of Trafalgar that cost the Spanish and French most of their naval vessels in a terrible defeat at the hands of the superior British Navy.

The repercussions of this disaster were far-reaching, but one of the immediate results was a British blockade of the Iberian peninsula. This, coupled with the fact that Spain no longer had a viable fleet with which to sail to the New World to administer its empire, effectively isolated the Spanish Latin American colonies in the Americas from almost all contact with their Spanish mother country. But the Spanish colonies found that they did quite well politically and economically in governing themselves in the absence of contact with faraway Spain.

In 1806 Spain joined other continental European powers in supporting the Berlin Decree, which was Napoleon's economic plan for a boycott against all British goods, and an attempt to isolate Britain from all influence and activity on the European continent. All of the continental Western European nations endorsed the plan with the exception of Portugal, which relied heavily on British shipping, trade, and maritime protection. Napoleon was furious with the Portuguese for refusing compliance, and planned an invasion to bring them under his control. However, since France had lost the bulk of its naval fleet at Trafalgar, Napoleon had only one viable option for placing troops in Portugal—he had to march them through Spain.

In 1807 Napoleon received permission from Spanish First Minister Godoy to march his troops across Spain *en route* to Portugal. In the controversial Convention of Fontainebleau of 1807 Godoy agreed to Napoleon's terms, hoping to ingratiate himself to Napoleon, and perhaps acquire some Portuguese real estate for himself in the deal. However, when Napoleon's army reached Lisbon, they discovered that the entire Portuguese court including the royal family, treasury, and several thousand courtiers had taken passage on British ships bound for Brazil.

Frustrated, Napoleon returned to Spain which he found in political chaos. Riots aimed at removing Godoy had become increasingly frequent and progressively more violent. Napoleon offered King Charles IV, Prince-regent Ferdinand, and First Minister Godoy all the chance to come to France to work out their differences under his supervision. None of them saw the hook in his offer, and in 1808 they all traveled to Bayonne where they were immediately put under house arrest and forbidden to leave France. Then, Napoleon placed his brother Joseph Bonaparte on the Spanish throne to rule in the absence of a legitimate Spanish monarch. The results in Spain and the New World were immediate. The population divided between support of the French government and the Spanish monarchy in exile, and the resultant civil war in Spain lasted until 1815 when Napoleon was banished from the continent and his brother Joseph was removed from the Spanish throne.

THE CATALYST FOR INDEPENDENCE IN LATIN AMERICA

With the Spanish leadership under Napoleon's control in France, Spain now had to deal with the touchy dilemma of sovereignty, not only in Spain, but also in the Spanish American colonies in Latin America that were becoming increasingly self-reliant politically, and progressively dependent on the United States and Britain economically. Because of the loss of its fleet, Spain could not maintain frequent and necessary contact with the Latin American colonies. Therefore, self-government in the name of the absentee king became one of the only viable political options available to the Spanish American colonies.

When the Spanish colonies realized that Napoleon controlled Spain, many began to govern themselves in the name of Ferdinand VII. But some Latin American Creoles began to wonder what the difference was between governing themselves in the name of a prisoner-king several thousand miles away with whom they had no contact, and governing themselves in their own name. Here then was the birth of Latin American independence; born, as was the United States, in the chaos of revolutionary Western Europe. It was only a matter of time before the Latin American colonies followed the example of the United States to the north in throwing off the yoke of colonialism and imperialism.

In 1815 when Napoleon was banished from Europe, Charles IV, Maria Louisa, Manuel Godoy, and Prince Ferdinand all returned to Spain. Charles abdicated his throne in favor of his son, and Ferdinand VII began to rule the crumbling Spanish Empire.[8] Ferdinand VII was arguably the worst king in Spain's history. He was out of touch with his kingdom at home, and with his empire abroad. He was seen as weak by his enemies, and he did not maintain the support of loyal Spanish citizens. He envisioned returning Spain to the old glory days of absolute rulers and grateful citizens that had existed prior to the French Revolution. But in the absence of strong rulers in Spain over the previous years, a radical element had managed to seize control of parts of the population.

Back in 1812, while the Spanish monarchy was still in captivity in France, liberals in Cadiz had drafted a new Spanish constitution designed to transform the government into a constitutional monarchy. When Ferdinand returned from exile and became the Spanish king, this Constitution of 1812 was placed before him for ratification, which he vehemently refused, fearing it would infringe on his absolutist designs. Instead, Ferdinand instituted a system of rule based on the French model of Royal Absolutism. However, by 1820, the more liberal elements of the Spanish government began to seriously consider removing Ferdinand from power in order to achieve their objectives.

It was during these precarious circumstances that Ferdinand attempted to reestablish contact and control with his New World colonies. He purchased some old ships from the Russian Baltic fleet, and proposed using these vessels to send troops to the New World to reestablish and shore up his control in the western hemisphere. But Spanish sailors believed these ships to be hardly seaworthy, and some of the military personnel who were intended for the voyage united under Colonel Rafael del Riego in a minor revolution against the crown. Whether or not their motives were simultaneously at attempt to preserve life and limb, the Riego Revolt of 1820 had two major repercussions. The first was yet another serious civil war, and second, and perhaps more important, was King Ferdinand's capitulation regarding the Constitution of 1812 which he signed with great resignation in March of 1820, to the delight of most of the Spanish populace.

When word reached the Spanish colonies in Latin America that Ferdinand VII had opposed the Constitution of 1812 and initially refused to ratify the document and rule the Spanish Empire under its guidelines, many colonial leaders in Latin America began to contemplate more seriously a complete break from the mother country. Later when word finally arrived in the western hemisphere that Ferdinand had capitulated and ratified the document after all, the damage was already accomplished and many local Creoles throughout Latin America were unwilling to put their revolutionary ideas aside. The liberal Creole population saw events in Spain as an opportunity to acquire more power, status, and influence in Latin American government and politics.

As early as 1810, some areas in the Spanish Empire had already experienced revolutions born of the previous years of chaos and uncertainty in Spain. Buenos Aires was one area in particular that revolted early on—not against Spain per se, but against Napoleon's control of Spain—and never quite returned to Spanish control. Soon, revolutions in Mexico, Venezuela, Argentina, and Chile would bring the power of the Spanish Empire in the New World crashing down.

CONCLUSIONS

The earliest relationships between Latin America and the United States were informal, tentative, and almost never official. Early trade opportunities between the United States and Latin America resulted from the needs of the former after winning independence from the British, and the needs of the latter which was denied communication and trade with Spain because of conflicts and problems on the European continent.

But this growing hemispheric association between the United States and Latin America was not only the product of economic necessity. Latin American revolutionary leaders paid close attention to the manner in which the United States had won its freedom from Britain, and also the republican form of government that the United States had created to govern itself after the expulsion of the British from the colonies in North America. Documents such as the Declaration of Independence and the U.S. Constitution would eventually have a profound effect on similar proclamations of freedom in Latin America, and the newly formed U.S. government would be held up again and again as a paradigm worthy of emulation by nascent Latin American countries.

3

The Independence Movements in Spanish Latin America and Brazil

Among the popular and representative systems, I do not favor the federal system. It is overperfect, and it demands political virtues and talents far superior to our own.... I say: Do not adopt the best system of government, but the one that is most likely to succeed.   – Simón Bolivar

There is no good faith in America, nor among the nations of America. Treaties are only scraps of paper; constitutions only printed matter; elections, battles, freedom, anarchy, and life all a torment. America is ungovernable. Those who have served the revolution have plowed the sea.   – Simón Bolivar

In 1955, historian Hubert Herring penned the following words in his well-written history of Latin America:

> The severing of the ties between the Iberian kingdoms and their American colonies was inevitable. It is not within the nature of man to accept forever the status of a dependent. *The wonder is not that the emergence of the free nations of America came so soon, but rather that it came so late.* Neither Spain nor Portugal...ever understood why her American colonies broke away.... The Iberians argued with good conscience that they had poured their best blood and treasure into their kingdoms overseas, that the colonies were morally beholden to the motherlands and had no right to abandon them so abruptly. But in reality there was nothing abrupt about the wars for Latin American independence. The blows which were finally struck reflected the accumulated angers and ambitions of three centuries.[1]

Herring argues that the events in early nineteenth century that culminated in independence for most of Spain's New World colonies and all of Portugal's, came as the unavoidable result of over 300 years of Iberian colonialism and imperialism that created insurmountable tensions and problems in the New World.

Part of the formative experience for Latin American independence occurred during the final years of the eighteenth century: two violent revolutions for freedom and equality born of the European Enlightenment. One of these revolutions, the French Revolution, was responsible ultimately for unsettling the Spanish Empire at its core by destabilizing the Spanish monarchy. The other, the American Revolution, occurred in the New World just north of the Latin American colonies. Latin American leaders viewed the emergence of the United States with both alarm and expectation. In less than fifty years, Latin America followed the French and the United States by staging their own revolutions for independence and freedom. But the revolutions for independence in Latin America were very different from the American and French Revolutions. Latin American revolutionaries were not prepared for the drawn-out nature of the fighting, or the implications of self-rule after they won their freedom.

Other differences are also telling. For example, the United States had formerly existed as colonies of England from the founding of Jamestown in 1607 to the end of the American Revolutionary War in 1783, a period of 176 years. By contrast, the Latin American colonies had been controlled by Spain from roughly 1492 when Columbus first colonized the island of Hispañola to 1825 when the country of Bolivia was created by Simón Bolívar, a period of over 330 years.

The significance of the fact that Latin America had a much longer colonial experience than the United States is found in the mentality of the populations. The United States emerged from colonialism ready to govern itself and move forward. U.S. citizens were less diffident about creating new governing structures and breaking with the traditions of the British political system. By contrast, Latin American rulers fifty years later reenacted the same governing structures they had experienced for generations. Instead of creating federal systems based on equality and representation, Latin American governments took shape under a series of military dictators who wielded varying degrees of absolute power based on military control and economic manipulation. And even though the new Latin American governments were loosely labeled democratic republics with written constitutions, many were dictatorships that more closely resembled the monarchical systems of government found in Europe.

BACKGROUND ON INDEPENDENCE

There are dozens of reasons for explaining the Latin American independence movements during the first two decades of the nineteenth century.

Some of the chaos and turmoil resulted from the problems that Western Europe endured during the late eighteenth and early nineteenth centuries. In addition, the tensions between Creoles and Peninsulars in Latin America over local and regional political and religious control only exacerbated the situation. Furthermore, many Latin Americans resented the attempted reintroduction of oppressive royal absolutism by Spanish King Ferdinand VII following his return from French imprisonment in 1815. Latin America had grown tired not only of Spain's inability to maintain and control the commercial aspects of the empire, but also of the often nonsensical commercial restrictions imposed on the colonies by the mother country. Furthermore, the United States, Britain, and France all continued to trade illegally with the Spanish New World colonies which bolstered the economies of all involved.

Another factor that led Latin America to seek independence from Iberia was a general weakening of the Catholic Church's authority because of the growing influence of the Enlightenment in the New World. Moreover, the inept behavior of inadequate kings such as Charles IV and Ferdinand VII further damaged Spain's political control at home and abroad. The Enlightenment slowly cankered relations between colonies and the Iberian mother countries. Corruption in local Latin American governments led to not only a desire for fewer restrictions and less oversight, but also a yearning in the colonies for self-control without the crown watching and directing the activities of the colonies.

Finally, the American and French Revolutions added incentive and determination to those in the Spanish colonies who desired a break from Iberia, even if it had to come through violence. Latin American political officials were highly intrigued by the newly drafted U.S. Constitution. They did not fully understand the document, but they were impressed with its implications nonetheless. The French Revolution and its Declaration of the Rights of Man presented an equally dangerous threat to Spanish and Latin American cultural and political solidarity because French culture was much more familiar to Spain and Portugal and their colonies than was the culture of Britain and the United States.

One of the most important issues for those Latin Americans who sought freedom from Spanish control was the fact that Spain's imperially imposed economy had become unbearable in the colonies. Many Latin Americans found that they could tolerate the fact that they were governed by a king who resided several thousand miles away. But what they desired more than political freedom was economic self-determinism. Under Spanish mercantilism, the colonies were required to ship their raw materials and bullion away to Spain.

Spanish mercantilism was not as economically mature or even profitable as the British mercantilistic system had been in North America. Under the British system, colonies exported raw materials back to Britain where these products were turned into finished products through British industrialization. These finished goods were then returned to the North American colonies and elsewhere where they were sold for a profit.

The Spanish system differed in one key element. The raw materials that were shipped to Spain were only a small percentage of the cargo; bullion (mostly silver and some gold) comprised the bulk of Spanish colonial exports. Then instead of producing a finished product in Spain for reexport or sale, the Spanish sent raw materials off to England or the Netherlands for production, which they paid for with bullion. The long-term result for Spain was a crippling dependence on cash, inflation, and a failure to industrialize. So while all of the reasons for Spanish American independence listed above were vitally influential in promoting Latin American independence in the early 1800s, their principal motivations were mainly for economic changes.[2]

Politically, the balance of power in the Spanish American colonies was divided three ways: the colonial political administration (comprising mostly Peninsulars), the Catholic Church hierarchy (made up of both Peninsulars and Creoles), and the local landed elites (mostly Creoles). At first glance, it might appear that the most powerful segment of society was the Peninsular political leaders. After all, they managed to control the legal and juridical aspects of colonial life. However, another look at the situation yields a different possibility, that the Catholic Church was very likely the most powerful entity in colonial Latin America because it had the ability to save the souls of elites and peons, Peninsulars and Creoles alike.

Nevertheless, in reality, neither political administration nor ecclesiastical organization were ultimately as powerful as the local Creole elites. These were individuals who owned vast tracts of land throughout Mexico and South America. They exercised much control over local economics and commerce because of their huge land holdings. And finally, they dominated most of the military and militia groups in towns and villages throughout Latin America because of the size of their estates and their greater population. Many large landowners—also occasionally known as *caudillos* or strongmen—controlled their own local militia groups. They also employed hundreds, and in a few cases, thousands of laborers on their huge *hacienda* estates. They controlled the local politics by swinging public opinion in the directions that most benefited them and their property. In addition, they occasionally constrained or attempted to control to varying degrees, the access that the Church had to their estates and the people who lived there.

But one of the most powerful motivating factors driving Creole behavior in early nineteenth-century Latin America was a growing sense of nationalism. Creoles began to analyze the realities of their colonial existence. The Latin American colonies were all much more wealthy in terms of natural resources than Spain was. Many Latin American colonies had much greater populations than Spain did. Latin American Creoles far outnumbered the Peninsulars who were sent from Spain to govern them. Latin

America was thousands of miles away from the mother country with an ocean in between. For all of these reasons, Latin American-born Creoles began to think of themselves not as Spaniards, Latin Americans, or even Creoles. They began to see themselves as Mexicans, Venezuelans, Chileans, Argentineans, Colombians, and so forth. This mentality also led the Creoles to view the Peninsulars as outsiders, transplants, and unwelcome overlords who represented a decrepit order of Old World imperialism. The time had come to act, and the wars for independence finally ignited throughout Latin America.

INDEPENDENCE IN SPANISH LATIN AMERICA

Because the independence movement in Brazil was so drastically different from those in Mexico and Spanish South America, it will be examined separately. The chaos and mismanagement of the Spanish Empire during the closing years of the 1700s created a power vacuum in Latin America that was filled by charismatic individuals and liberal governing bodies called *juntas*. These individuals rose up and threatened the traditional Spanish authorities in the New World and ultimately tried to drive the Spanish Peninsulars completely out of the hemisphere. The spark of independence that swept the regions of Latin America was fanned to flame as early as 1790 by the successful slave revolutions in Haiti which became the second freely independent country in the hemisphere, following the United States.

Haiti

In 1791, a free African coffee plantation overseer named Toussaint L'Ovuerture led a bloody revolution in Haiti (the French portion of the island of Hispañola) because the ideals of the French Revolution—liberty, equality, fraternity—were not transferred to the slave populations in France's colonies in the Caribbean. Over the next decade L'Ovuerture and his slave revolution devastated the entire colony. Much of the island was burned, the sugar plantations were destroyed, and thousands of individuals were slaughtered.[3]

By 1801, L'Ovuerture controlled the entire island including the eastern portions claimed by Spain. He then drafted a constitution and freed all the slaves. But in 1802, L'Ovuerture was captured by French soldiers and sent back to Europe to rot in a French prison. Nevertheless, the Haitians did not give up. They succeeded in driving the French out of Haiti and declared themselves an independent nation in 1804.[4]

Haitian independence, coupled with the successful American Revolution, set the stage for Latin American revolutions. But the United States was reticent to support the newly formed country of Haiti because of slavery issues in the American South. And throughout Latin America, the Haitian Revolution was viewed with distaste as well because of the Spanish ideals of caste and social hierarchy that had been embedded in Latin American culture from its inception. So even though Haiti won its freedom from colonial status earlier than any other Latin American nation, the only inspiration that Latin American revolutionaries drew from the Haitian experience was the opinion that if Haitian slaves could defeat and drive out the French, then certainly the Latin Americans could do the same to Spain.[5]

Mexico

Independence in Mexico was a long, drawn-out, bloody affair that lasted for over a decade. Mexican independence was initiated through the efforts of a priest, Father Miguel Hidalgo. On September 16, 1810, Hidalgo issued his declaration of Mexican independence, the *Grito de Dolores*, and started a race war that he tried unsuccessfully for the rest of his life to transform into an ideological conflict for Mexican independence.[6]

Hidalgo's revolutionary plan was simple. He had been meeting for months with another young Mexican Creole, Ignacio Allende. Under the guise of meeting as a literary society, Hidalgo, Allende, and others plotted the overthrow of Spanish authority in Mexico, and the creation of a Mexican Creole government. They planned their revolution for December 8, 1810. But as often happens, someone leaked the information and the date to local authorities.

On September 14, 1810, the Mexican viceroy, Francisco Javier de Venegas, was informed of the revolution that Hidalgo and Allende were planning. So Venegas immediately ordered the arrest of everyone involved. To this end he dispatched troops north to the towns of Dolores and Querétaro to apprehend Hidalgo and the other conspirators.

On the evening of September 15, Hidalgo and Allende discovered that their conspiracy had been compromised and they would soon be arrested and tried for treason. Hidalgo decided that given the circumstances, they had nothing to lose and should move the date of their revolution forward. Early in the morning on Sunday, September 16, Hidalgo rang the church bells in Dolores, called the Indian and Mestizo inhabitants to the church, and issued his famous sermon, the *Grito de Dolores*. He pleaded with the people to recover their stolen lands from the Spaniards and to take up arms against their enemies.[7]

Hidalgo's intention was to raise an army. His movement was supposed to supplant the Peninsulars with a Creole ruling elite. But the only support he could muster on such short notice were Indians and Mestizos. So instead of a Creole militia determined to topple the Mexican government, Hidalgo inadvertently created a mob that was determined to slaughter white Spaniards; Hidalgo had started a race war.

Between September of 1810 and early January of 1911, Hidalgo's forces swelled to over 80,000. He marched them through the mining district of north-central Mexico in a perpetual orgy of brutality and violence. Then as Hidalgo approached Mexico City, he divided his forces and, for some reason, did not sack the capital. Instead they turned toward Guadalajara where the violence and slaughter continued. In the autumn of 1810, the Spanish military began to recover some of the towns that Hidalgo's forces had sacked. Hidalgo began to lose hundreds of men to desertion, and his revolution lost much momentum. In January of 1811, as Hidalgo tried to escape through northern Mexico—possibly intending to cross the border into the United States—he was captured by the Mexican military. He was subsequently defrocked, tried, condemned, and shot.

Following Hidalgo's death, leadership of his revolution passed to a fellow conspirator, José Maria Morelos, who was also a priest. But unlike Hidalgo, Morelos was a Mestizo, not a Creole. Morelos attempted to do what Hidalgo had refused to do by laying siege to Mexico City. Morelos even began to draft a new constitution for an independent Mexican nation should they succeed. But he eventually was captured in 1815 on the outskirts of Mexico City and suffered the same fate that had befallen Hidalgo.[8]

After Hidalgo and Morelos had failed to achieve independence, Mexico was left in ruins. Thousands had died and the nation had become economically stagnant. It seemed that Hidalgo's revolutionary movement had utterly failed and Mexico would remain a Spanish colony. At this critical time, a charismatic Creole military commander named General Augustine de Iturbide succeeded in forming a massive army, putting an end to the popular uprisings that emerged from Hidalgo's movement, and then declaring Mexican independence from Spanish control in 1821.

Between 1816 and 1820, following the death of Father Morelos, the viceroy commissioned General Iturbide to command an impressive army that would eradicate the remnants of revolution in Mexico once and for all. However, Iturbide sensed that the time had come to throw off Spanish hegemony in Mexico—and he very likely saw a position for himself at the pinnacle of any new Mexican government once Spain was removed from the hemisphere. So he used his army, not to destroy the rebels that were left over from Hidalgo's revolution, but instead to join with them. Soon, Iturbide found himself in control of an even larger military force, and he rapidly marched his army into Mexico City, threatened the Spanish government, and then graciously accepted the surrender of the last Spanish viceroy, Juan O'Donojú, on February 24, 1821.[9]

During the ensuing months between July 1822 and March 1823, Iturbide named himself Agustin I, Emperor of Mexico, and ruled Mexico as an absolute monarch in a catastrophic tenure of office that lasted less than a year. During his brief rule, Iturbide managed to bankrupt the country and aggravate relations between Mexico, Europe, and the nations of Central America (which he annexed to Mexico in 1822) before he was finally driven from the country into exile in 1823.

Central America

With regard to Central America, leaders there had declared their independence from Spain in 1821, but in 1822 Iturbide had appropriated all of the Central American territory between Guatemala and Costa Rica. Once Iturbide was driven from power in Mexico in March of 1823, the Mexican government recognized Central American independence. In July of 1823, prominent statesmen from the different regions of the Central American isthmus proclaimed the creation of a new country, the United Provinces of Central America (UPCA) which included Guatemala, Honduras, El Salvador, Nicaragua, and Costa Rica.

Tragically, neither the UPCA nor Iturbide's exile lasted very long. During the last years of the 1830s, the UPCA fragmented into regional units and civil wars broke out in Honduras, Guatemala, and Nicaragua. Then between 1838 and 1841 all five of the states declared their independence and the UPCA dissolved. As for former Emperor Iturbide, after leaving Mexico he traveled through Europe where he spoke about the tragedy of his abdication to all who would listen. Then about a year after he had gone into exile, Iturbide returned to Mexico in an attempt to regain his political power. He was promptly arrested and shot.

Spanish South America

The independence movements in South America were accomplished in roughly the same amount of time and generally during the same chronology of years as independence in Mexico and Central America. The wars for independence in South America lasted roughly fourteen years, from 1810 to 1824. And just as in Mexico, the South American Creoles wanted greater independence from the oversight of the Spanish monarchy and the Peninsular governors so that they could make more of their own economic and political decisions. One of the major differences between Mexican and South American independence from Spain was the sheer size of the South American continent. This geographic factor alone made South American independence difficult and costly for the Creole revolutionaries.

A Venezuelan named Simón Bolivar was influential in achieving independence in Venezuela, Colombia, and Ecuador. At the other end of the continent, an Argentine named José de San Martín played major and minor roles in the liberation of Argentina, Paraguay, Uruguay, and Chile. Both of these men worked simultaneously on different ends of South America, and then met in the middle to liberate Peru together.

Simón Bolívar

Simón Bolívar's story is exceptionally interesting. Like Father Hidalgo in Mexico, Bolívar was a Creole, born in Venezuela in 1783. Young Bolívar entered the Venezuelan military at the tender age of 14 and thus was launched the career of the man who would eventually earn the moniker The Liberator.[10]

After the turn of the nineteenth century, Bolívar took a leave of absence from the Venezuelan military, and between 1802 and 1807 he traveled extensively through Spain, France, and other areas of Europe, and eventually made it to the United States of America.. But in 1807 when Napoleon invaded Portugal and Spain, Bolívar returned to Venezuela to prepare for his liberation movement. On July 5, 1811, Bolívar and other Venezuelan liberals declared their political freedom from Spain, and the formation of a new Venezuelan government, even though the Spanish had not been driven from the colony. Bolívar fully expected the United States of America to extend its full support to his revolution against Spain, but American support was slow in coming.

Between 1812 and 1819 Bolívar suffered several defeats at the hands of the Spanish military in Venezuela before he finally achieved victory on August 7, 1819, when he crushed the Spanish and drove them out of the region, liberating the territory that would eventually become the modern nations of Colombia, Venezuela, and Ecuador.[11]

At this point, Bolívar's ambitions demanded that he march south and liberate Peru as well. However, because Peru was one of the most closely guarded and heavily fortified areas of Spanish power in South America, Bolívar could not accomplish this task alone. It is at this point that the stories of Simón Bolívar and José de San Martín intersect. General San Martín unshackled most of southern South America while Bolivar was doing the same in the north, and they then met briefly in Ecuador where they joined their armies and planned their assault on the last remaining Spanish forces in Peru.

José de San Martín

José de San Martín was born in Argentina in 1778. At the age of 11 he and his father traveled to Spain where San Martín began his military career. Like Bolívar, when Napoleon invaded Spain in 1807, San Martín returned to the land of his birth where he became a general in the Argentine military. With the help of San Martín, the province of Buenos Aires defeated and drove the Spanish out of the region by the early months of 1813.[12]

Leaders in Argentina then became interested in exercising some economic and political control in nearby Uruguay and Paraguay, and began to send troops into these regions. In 1814 Argentina had some success fighting against the Spanish in Uruguay, but leaders in Paraguay had declared their emancipation from Spain as early as 1811. And as Argentina's designs in Uruguay and Paraguay ultimately crumbled, José de San Martín was given the assignment of taking his army to Peru instead.[13] He decided that because the Spanish royalist forces in Peru would expect him to approach from the southeast, and since the Andes mountains were such a formidable barrier separating Argentina and Chile, the easiest way to liberate Peru would be to do the unexpected by first liberating Chile from Spanish control, and then traveling north into Peru from Chile.

In 1817, San Martín marched his army across the Andes mountains into Chile in a military maneuver comparable to Hannibal's crossing the Alps during the Second Punic War between Rome and Carthage at the end of the second century BC. Once in Chile, San Martín found himself in a civil war between liberal Chileans who favored Chilean nationalism and conservatives who supported royalist Spain. San Martín added his military might to the cause of the liberals who were led by Bernardo O'Higgins, and together they quickly defeated the royalist army in February of 1817.[14]

Once Chile was free from Spanish control, San Martín used Chile as a base from which to liberate Upper and Lower Peru. He believed that if he could capture and hold the city of Lima on the coast, Spanish control of Peru would eventually crumble. In 1820 he sailed north along the Chilean Pacific coast and landed near Lima, and by 1821 he had declared Peruvian independence. But Spanish forces still occupied other parts of Peru.

On July 26, 1822, José de San Martín met with Simón Bolivar in Ecuador to discuss the end of the fighting and the creation of a new Peruvian government. They spoke for a total of around four hours and disagreed on most things including the type of government to establish in Peru once it was liberated. Sometime that evening, General San Martín decided to resign from the campaign rather than argue the point, and let Bolívar be responsible for the rest of the Peruvian revolution. So San Martín sailed back to Argentina, while Simón Bolívar rallied both armies and prepared for the final battles with the Spanish Royalist forces.[15]

By 1824 Bolívar succeeded in driving the Spanish out of Peru, and he declared the entire continent of South America free of Spanish control. In 1826, Bolívar tried to form a united South American confederation for hemispheric solidarity at a conference held in Panama. But because of mistrust, geographic isolation, and the massive distance between cities and countries, Bolívar's attempts at Pan-Americanism dissolved in chaos and suspicion.[16]

Brazil

Brazilian independence was drastically different from the independence movements in other locations in the hemisphere. Napoleon Bonaparte was partially responsible for the separation of Brazil from the Portuguese Empire, and because of the Napoleonic invasion of Portugal in 1807, Brazil's independence was swift and virtually bloodless. But Napoleon does not deserve all the credit. Between 1750 and 1800 Brazilians began to experience the same sense of nationalism that infected Spanish Latin Americans. They began to see Portugal as a backward mother country that was economically, politically, and militarily weak. Furthermore, to compensate for these weaknesses, Portugal relied very heavily on Great Britain for commercial and military support.[17]

In 1807 when Napoleon demanded that Portugal sever its ties with Britain, Portugal refused, sparking the Napoleonic invasion of both Portugal and Spain. In response to Napoleon's plan to conquer Portugal, on November 29, 1807, between 10,000 and 15,000 people fled from Portugal aboard British and Portuguese ships. Among the passengers was the entire royal family of Portugal, including Maria I the Queen and Dom João the Prince Regent. Also among the escapees were the entire Council of State, the ministers, military leadership, church hierarchy, treasury officials, court justices, some businessmen, some aristocratic families, hundreds of courtiers, servants, and some local citizens as well. Finally, they also carried with them several libraries, a printing press, the entire Portuguese royal treasury, and most of the governmental paperwork and files. To call this migration an enormous undertaking would be a gross understatement.[18]

The ships arrived in Brazil on January 22, 1808. Of course, Napoleon kept Portugal for himself, but the Portuguese overseas empire continued to function under the direct rulership of the Portuguese royal family from Brazil. The only difference was that instead of ruling the empire from Lisbon, they did so from Rio de Janeiro. And all of a sudden, Brazil became a very important place. The colony immediately benefited from such luxuries as printing presses, banks, universities, libraries, theatres and museums, and thousands of immigrants over the next several years.

Brazil went from colonial status to kingdom status overnight. Brazil's ports were opened to trade with the United States and the rest of the world after 1808, and by 1815 Brazil was no longer considered a colony, but a coequal kingdom with Portugal. Instead of continuing the practices of mercantilism, Brazil began to keep its natural resources and use them for manufacturing at home. Conditions were so positive that many Brazilians began to wonder why they needed their historical ties to Portugal at all.

In 1816 Queen Maria I died and the Crown Prince became João VI, King of Portugal. By this time Napoleon had been banished from Europe, and the nobles and aristocrats who had remained behind in Portugal demanded that the royal family leave Brazil and return home where they belonged. Some of the more liberal Portuguese nobility even threatened that if João VI did not return, they would do away with the monarchy all together and form a republic. King João VI was intelligent enough to comprehend that he could not keep both Portugal and Brazil for himself. If he remained in Brazil, he would lose Portugal. If he returned to Portugal, he was quite sure he would lose control of Brazil because the Brazilians would not stand for returning to colonialism after nearly fifteen years of coequal kingdom status.

So in 1821, João VI made his decision and returned to Portugal where he was received as the king of the entire empire including the Brazilian colony. However, King João's son, the Crown Prince of Portugal Dom Pedro, remained in Brazil. What the Portuguese aristocracy did not know was that Dom Pedro had been left behind intentionally by his father to act as a viceroy representing the people of Brazil for the crown in far-off Lisbon.[19]

When João VI returned to Lisbon without his son, the nobility predictably demanded that Pedro also return as soon as possible. When word reached Pedro that the Portuguese nobles and aristocrats of his father's court demanded his return, according to their preconceived plan, he declared Brazil a free and independent country on September 7, 1822, in his famous speech, the *Grito do Ypiranga*.[20]

Obviously, the most immediate question in Brazil was now one of sovereignty. No one in Brazil really questioned that Pedro was in control; but what kind of government should they form? Many wanted a familiar, monarchical system resembling the Portuguese structure they were accustomed to. But other more liberal thinkers began to argue that the people of Brazil should actually be sovereign and form a republic in emulation of the government established in the United States to the north nearly forty years earlier. The only problem with this plan was the fact that those who advocated republican democracy were the educated middle class who constituted only a small minority of the population. Therefore, reflecting the wishes of the greatest number of Brazilians, in 1824 a new constitution was drafted and put into effect that created a constitutional Brazilian monarchy with Pedro I as Emperor.

Brazilian independence differed from that of Spanish Latin America in at least three essential regards. First of all, and most noticeably, Brazilian independence was largely bloodless. With the exception of a few minor revolts, Brazil abandoned colonialism with almost none of the destructive bloodshed that plagued Mexico and Spanish South America. Second, because the Portuguese royalty had lived in Brazil for almost a decade and a half—and indeed because of the fact that Dom Pedro remained in Brazil to lead it after independence—there was very little political, economic, or social disruption at all. Things continued much the same as they had before Pedro's declaration of independence. Finally, Brazil did not have to create a new political system like Mexico and Latin America did. In fact, Brazil became the only former Iberian colony in the new world to retain a monarchical system of government after independence—a fact that disturbed the United States greatly until Brazil also declared an end to its monarchy and became a republic in 1889.

THE UNITED STATES AND THE INDEPENDENCE OF LATIN AMERICA

The United States did not get overtly involved in the Latin American wars for independence for several reasons, but predominantly because of a fear of reprisal by the British. Some might argue that the United States had more to fear from Spain or Portugal by way of retribution than the British.

But Great Britain represented a much greater threat to the United States than the decrepit Spanish and Portuguese Empires. And given the fact that the United States and the British had just recently concluded fighting each other in the War of 1812, the United States did not want to provoke Britain any further.[21]

To further complicate things, the British desired to control economic markets in the newly formed Latin American countries, and did not look kindly on U.S. interference. Additionally, the long relationship between the British and Portuguese empires translated into a sense of British responsibility and paternalism in Brazil that the United States could not easily duplicate. Finally, the British were obviously perfectly happy with Brazil's monarchical system and were eager to continue to grow economic trade relations with Brazil.

But many statesmen in the United States were enamored with the idea of a hemisphere of republics in the west to counter the hemisphere of monarchies in the east, a hemisphere that could be influenced politically and economically. But the United States also realized that it was not the only government vying for power in the hemisphere, and that it would have to compete with Great Britain and France. Finally, the United States hesitated to get involved in the Latin American independence movements because at first it appeared very likely that the Latin Americans might not even succeed.[22]

So given all of these factors that created a reticence in the United States for open involvement in the Latin American revolutions, what did the United States actually do in Latin America during the early years of the nineteenth century? During the wars for independence in Latin America, the United States sold munitions and supplies to groups of revolutionaries, sent emissaries to observe and comment on their plans and preparations, and even permitted some of the Latin American leaders to plot from inside the United States itself.[23]

But in the end, the reasons that kept the United States from fully allying with the Latin Americans against Spain turned out to be the same reasons for which the Latin Americans did not immediately embrace the United States after their revolutions were concluded. Britain was simply too powerful militarily and commercially to risk provocation. Furthermore, the British offered better trade opportunities and represented greater political and economic stability for the newly created Latin American countries than the United States, which was only half a century old.

So immediately after most of the independence movements were concluded in Latin America, the United States realized that if the hemisphere was to be protected from British exploitation, some things would have to change. To this end, in 1823, while Bolívar's forces continued to fight the Spanish in Peru, the President of the United States, James Monroe, delivered his famous words, that were later called the Monroe Doctrine, which changed U.S.–Latin American relations forever.

4

The Monroe Doctrine, Manifest Destiny, and the Mexican War

The American continents, by the free and independent condition which they have assumed and maintain, are henceforth not to be considered as subjects for future colonization by any European powers.... We could not view any interposition for the purpose of oppressing them, or controlling in any other manner their destiny, by any European power in any other light than as the manifestation of an unfriendly disposition toward the United States. — James Monroe

All new states are invested, more or less, by a class of noisy, second-rate men who are always in favor of rash and extreme measures, but Texas was absolutely overrun by such men. — Sam Houston

I shall lead my compatriots by the hand to the margins of the San Jacinto and there among the very ruins where they wish to bury my glory, in the very deserts where it is said that its luster was dimmed, by the deep rivers still tinted red with the blood shed in a righteous war by Mexicans and the invaders of Texas... I will show them how far I steered from that treacherous path imputed to me. Santa Anna, whether conqueror or conquered, whether free or in chains, yea, I swear it before the world, did not in Texas debase the Mexican name in which he glories and takes pride. — Antonio López de Santa Anna

Following the Latin American wars for independence in the early 1800s, U.S.–Latin American relations entered a new phase and quickly got off to a troubled start. American statesmen tended to view Latin America in general as a backward, inferior, and underdeveloped region in constant need of supervision and oversight. On the other hand, the new Latin American countries were somewhat ambivalent about the United States at first, and truth be told, they were just a little apprehensive about American intentions in the hemisphere. After all, the basis for the relationship between Latin America and the United States up to this point had been predominantly economic in nature, and somewhat surreptitious.

But now the United States and the countries of Latin America were independent and free from colonialism. They could set their own foreign policy and economic agendas. And, despite their differences and apprehensions, there was a common goal between the United States in the north and Latin America in the south: namely the restriction of European political power in the entire western hemisphere. The United States saw Europe as a challenge and even threat to its designs in the hemisphere, and Latin America saw Europe as a potential menace to its future economic and political sovereignty and development.

From the U.S. perspective, Latin America needed supervision; many American statesmen saw Latin American civilization as backward and diffident. For the United States, Latin American countries were at a disadvantage because of their cultural and social ties to concepts and institutions such as the perceived degeneracy of the Spanish Empire, the role Roman Catholicism had played in dominating Latin America's social and political ideas, and the evils of the monarchical system of government which Latin America seemed to have difficulty overcoming. In the eyes of many U.S. citizens, Latin America needed to compensate for each of these deficiencies, and was simply not up to the challenge.

As for perceptions in Latin America, most citizens of Latin American countries did not necessarily view the United States as stronger or weaker. Neither side had yet demonstrated its military superiority against the other, and neither would be proved more or less powerful until after the Mexican War of 1846. But even prior to the independence movements in the 1820s, Latin Americans had viewed the United States as a potentially antagonistic and expansionistic neighbor. And therefore, following their independence from Spain and Portugal, Latin American countries did not relish dealing with the impending problems that could ensue in a future clash with the United States. When the conflicts finally did come, the United States quickly demonstrated its proclivity for steering the hemisphere where it wanted, much to Europe's irritation, and much to the dismay of most Latin Americans.

U.S. EXPANSION

As discussed in Chapter 2, the United States purchased Louisiana from Napoleon in 1803. After U.S. statesmen began to comprehend the secrecy and clandestine diplomacy that had occasioned the earlier transfer of the Louisiana territory back and forth between Spain and France over the previous century, the United States did not want to deal with future European arrangements that involved the reassignment of territory in the Americas, secret or otherwise.

By 1810 the United States had to solidify its attitudes regarding European-controlled territory in the hemisphere because at that time many American citizens lived in west Florida in the area of modern Alabama and the panhandle, a territory technically still governed by Spain. These settlers were not disposed to Spanish rule in the region and asked for annexation and admission into the Union. The U.S. government did not act immediately because it feared reprisals from both the Spanish and the British. However, it quickly became apparent that if the United States did not act swiftly, Spain might cede the Florida territory to Britain.

So on January 3, 1811, in order to prevent the transfer of Florida to another European power, President James Madison took formal possession of the Florida territory and issued a statement which has since become known as the No Transfer Resolution. This declaration became the first official policy statement by the U.S. government regarding Latin America and its territories, and was the first in a series of documents drafted in the United States that would direct U.S.–Latin American relations for decades, if not centuries. In the No Transfer Resolution, President Madison stated that the United States simply would not tolerate Spain passing any part of the Florida territory to any foreign power, and in order to safeguard the area, the United States formally occupied the region. By 1813, the United States officially annexed west Florida and made it a part of the United States of America.[1]

Why was Florida such an important island in U.S.–Latin American relations? Simply because the Florida territory controlled access to the Mississippi River, the Caribbean Sea, the Gulf of Mexico, and the southeastern portion of the North American continent. The United States was unwilling to permit any other power—especially a European power—to have the ability to control the Florida peninsula for national security reasons. The No Transfer Resolution sent a strong message to the rest of the hemisphere and to Western Europe that the United States would not condone what it considered security threats, and would act aggressively in standing up for its own interests in the hemisphere.

The rest of the southern Florida peninsula that had not been annexed by the United States in 1813 was eventually acquired in 1819 by the Treaty of Adams-Onís between the United States and Spain. This treaty was the result of negotiations between John Quincy Adams and Luis de Onís, the Spanish ambassador. In exchange for the rest of the territory of Florida, the United States pledged to pay Spain $5 million, and not threaten or claim any of Spain's Texas territory in northern Mexico.

In the 1820s, with the small episode of national security in Florida solved, the U.S. Congress allocated funds to support diplomatic representation in several of the newly formed Latin American nations. By extending official diplomatic recognition to the new countries of Latin America, the United States ensured that the Latin Americans could not simply turn their backs on U.S. aid and guidance. And the Latin American nations really had no other good alternatives because the Western European nations of Spain and Portugal were still angry over the loss of their former colonies, and it appeared that France and Great Britain had hegemonic aspirations of their own in Latin America.

THE MONROE DOCTRINE

In Europe, the heads of state had not been very impressed with the American Revolutionary War and Britain's loss of its North American colonies at the end of the eighteenth century. At the beginning of the nineteenth century, they were equally unimpressed with Spain's loss of its New World colonies, and with the rapid U.S. diplomatic recognition of the new Latin American states. Europe saw all of these events as indicative of its own increasing weakness and possibly the growing strength of the United States—a mounting threat and economic, political, and even military competitor in the western hemisphere.[2]

Therefore, several European nations organized a union of sorts called the Holy Alliance. They intended to crush the fragile new Latin American states, reestablish European economic and political control over the western hemisphere, and eliminate the threat of U.S. expansion and growth throughout the region. The initial nation-members of this European coalition were Russia, Austria, France, Prussia, and Britain. Spain and Portugal were also interested in the success of the Holy Alliance, but were in the midst of fighting for control of their colonies in the early 1820s and could not fully participate in the Holy Alliance.

By 1821 the leaders of the Holy Alliance had decided on a course of action for counterrevolutionary intervention in the western hemisphere. Their objective was to destroy liberalism and republicanism. Their intention was to intervene in states that had recently experienced revolutions and might therefore represent a threat to other states in surrounding regions. Although their intentions were summarily vague, their actions soon became very clear.

Tsar Alexander I of Russia soon declared that no foreign vessels would be permitted to approach the Alaskan coast closer than 100 miles. When questions arose about what exactly constituted the Alaskan coast, Alexander defined it as stretching from the northern tip of Alaska, all the way to California north of modern San Francisco. By itself, Tsar Alexander's decree was not much to get excited about, but U.S. leaders believed it was designed as a ploy by the Holy Alliance to both restrict and harass the United States and the new nations of Latin America.

So in response, U.S. President James Monroe chose to speak of the issue in his State of the Union address before the U.S. Congress on December 2, 1823. His statement very clearly separated the western hemisphere from Western Europe, and warned Europe that the United States would not tolerate any further incursions into the hemisphere. Furthermore, Monroe used very unambiguous language to forecast that any threat to the nations of Latin America would, by default, be considered a direct threat to the interests and security of the United States. In other words, the Monroe Doctrine essentially proclaimed the western hemisphere off limits to European colonization; it was more or less an assertion that as far as Europe was concerned, they should adopt a "hands off" approach to the hemisphere.[3] President Monroe stated,

> It is impossible that the allied powers should extend their political system to any portion of either continent without endangering our peace and happiness; nor can anyone believe that our southern brethren, if left to themselves, would adopt it of their own accord. It is equally impossible, therefore, that we should behold such interposition in any form with indifference. If we look to the comparative strength and resources of Spain and those new Governments, and their distance from each other, it must be obvious that she can never subdue them. It is still the true policy of the United States to leave the parties to themselves, in the hope that other powers will pursue the same course.[4]

In general terms, the most explicit purpose behind President Monroe's statement was to maintain the independence and freedom of the newly emerging nations in Latin America. However, President Monroe's personal reasons for issuing the statement were not motivated by the same incentive. The most important reason for issuing such a statement was to safeguard the interests of the United States in the hemisphere. In other words, the primary concern of the Monroe Doctrine was to protect the interests of the United States. Latin American independence was important, but of a secondary nature to the United States in the overall scheme of things.

One thing the Monroe Doctrine did *not* do was encourage any change of status with regard to *existing* European colonies in the hemisphere. In other words, Russian Alaska, French Guiana, Spanish Cuba and Puerto Rico, and the British presence in Jamaica and Belize were supposedly not affected by the doctrine because they were preexisting colonies that had been owned and administered prior to 1823.

At first, President Monroe's speech to the Congress was not called specifically the Monroe Doctrine. It would not gain this title for several decades, until it was used by future presidents and statesmen to further the U.S.

position in the hemisphere. However, the implications of President Monroe's statement were immediate. The United States had *ipso facto* declared itself the predominant military, political, and economic force in the hemisphere. Future statements that built on the foundation of Monroe's words would extend the self-appointed authority of the United States even further, but for the moment, the statement was incredibly bold.

It was also somewhat foolish. In 1823, the U.S. government had no means of defending the entire hemisphere from European expansion and colonization. The United States could barely defend its own borders with the naval vessels it owned. There was little question that the United States was no match for a combined and unified European association such as the Holy Alliance, either militarily—strictly in terms of naval power—or commercially. Furthermore, in 1823 Britain was both the economic and political powerhouse throughout much of Latin America. British economic and military sovereignty far outweighed that of the United States.

Perceptions of the Monroe Doctrine in Europe were interesting. Europeans were generally surprised and at the same time quite condescending. The king of France, Louis XVIII, reacted in a particularly bellicose manner. He argued that President Monroe had no business making the statement in the first place because while he was indeed the president of the United States, his term in office was temporary, diminishing his overall authority in the eyes of the monarchs of Europe whose terms of office usually ended with their deaths. Furthermore, by what right did this temporary president claim responsibility over an entire hemisphere when the United States of America occupied only a portion of North America? The other European nations reacted in a similar, if less vociferous, manner over what they perceived to be the ridiculous proclamations of an impudent and momentary president.[5]

In Latin America, the reaction was much as could be expected. Latin American governments and revolutionaries were not very excited about the prospects the statement seemed to avow. They generally saw Monroe's announcement as an overreaction by the United States, which further contributed to Latin American suspicions of U.S. motives. It was true that the emerging Latin American nations did not desire to face renewed threats to their sovereignty from other European nations, but they were also equally concerned about the manner in which the United States would undertake to defend the hemisphere in the eventuality that the United States saw a need to do so. So while the Monroe Doctrine was both bold and decisive in its language, Latin Americans were equally uncomfortable with the things Monroe's statement did *not* say, such as the cost to Latin American nations if the United States decided to intervene in hemispheric events, the potential avenues the Americans might take in such interventions, and the long-term results of these future actions.

Some of the incredulity regarding the Monroe Doctrine in Europe and Latin America came from the fact that the declaration in and of itself had no real authority or bearing in the international community. It was delivered to the U.S. Congress as President Monroe's State of the Union address. According to the U.S. Constitution, the purpose of the State of the Union address is simply to inform the Congress and recommend that they consider certain important decisions and actions regarding the well-being of the United States. In no place does the U.S. Constitution state that the State of the Union address is a legal, codified, ambassadorial, or otherwise binding tool of U.S. foreign policy or diplomacy. So it is not hard to understand the dismay and astonishment that were demonstrated in Latin America and Europe when Monroe read the document to the Congress in 1823. It also follows that if the document had no legal binding power on the United States or the hemisphere, it was fundamentally noncompulsory in any legal or diplomatic sense.[6]

But despite the fact that the Monroe Doctrine was more or less unenforceable in 1823, and even though it was very unhappily received in Europe and only slightly less so in Latin America, it served as a rallying cry to the citizens of the United States, and American nationalism continued to grow while U.S. citizens looked to the future with high hopes. Americans were pleased that President Monroe had defended the interests of the United States, and were less concerned about what the Europeans and Latin Americans thought.

In the long run, the significance of the Monroe Doctrine cannot be overstated. It became the foundation for U.S.–Latin American diplomatic and military interactions for the rest of the nineteenth century and most of the twentieth century as well. And even though it did not prevent the powers of Western Europe from interfering in the western hemisphere, it did serve as a vehicle for emergent U.S. imperialism because it could be—and indeed was—modified frequently by U.S. leaders according to the needs of the moment.

Nevertheless, soon after Monroe's statement was issued, and the fallout quieted down, the issue and indeed the statement itself were both forgotten about for several decades. The document was not called the Monroe Doctrine until the 1840s and 1850s, and not seriously and systematically implemented until after the U.S. Civil War. Even so, this statement in 1823 was the first major step taken by the United States to establish itself as a major hemispheric and world power.

THE MAKING OF MANIFEST DESTINY

During the early 1800s Americans began to develop a keen sense of their own importance in world affairs. Perhaps this developing sense of consequence in the United States further explains why a U.S. president would dare to make such a bold statement as the Monroe Doctrine. Another direction that these attitudes took was down the path to what was referred to then and now as Manifest Destiny.

Prevalent at the time in the United States was the idea that the American people were destined to fulfill some future greatness—the notion that racially, religiously, economically, and certainly politically, the United States of America represented the vanguard of a brave new world, and all nations would benefit from interaction with the United States. This thinking was not unlike the notion that would be given a name by the end of the century in Rudyard Kipling's famous poem entitled "The White Man's Burden."

But more importantly, these early notions of Manifest Destiny colored and influenced early U.S.–Latin American relations because Manifest Destiny created a sense of benevolent paternalism in the United States, the diffusionist notion that all contact between Latin America and the United States would be advantageous to the Latin Americans and would ultimately be for their own good.

Manifest Destiny and U.S.–Latin American Relations

The term "Manifest Destiny" began to appear in print around the 1850s in the United States. John L. O'Sullivan is given credit for coining the phrase in an editorial on the annexation of Texas in 1946 when he argued that "other nations" had no business intruding into the affairs of the United States to hinder "the fulfillment of our manifest destiny to overspread the continent allotted by Providence for the free development of our yearly multiplying millions." Later in the same editorial, O'Sullivan echoed these words by arguing that the rapidly growing population of the United States "is too evident to leave us in doubt of the manifest design of Providence in regard to the occupation of this continent."[7]

At the time, the phrase "Manifest Destiny" meant simply that the United States had the right—granted by God (thus the word "destiny")—to spread across the entire North American continent. The religious sentiment of nineteenth-century Americans in general should not be underestimated. Many believed that the United States was sacred land that had been given to them by God.

Another interesting phenomenon besides religion in shaping the notion of a predestined expansion over the continent was the fact that since the founding of the thirteen British colonies, there had been really only one geographical direction to go: west. So throughout its early history, the United States had practiced territorial expansion long before they began to call it Manifest Destiny. The United States had extended its borders in Florida and Louisiana even before Latin America won its freedom from Spain. Other expansions that fell directly under the guise of Manifest Destiny would eventually include Texas, California (and all the land in between), Puerto Rico, the Philippine Islands, Alaska, and Hawaii—although by the time the United States acquired Alaska and Hawaii, some had dropped the phrase Manifest Destiny and replaced it with a shorter one: Imperialism.

But back in the 1820s, the fledgling notions of America's destiny to spread out led over and over again to American settlers moving outside the territorial boundaries of the United States. In almost every instance, American settlers who departed from the territorial United States entered and settled in Latin American territory. The two most blatant examples were the regions of Texas and California, both of which were owned by Spain prior to 1821 and by the sovereign nation of Mexico after 1821. By 1848 they would both become part of the United States of America.

Frederick Pike has demonstrated that perceptions in the United States about land ownership and expansion were very fundamentally different from attitudes in Latin America. He argues that while Americans were self-made and adaptable, Latin Americans tended to hold onto their traditions and customs in a very nonflexible manner. Nineteenth-century Americans believed that God would bless them, and therefore they went out and won his blessings through the sweat of their own work. Conversely, Latin Americans believed that if God wanted them to be blessed in a certain way, he would provide the appropriate blessing despite—or in some cases in spite of—their actions. These differences, according to Pike, made Latin America ripe for manipulation by the industrious and blatantly aggressive North Americans.[8]

Furthermore, Latin American peoples tended to believe that they were bound and obligated to fulfill the destiny that had been assigned to them at birth. By contrast, Americans saw themselves as obligated to take the benefits and aptitudes they had been granted, and then through hard work and the shrewd exercise of control, achieve even better results throughout the course of their lives. So while the Americans practiced Manifest Destiny by conquering and swallowing up more and more territory—mostly at the expense of Mexico—Latin Americans tended to wonder why God had treated them with so much indignity as to permit the United States to manipulate and take advantage of them.[9]

So during the early years of the nineteenth century, the United States began practicing imperialism through territorial expansion across North America. But because the United States expanded into territory that was either already owned by Mexico or Spain, or was eventually purchased from them, the actions of expansionistic American presidents were not viewed predominantly as blatant imperialism or colonialism in the United States or in Europe. Furthermore, the existence of a frontier into which the United States could expand became a safety valve that kept the United States from reverting to the economic stagnation and political problems evident in Europe at the same general time. However, the fact that the United States had a buffer zone for further expansion actually contributed to European jealousy at this time. European nations had no such luxury, and European empire building actually increased throughout the world, despite the loss of colonies in the western hemisphere by England, France, Spain, and Portugal. So when the

United States and Mexico began to disagree on the status of the Mexican territory of Texas, Europeans sat back to enjoy the show. Surely Mexico was on the verge of teaching the upstart Americans a valuable lesson.

THE TEXAS QUESTION

In the early 1830s, Mexico began to suspect, anticipate, and even fear U.S. territorial expansion and aggression along the northern Mexican frontier, and especially in Texas. Mexicans had watched as the United States acquired Louisiana in 1803. Mexicans observed as the United States slowly took all of Florida by 1820. Justifiably, Mexico began to fear that Texas might be next on the list of U.S. expansion possibilities. At this time Mexico was led by President Antonio López de Santa Anna. He became the president of Mexico in 1833 and remained in power more or less until 1855 when he was forcibly pushed into exile by the Mexican people. To state that this period of Mexican history was problematic would be a considerable understatement. Chaos and disorder caused much hardship, and the political and economic well-being of Mexico was seriously undermined.[10]

Part of the problem in Mexico was Santa Anna himself. As Michael Meyer, William Sherman, and Susan Deeds state in their well-written history of Mexico, "Between May 1833 and August 1855 the [Mexican] presidency changed hands thirty-six times, the average term being about seven and a half months. Santa Anna occupied the presidential chair on eleven different occasions, and his whim was Mexico's imperative. Even when he was out of office he was a force to be reckoned with."[11]

But Santa Anna was not Mexico's only problem. The coming years would be among the darkest Mexico had endured since the Spanish conquest in the early 1500s. In 1829 Spain pulled off a half-hearted invasion of Mexico in a vain attempt to reassert control over its one-time colony. In 1836 the Texas situation came to a head. In 1838 France briefly landed troops in Mexico to protest the treatment of French pastry chefs. In 1846 the United States declared war on Mexico, and by 1848 succeeded in acquiring almost half of the total northern Mexican territory. Santa Anna played a significant role in all of these tragedies.

The problems in Texas that eventually culminated in Mexico's loss of most of its northern territory began as early as 1803 with the Louisiana Purchase. With Louisiana territory in U.S. control, the international border in North America lay between the Spanish Empire and the fledgling United States. As a colony of Spain at that time, Mexico was nevertheless concerned about several potential threats along its northern borderlands including encroachments by Russia and Britain in the northwest and by United States in Texas and California.[12]

By the early 1820s, Mexican government officials including Santa Anna decided that the best way to strengthen the northern Mexican border was to send as many Mexican settlers there as possible. However, the problem with this solution became immediately apparent. Most of the young men who would have been sent north as settlers to fortify the new border between Mexico and the United States had died in the decade-long struggle for Mexican independence. There were simply not enough young men to send north because they were needed in Central and Southern Mexico to keep the Mexican economy growing.

So Mexico implemented perhaps one of the strangest solutions in the history of Mexican American relations. They decided to invite and encourage foreign immigration in Texas as a way of quickly populating the area. And the foreign nation that provided almost all of the settlers for Texas was none other than the United States. Scholars have argued this decision, and the *non sequitur* nature of the logic, countless times in the recent and not so recent past. After all, if one of Mexico's principal dilemmas was finding a way to prevent the occupation and eventual annexation of Texas by foreign powers—*especially* the United States—it seems quite strange to approach the United States and offer to let thousands of settlers from the United States enter the territory.

Nevertheless, the decision was made and the United States responded eagerly. Many statesmen and politicians in the U.S. government had looked west to Texas as a primary option for American expansion on the continent. So when Mexico appeared amenable to the settlement of Texas by Americans, the United States saw it as nothing less than destiny.

In 1821 an American citizen named Moses Austin received permission from the Mexican government to bring around 300 families into Texas from the United States for purposes of settling and populating the territory. However, several provisos were imposed on Austin's group by the Mexican government, and these stipulations would apply to not only Austin and his followers, but to most of the American settlers who desired to move into the Texas territory thereafter. First of all, the U.S. citizens were required to either profess Roman Catholicism or convert to Catholicism after arrival in Texas. Second, they had to agree to abide by the laws of Mexico while in Texas—U.S. law would have no bearing on their lives there. Third, they were forbidden from settling on lands that were deemed "too close" to coasts, waterways, or international borders, and in most instances were restricted from obtaining more than 70 square miles of Texas land. Finally, they were encouraged to apply for Mexican citizenship. There was an economic benefit attached to the deal as well: settlers in Texas were exempt from paying taxes for up to four years.[13]

Unfortunately, Moses Austin never made it to Texas; he died soon after striking the deal with the Mexican government. However, his son Stephen F. Austin carried out the original plan and moved the group of settlers across the border into Mexico. Not long afterwards, literally thousands of *Norteamericanos* began to settle in Mexican territories between Texas and California. The majority of Americans who flooded across the border into Mexico were illegal immigrants. They began to farm and ranch, to build houses, and interact with the Indians and locals. The problem with this situation was soon clearly apparent—these illegal American settlers lived in communities and regions where other legal settlers had established themselves, but they themselves refused to be held to the same laws and statutes established by the Mexican government.

And for Mexico, American migration into Texas posed yet another serious problem. In 1821 when Stephen Austin and his group of settlers began to homestead in Texas, there were only around 2,000 Mexican citizens residing in the territory in addition to the Indian groups that had lived there for centuries. Within a decade, the number of Mexican settlers had not increased dramatically, but the number of American settlers had jumped to more than 7,000. By 1834 the number of Americans was estimated at around 20,000, and two years later it climbed to around 40,000 Americans in Texas. The implications of this rapid influx of American ranchers and farmers into Mexican Texas were staggering. This meant that the predominant language spoken in Texas was English, not Spanish. This meant that the predominant religions practiced in Texas were Protestant, not Catholic. This meant that the U.S. institution of slavery was being practiced in the Mexican state of Texas.[14]

The original Mexican plan that permitted Americans to settle in Texas, become Mexican citizens, and thus fortify the northern border between Mexico and the United States had failed. Mexico attempted to allow U.S. emigration on condition that the settlers would be assimilated into Mexican culture and society. But this plan backfired dramatically in Texas. There was no American assimilation in Texas. How could Americans assimilate with the Mexican population in Texas? The American population in Texas was around twelve times greater than the Mexican population. If anything, social and cultural assimilation in Texas went the other way.

So Mexico began to attempt to control the population of Texas in other ways than simply demanding that they become Mexican citizens and convert to Roman Catholicism. But Mexico had to be cautious; Mexico had to find a way to control American settlers in Texas without antagonizing them. Mexicans knew that if they antagonized the Americans, Texas would likely try to secede and join the United States.

In 1829 Mexico abolished slavery and emancipated all slaves living in Mexican states and territories. This was an attempt to curtail the number of American settlers who were crossing the border illegally and bringing black slaves with them. Then, in 1830 the Mexican government ordered a cessation of all U.S. emigration into the Mexican state of Texas. Americans were still welcome to settle in other Mexican territories, such as California, but Texas was now off limits to U.S. citizens. But this plan also failed. As a result of this 1830 restriction, the U.S. settlers who would have fortified the

Texan economy were restricted from entering legally. But the criminals and other undesirables who had entered Texas all along continued to cross the border illegally.[15]

When these attempts at controlling the situation in large measure failed, the Mexican government reverted to a practice that had achieved limited success years earlier under the Spanish Empire: they constructed presidios (small military outposts) across the borderlands and stationed military garrisons in remote areas whose responsibilities included keeping the peace, contending with Indian groups, monitoring the activities of American settlers, and preventing new illegal immigrants from settling down in Mexican territories.

When these presidios also failed to produce any meaningful results, Mexico made perhaps their wisest move in the whole Texan situation. The Mexican government formally combined the Mexican states of Texas and Coahuila into one territorial political boundary; in effect, Mexico created one state out of two preexisting territories. This was a very shrewd, albeit defensive maneuver on the part of Mexico. If the Americans tried to remove Texas from Mexican sovereignty, the Mexican government could claim that Texas was in fact half of a state and could not be divided in such a manner. And even though this move was an intelligent, defensive plan, it came too late to stop the aggressive American Texans from eventually seceding from Mexico.[16]

At this point, Mexican President Santa Anna and his government must have reached the end of their creativity, because they tried a couple of solutions that lacked serious foresight or practicability. For instance, Mexico attempted to round up all illegal settlers and send them back to the United States. When this failed miserably, Santa Anna tried to make it illegal for American settlers in Texas to own firearms. Again, this solution was impossible to enforce, and it would have rendered the Texan settlements defenseless against aggressive Indian groups.

Texans who were fed up with Mexican oversight and the political maneuvering of Santa Anna decided to fight for greater self-sufficiency by asking the Mexican government to grant them independent statehood by separating them from Coahuila. To this end, in 1833 Stephen Austin traveled to Mexico City to deliver the petition in person on behalf of the Texans. The Mexican government responded in 1834 by charging Austin with insurrection and throwing him in prison where they left him for over a year.

The sparks flew a couple of years later when Santa Anna used troops to quell an uprising in another northern Mexican state, Zacatecas. When that rebellion was put down, Santa Anna believed that the Texans would soon mount their own insurgence against the Mexican government, so he marched his troops north. In fact, Texas had *not* been planning a revolution or a secession from Mexico at that time. But Texans—or Texians as they began to call themselves—did want to govern themselves as a free Mexican state.

When word arrived that Santa Anna was marching an army north to make sure they did not rebel, they did just that. On October 1, 1835, Texans revolted against the Mexican government. Their decision was partially based on the fact that they wanted to govern themselves under Mexican law and not have Mexican governors sent to watch over them. But also at stake was the fact that Santa Anna had recently toppled the central Mexican government, again, and thrown out the old Mexican Constitution of 1824. Texas refused to accept Santa Anna as a dictator who ruled arbitrarily with no constitutional authority.[17]

In 1836, the Mexican military leaders in the San Antonio area demanded that settlers in the surrounding communities surrender their firearms to the military garrisons. The Texans in nearby Gonzales refused. So the Mexican troops attempted to disarm the Texans by force. The Texans responded by firing on the Mexican troops and eventually driving them out of the area. Soon, Texan fighters rallied behind Stephen Austin—who had recently returned from jail in Mexico City in 1835—in the fight for Texan freedom from Mexican oppression. On March 2, 1836, Austin and others declared Texas a free and independent nation with a new constitution and a new president, David Burnet. But Santa Anna and the Mexican military determined that the Texans would not tarnish Mexican honor by seceding from Mexico.

"Remember the Alamo" and the Republic of Texas

The confrontation between Americans and Mexicans at the Alamo, which has become something of an epic in U.S. history, occurred in the crumbling adobe missions of San Antonio. One of those missions, called the Alamo by the Texans, was the location where around 1,500 of Santa Anna's Mexican military engaged the 180 Americans inside the Alamo. When the fighting concluded, all 180 of the Americans were killed, while Santa Anna lost less than 500 soldiers. This event has taken on near mythic proportions in U.S. history; books and movies have tried to recreate these events several times, and some have succeeded better than others.[18]

The immediate events that led up to the actual Battle of the Alamo took almost two weeks. On February 24, 1836, Santa Anna's military forces—which numbered as many as 1,500—began a siege of the Alamo with the intent of forcing the Texans into submission. During the following thirteen days, several groups of Texans managed to get either into or out of the Alamo carrying messages and bringing needed supplies and munitions.

The final battle occurred on March 6, 1836, around 5:00 in the morning when the Mexican army began a coordinated assault on the compound. The actual fighting was over in less than two hours. The final stages of the conflict were conducted in the close quarters of the Alamo compound where several famous or soon-to-be famous men died including William Barrett Travis, James Bowie, and David Crockett.[19] Six weeks after this slaughter in San Antonio, Texans at nearby San Jacinto fought with Mexican troops on April 21 while shouting "remember the Alamo!" This appears to be the first recorded uttering of the now famous phrase, although historians are unable to attribute the statement to any specific individual.[20]

Several weeks after the massacre at the Alamo, General Santa Anna ordered the execution of around 300 more Texan prisoners of war who had been captured at the nearby town of Goliad. Texans were enraged. Hundreds rallied to the Texan army now under the leadership of Sam Houston. Despite all the disadvantages suffered by the Texans during the fighting, they had the advantage of defending their own homes and their families.

Under Houston's command, the Texans finally defeated Santa Anna's forces on April 21, 1836, at the Battle of San Jacinto. Not only was the Mexican military soundly defeated during the fighting, but Santa Anna himself was captured by Texan troops and forced to surrender. Sam Houston eventually sent Santa Anna off to Washington, D.C., where he was mildly interrogated by President Andrew Jackson and then permitted to return to Mexico in early 1837.

Now that Texas was a free and independent nation, the Texan citizens petitioned for annexation into the United States of America. However, the sheer size of Texas, coupled with the problems over the issue of slavery, postponed Texan admittance to the Union. Antislavery advocates in the United States could not swallow the prospects of admitting another slave state to the Union, especially one as large as Texas. So in 1837 the U.S. government simply extended diplomatic recognition to the new Lone Star Nation and told them to be patient. It would take almost a decade before Texas could be admitted as a slave state into the Union.[21]

THE MEXICAN WAR

Mexico was bitter over the loss of Texas. Mexico also became distressed when the United States unashamedly recognized the new nation of Texas. Mexico claimed that the aggression of the American settlers, coupled with U.S. notions of Manifest Destiny, was to blame for the loss of the Texas territory. But Mexico had always had problems with the northern territories along the Spanish borderlands. Even during the colonial years, Spanish officials and viceroys in Mexico City were usually at a loss about how to populate the northern borderlands and subdue the Indian nations that had lived along the borderlands for centuries. Now the nation of Mexico had finally lost Texas to the antagonistic *Norteamericanos.*

In the United States the Texas issue became a problem for the U.S. government. Patriotic American settlers and farmers, mixed with belligerent toughs and roustabouts, flocked into Texas to defend the Americans living there from Indian hostilities and ongoing Mexican raids that continued even after 1837. Many of these new comers were from Tennessee and Kentucky, which were slave states; they brought their values and beliefs on slavery into Texas with them.

Meanwhile the question of slavery in Texas continued to be debated in the U.S. Congress. Many northern congressmen argued that the South was deliberately using the Texas issue to generate support for the institution of slavery. On the other hand, several southern congressmen claimed that if Texas were not quickly brought into the United States as a state, the British or even the Mexicans would very likely try to gain or regain control of it. While the debate continued, conditions in Texas worsened. Economic depression and increased hostilities in Texas promised to produce a crisis if some action were not taken soon.

In 1844, James K. Polk was elected president of the United States. His platform consisted mostly of promises in the name of Manifest Destiny. He was born in North Carolina and had served in the Tennessee legislature and later as the governor of the same state. During the presidential election campaign of 1844, Polk claimed that U.S. expansion should be given greater attention, especially in the territories of Texas, Oregon, and California. When European powers, especially the British, questioned his intentions in the Oregon territory—where they also had considerable interests— Polk pulled out the 1823 Monroe Doctrine, dusted it off, and claimed that the document was all the justification the United States needed to expand into any area in North America (including annexing Texas or claiming the Oregon territory to keep the British out).[22]

Early in 1845, the U.S. Congress approved a treaty of annexation between the United States of America and the sovereign nation of Texas. The Texans voted in favor of becoming a U.S. state in December of the same year, and Texas was admitted as the twenty-eighth state in the union and the fifteenth slave state. The situation in Oregon Country between the United States and the British was also quickly resolved without violence.

Next, President Polk shrewdly saw an opportunity to acquire more territory from Mexico. In 1845, Polk appointed John Slidell as a special diplomat to Mexico, and sent him there to negotiate the sale of the California and New Mexico territories to the United States. The United States was willing to pay up to $20 million for the territory that lay between Texas and the Pacific coast of California. However, Slidell was rebuffed by the indignant Mexican politicians and sent home. The Mexican government had threatened that if the United States annexed Texas it would lead to war between the two nations. When the United States went ahead with the treaty of annexation in 1845, Mexico had broken off all diplomatic relations with the United States and therefore could refuse to interact with Slidell as a U.S. ambassador.[23]

Years later, after the Mexican War was over, the United States tended to view the conflict as the unavoidable consequence of a shared national border between a powerful expanding nation and an irresponsible and irrational one. Whether or not the Mexican War was inevitable, the Mexicans saw the situation very differently, viewing the Americans as overly aggressive and taking by force what they had no business offering to purchase in the first place.

The actual fighting of the Mexican War began over a technicality. When Texas seceded from Mexico and was subsequently annexed into the United States, the border between Texas and Mexico was never bilaterally agreed upon. Texas and the United States argued that the border between the two areas was the Rio Grande River. On the other hand, Mexico contested that the border was actually the Rio Nueces River, to the north. In the spring of 1845, President Polk sent troops into Texas under the leadership of General Zachary Taylor (who eventually became president of the United States himself). Taylor's troops slowly worked their way down the Texas coast, and when word came early in 1846 that Mexico had refused the offer delivered by special envoy Slidell, Taylor was ordered to move his troops across the Nueces River and approach the Rio Grande.

When Taylor marched his troops through this "no-man's-land" approaching the Rio Grande, Mexico saw this action as an aggressive act of war—technically, according to the Mexicans, a U.S. military force had entered the sovereign nation of Mexico when they crossed the Nueces River. So Mexican General Mariano Arista sent his own soldiers across the Rio Grande to meet the belligerent American troops, all the while claiming that he was still on Mexican soil. The first shots were fired on April 25, 1846, in this no-man's-land between the two rivers—each power claiming they were on their own territory.[24]

When news of the fighting reached Washington, President Polk told the U.S. Congress that American blood had been shed on American soil by an invasion army from Mexico. The Congress declared war on Mexico immediately on May 13, 1846. By that time, General Taylor had managed to drive the Mexican forces back across the Rio Grande and had begun to pursue them into Mexico.

The Mexican War that ensued would be fought on three major fronts over the next two years. Both sides were admittedly unprepared for the war, and both sides were economically ill-equipped to wage a drawn-out conflict. But Europeans believed that Mexico had the added advantage of over 300 years of experience in North America. In their eyes the Americans did not stand a chance. Many European rulers were confident that the United States would receive a good and well-deserved beating from the more disciplined and experienced Mexican military.

Texas and the Northern Mexican Expedition

Northern Mexico was quickly and literally conquered by General Taylor's forces. He eventually occupied several key Mexican cities and defeated Santa Anna's forces in a few major engagements. Taylor also managed to draw much press attention to his exploits in northern Mexico, which aided his presidential campaigning in 1848, the same year the Mexican War ended.

Mexican forces were initially confident in their ability to not only defeat the American military in Texas, but to fully reconquer and subdue Texas as well, returning it to the sovereign nation of Mexico where it belonged. The Mexicans had believed that their larger numbers and hundreds of years of proud European military heritage would be enough to defeat the Americans. But after several engagements with the American troops, Mexican military leaders realized that they would need to exert all of their military might just to survive.

Early in May of 1846, Taylor's forces reached Matamoros just across the Rio Grande. After several months of planning and supplying his troops, Taylor began preparing to march against the next Mexican stronghold in northern Mexico, Monterrey. On September 21, 1846, Taylor's forces attacked the city of Monterrey. They were outnumbered and outgunned, but after four days of fighting they took the city as the Mexican troops withdrew. By the middle of November, Taylor's forces captured the nearby city of Saltillo. Here in the newly won northern Mexican territories, General Taylor and his forces prepared to meet the even larger armies of Mexico which were marching north to stop them in their southern progress.[25]

California and New Mexico

While General Zachary Taylor was slowly pushing south toward Mexico City, other American military commanders made their way into the northwestern Mexican territories. One of President Polk's greatest ambitions was to be the president who took California. As a result, the Mexican territory between Texas and California would, of necessity, need to be part of the complete package. Therefore, even though the most important fighting was taking place in northern Mexico, American troops were sent to these other areas to claim and maintain them for U.S. occupation after the war.

By mid-year 1846, U.S. troops under the command of General Stephen W. Kearney and Brigadier General Alexander Doniphan entered the New Mexico territory. After the Americans succeeded in overwhelming the unprepared Mexican troops in Santa Fe on August 18, General Kearny took most of the troops and continued west toward California, while General Doniphan remained in Santa Fe as the commanding officer of the remaining U.S. soldiers in the New Mexico territory.

However, Doniphan did not remain in New Mexico long. By early 1847 he marched his troops southeast toward El Paso and modern-day Ciudad Juarez. By February 1847, Doniphan and his soldiers began a direct march into the Mexican state of Chihuahua, which was also quickly subdued. With New Mexico and Chihuahua under U.S. control, Doniphan moved his troops to southeast to Saltillo and Monterrey to fortify General Taylor's forces in that area.

Meanwhile, General Kearny and his troops had set out for California back in September of 1846. Unknown to them at the time, an American explorer named John C. Frémont had journeyed to California in 1845 and fomented an insurrection among American settlers in California, encouraging them to rebel against the Mexican government. In July of 1846 U.S. Commodore John D. Sloat sailed into Monterey harbor on the California coast intending to capture California for the United States.

By the time General Kearney and his forces arrived in California at the end of 1846, Commodore Sloat's U.S. naval forces and Frémont's rebels were engaged in skirmishes with Mexican troops in several locations along the California coast. Kearney's forces managed to humiliate the demoralized Mexican soldiers in several key battles near Los Angeles, and Mexican military commanders finally surrendered the territory in January of 1847.[26]

The Gulf of Mexico and the Southern Expedition

While Taylor, Kearney, Doniphan, and Frémont occupied Northern Mexico, California and New Mexico, another prong in the U.S. attack of Mexico began to fall into place. And even though the U.S. troops based between Texas and California were important to the war effort for the United States, some of the most important events of the entire war occurred in the Gulf of Mexico and along the Mexican east coast. And since most of the northern campaigns in the Mexican War had gone very badly for Mexico by this time, the Mexicans began to feel somewhat desperate.

In 1846 the Mexican government turned to and accepted help from the one source that was just fanatical enough to try to fight the United States against surmounting odds. They agreed that former president Antonio López de Santa Anna could return to Mexico from his Caribbean exile. Because of his duplicity after being captured in the aftermath of the Alamo massacre years earlier, the Mexican government had exiled Santa Anna to Jamaica where he had remained between 1844 and 1846. When the Mexican government began to collapse and the American military seemed assured of victory, former President Santa Anna decided to return to Mexico to rule the nation and drive the Americans out. Santa Anna may have felt that this war with the United States provided an excellent opportunity for him to reverse the embarrassments he had suffered in Texas a decade earlier when U.S. troops captured and humiliated him.

After spending time in Jamaica, Santa Anna had relocated to the larger island of Cuba which was still a colony of Spain. Santa Anna was willing and even eager to return to Mexico, to fight the Americans, and to reclaim some of his lost honor. But U.S. General Winfield Scott, who had accepted command of the southern expedition that was charged with blockading the Mexican east coast, believed that if Santa Anna were permitted through the blockade and allowed to land in Mexico he would stir up resistance to U.S. troops. Nevertheless, Santa Anna persuaded President Polk that if he were permitted to land in Mexico he would encourage the Mexican government to submit to U.S. demands thus ending the war more quickly. Polk issued orders that General Scott and the U.S. Navy allow Santa Anna to pass through the blockade.

Santa Anna landed at Veracruz on August 16, 1846. He immediately proclaimed himself president of Mexico and received the approval of many of the politicians and much of the population, most of whom saw Santa Anna as a savior figure who would deliver Mexico from the aggressions of the United States. Then, instead of negotiating a truce between the United States and Mexico as he had promised, Santa Anna began to build a large military force to repel the American advance led by General Taylor in northern Mexico.

As Santa Anna began to march north to engage General Taylor's forces, Americans realized Santa Anna's duplicity and took immediate action. In March of 1847, General Scott landed several thousand troops on the Mexican east coast near the city of Veracruz. By March 28, the city surrendered and General Scott began his march overland toward Mexico City, following roughly the same route used by Hernan Cortes during the Spanish conquest of Mexico 328 years earlier in 1519.[27]

THE END OF THE WAR AND THE TREATY OF GUADALUPE HIDALGO

Early in 1847, Santa Anna began his northward march designed to repel American soldiers from proceeding further into Mexico. When General Taylor learned of Santa Anna's approach, he began to fortify his position in order to defend himself. On February 22, 1847, Santa Anna's army attacked the Americans just outside the city of Saltillo. The fighting was extremely bloody and almost 1,000 Americans were killed, while Mexican casualties numbered almost 2,000. Historians have argued that if Santa Anna had remained and engaged Taylor's forces, he probably would have defeated them. But he decided instead that it was more important to retreat to the south and engage General Scott's inexorable advance on Mexico City. General Scott reached Cerro Gordo in April of 1847 and found Santa Anna's forces ready for battle. The Mexican forces were routed and they fled to the west. General Scott then continued inland approaching the Mexican city of Puebla.

Santa Anna prepared to defend the capital city from invasion by General Scott. By August, Scott's forces arrived and the fighting outside Mexico City began. Several major battles occurred on the outskirts of the capital, and the Mexicans suffered heavy losses every time. Finally the conflict came to a conclusion at Chapultepeque. In September of 1847 the U.S. forces overran the Mexican fortifications that were, by that time, defended almost entirely by cadets impressed from the military college of Mexico. On September 12, 1847, American troops entered Mexico City. After five months of bloody fighting, the Mexican War had ended.

Santa Anna was forced into exile again by disgusted Mexican politicians and citizens alike, and the Mexican government began negotiations with the United States over terms of the peace treaty. The Treaty of Guadalupe Hidalgo—named after the small Mexican village where the treaty was signed—was officially endorsed by both sides on February 2, 1848. The treaty guaranteed that the state of Texas would remain a part of the United States of America, and that the official border between Texas and Mexico would remain the Rio Grande River. The treaty also formalized the transfer of California to the United States. Finally, the New Mexico territory was ceded to the United States because American troops had occupied it during the fighting.

The United States had gained all of the territory between Texas and California, including the future American states of New Mexico, Arizona, Nevada, Utah, Colorado, and Wyoming. Including Texas and California, this was a territorial increase of over 1 million square miles for the United States.[28] In return, the United States agreed to pay Mexico $15 million and to cancel all outstanding Mexican debts owed to the United States.[29]

CONCLUSIONS

Why did Mexico lose the Mexican War? As discussed earlier, several European nations believed that Mexico would soundly defeat the Americans. But Mexico was so disrupted and disjointed by internal economic and political chaos that they had very little unity. Mexico defeated itself before the war even started. The degree of difference between the social levels in Mexican society created poverty, despair, apathy, and indifference among the bulk of the Mexican population.

As a result of the Mexican War, Mexico suffered increased economic disruptions that resulted from creditor nations withdrawing their support from Mexico's increasingly unstable markets. Mexico also lost so many young men as casualties of war that the subsequent loss of manpower in Mexico was overwhelmingly debilitating. Finally, Mexico had to live with the ignominy of having suffered defeat to the United States. For perhaps the first time since Mexico won its independence from Spain, Mexicans and

Latin Americans in general realized that they were in fact far behind the curve in terms of political and economic development.

But perhaps the greatest conclusion Mexico drew from the Mexican War was the fact that they now realized that the United States was quickly becoming (if it had not already become so) the most powerful country in the western hemisphere. Mexico was weaker economically, politically, and certainly militarily than the United States, and it would be very difficult, if not impossible, to reverse this situation.

North of the Rio Grande, immediate reactions were joyful. The United States had gained an enormous expansion of territory and innumerable natural resources. They had gained new lands for development and territorial growth. But as time went on, some began to question the motives of President Polk and others in waging the war. American statesmen decades later would publicly question or criticize American actions during the Mexican War.

Some time after the war was over, U.S. politicians tried to assuage their consciences by arguing that the act of depriving Mexico of half of its territory was justified because it ensured the survival of democracy and republican government in North America. Other arguments defending American actions during the war bordered on the ridiculous by claiming that the war was actually a benefit to Mexico because now the Mexican capital, Mexico City, was more centrally located in the interior of the nation.

Meanwhile, Mexico tried to put things in order once again. In 1853 they called Santa Anna out of exile once again to serve as president. This would be his last term. Mexicans finally gave up on him in repugnance when he agreed to the terms of the Gadsden Purchase wherein he sold almost 30,000 square miles of territory on the southern border of New Mexico and Arizona to the United States for $10 million. His justification was that Mexico needed the money and did not need that territory for any useful purpose. Mexico exiled him again, this time to Colombia. He tried to return to Mexico at least twice more before his death in 1876, but both times Mexican authorities refused to even let him dock in Mexican harbors or come ashore.

In terms of U.S.–Latin American relations, the Mexican War was a turning point for all of Latin America, not just Mexico. These events were important in shaping the future of U.S.–Latin American associations. Most European nations had believed that Mexico would win this struggle. After all, Mexico had a longer history in the hemisphere, had a larger military, and had the advantage of fighting on their home territory. The U.S. victory stunned not only Mexico, but the rest of the world. Europe realized that the United States was quickly becoming a major power. Latin America became conscious of the fact that the United States might not stop with some Mexican territory.

And even though, as Lester Langley observes, Latin American society was rooted in a militaristic way of thinking following the wars for independence, they began to realize that their militarization would not be enough to stand up to the aggressions of the United States, which was militarily and economically stronger than any other Latin American nation.[30] As a result of the Mexican War, the United States was correctly viewed as an emerging world power by Latin America and Europe. Furthermore, Europe could no longer easily compete with the United States in terms of military might or economic influence in the western hemisphere because the territorial addition to the United States following the Mexican War gave the Americans almost unlimited natural resources and access to both the Atlantic and Pacific Oceans. The Mexican War changed the United States and its relations with the Latin America and the world forever.

5

Nineteenth-Century U.S. Imperialism and the Spanish American War

Unless a man believes that there is something great for him to do, he can do nothing great. Hence so many of the captains and reformers of the world have relied on fate and the stars. A great idea springs up in a man's soul; it agitates his whole being, transports him from the ignorant present and makes him feel the future in a moment. It is natural for a man so possessed to conceive that he is a special agent for working out into practice the thought that has been revealed to him. Why should such a revelation be made to him, why should he be enabled to perceive what is hidden to others—if not that he should carry it into practice?   — William Walker

During the year preceding the outbreak of the Spanish War I was Assistant Secretary of the Navy. While my party was in opposition, I had preached, with all the fervor and zeal I possessed, our duty to intervene in Cuba, and to take this opportunity of driving the Spaniard from the Western World. Now that my party had come to power, I felt it incumbent on me, by word and deed, to do all I could to secure the carrying out of the policy in which I so heartily believed; and from the beginning I had determined that, if a war came, somehow or other, I was going to the front.

— Theodore Roosevelt

Following the end of the Mexican War, the United States emerged as the major power in the western hemisphere. The United States had demonstrated that it had the ability—militarily and economically—to wage and win a war within the hemisphere. And although at first the United States was quick to defend its actions as retaliatory in nature against Mexican aggression, Latin

America's worst fears were confirmed in 1848 when the Treaty of Guadalupe Hidalgo was ratified. The United States was aggressive and expansionistic, and Latin America was in its sights.

Over the next fifty years until the turn of the twentieth century, several events occurred in the hemisphere that served to confirm this notion of the United States as an aggressive northern neighbor. Even though the United States would not be seriously viewed as a practitioner of blatant imperialism until after the Spanish American War in 1898, several incidents prior to that 1898 conflict served as precursors to U.S. hemispheric hegemony. One of the problems was that Europe and Latin America both believed they saw hypocrisy and duplicity on the part of the United States in the way it had handled the Mexican War. It did not help matters that within mere months of California becoming an official U.S. territory, gold was discovered there, sparking one of the greatest gold rushes in modern history.

The California Gold Rush of 1849 had an enormous influence on U.S.–Latin American relations, and not just because of resentments over the fact that the California territory had recently been confiscated from Mexico. All across the United States men tried to get to California as quickly as possible to gain the instant wealth they thought they would find there. But getting to California was not easy in 1849. There were basically three ways that gold-seekers traveled west to California. The first was to trek overland, or by river, or through a combination of both, from the east coast, the south, or the developing states of the Midwest. But overland expeditions were fraught with danger from exposure, harsh conditions, and American Indian tribes. And even if a traveler had the good fortune to not be particularly troubled by these dangers, the journey overland took as long as four to six months to complete.

The second option was to travel to California by sea. In 1849 this meant a likely prospector would need to depart from a port city on the U.S. east coast or Gulf of Mexico, sail down the Atlantic coast of South America, round Cape Horn in Argentina, sail north along the South American Pacific coast, and finally land in California. This option did not help men arrive in California any faster, and often it actually took longer to sail to California than to walk there; in some cases men arrived in California a year after they embarked. In addition, sailing was no less dangerous than traveling the overland routes, although the dangers were different and specific to sea life such as storms, poor food and water supplies, diseases, and other perils.

There was a third option that usually consisted of a combination of land and sea options, but the dangers and the travel time involved were not lessened by combining travel options in wagon trains and ships. However, some innovative explorers and businessmen realized that they could cut the travel time to California in half by just such a combination of water and land routes to the west. Ships began to carry would-be gold diggers to Nicaragua or Panama where they trekked across the narrow Central American isthmus.

They had to cut their way through dense jungles and navigate rivers on their way from one ocean to the other. Once they arrived on the Pacific side they could continue by ship to the southern California coast and arrive several months faster—if all went well—than by either of the previously mentioned two options.

The results of this search for the fastest route to California had several effects on U.S.–Latin American relations. Many more American men began to arrive in the gold fields in California, and many of them had traveled through the jungles of Central America. They began to interact with the peoples and governments of these countries. Often poor Nicaraguans and Panamanians were hired to guide Americans through the jungle passes and along the rivers. Many were paid as porters to carry supplies for American travelers.

This increased contact between Americans and Central Americans was the circumstance that led to the eventual ratification of several treaties between the United States, the nations of Central America, and Great Britain, which eventually changed the destiny of Nicaragua, Panama, Colombia, and other nations in the area. In the long-term, this early American presence in Central America eventually led to the creation of the nation of Panama and the construction of the Panama Canal in the early years of the twentieth century. It also led to certainly one of the strangest incidents in U.S.–Latin American relations in the 1800s, if not in the entire relationship between Latin American countries and the United States: the extraordinary episode of William Walker.

WILLIAM WALKER AND THE CONQUEST OF NICARAGUA

During the 1850s, one ambitious American changed the course of Nicaraguan history and U.S.–Latin American relations. This man was William Walker (1824–1860). Prior to the U.S. Civil War, Walker was a journalist in New Orleans. But Walker was not just a journalist. By 1848 he had successfully earned M.D. and J.D. degrees from accredited universities in the United States. After publishing several inflammatory and expository columns in a New Orleans newspaper related to slavery and U.S. desires to annex Cuba, he was driven out of town. He eventually found his way to California where he again took up journalism in San Francisco. His career as a journalist placed him in a position to not only be aware of current political trends and international developments, but to see how to exploit situations on the basis of historical events.[1]

At roughly the same time, the famous American entrepreneur and builder Cornelius Vanderbilt (1794–1877) was engaged in business transactions in Nicaragua which involved the construction of a rail line across the isthmus and the possibility of a canal as well. Vanderbilt made a lot of money transporting men to the gold fields in California, across the jungles of Nicaragua. Soon, Walker and Vanderbilt clashed in Nicaragua as they both got caught up in the diplomacy between the U.S. and British governments over canal rights in Central America.

At the time, Nicaragua was a particularly good location for a canal or railroad line because the San Juan River that separated Nicaragua and Costa Rica was navigable by fairly large vessels from the Atlantic Ocean side. The San Juan River emptied from the large Lake Nicaragua. This meant that the only place a cut would need to be made for a potential canal was a relatively small area (roughly 50 miles) between the southwest shore of the lake and the Pacific Ocean.

However, Vanderbilt's plans were ground to a halt because of a treaty the United States had entered into with Great Britain. The 1850 Clayton–Bulwer Treaty was named for U.S. Secretary of State John Clayton and British Ambassador Henry Bulwer. Because both the United States and Britain desired to use and even possess territories in Central America, the potential for hostilities and escalated violence between them in the region grew. The Clayton–Bulwer Treaty therefore proposed that neither the United States nor the United Kingdom could build a canal unilaterally in the region. Furthermore, if and when any canal was constructed in Central America, neither the United States nor the United Kingdom could militarily reinforce the canal zone, or formally colonize territories in Central America.[2]

The treaty specifically mentioned the vaguely defined coastlines of the Mosquito Coast in Honduras and Nicaragua as being off limits to such activities. In effect, the Clayton–Bulwer Treaty denied the United States the ability to construct a canal in Nicaragua—or anywhere in Central America for that matter—without joint effort and approval by the British. When Americans realized how they had been restricted as a result of the treaty, many were furious. They believed the United States had been duped by the British, and many Americans, including William Walker, saw the treaty as a threat to Manifest Destiny. A large part of the resentment Americans felt over the treaty grew out of the fact that the British already controlled large areas of land in Central America including the mouth of the San Juan River in Nicaragua. Even worse, the British claimed ownership of some contested territory in Guatemala that they called British Honduras, which they had possessed as early as the eighteenth century.[3]

So in 1853, in response to his frustrations over British hegemony and interference with U.S. Manifest Destiny, William Walker organized a quasi-military group of around fifty men and used them to invade Baja California just south of the U.S. California border. His motives were questionable, and his ability to influence U.S. policy in Central America was not clearly delineated by his expedition to Baja. However, he determined that the United States should not sit idly by while the British exercised more and more control over Nicaragua and the surrounding areas. Once in Mexico, Walker declared Baja an independent nation and fully expected the U.S. Congress to annex the territory, much the same way the United States had done in Texas several years earlier. But the U.S. government did not react in the way Walker desired.

When the United States did not immediately respond to Walker's impetuous act of conquest, Walker declared the neighboring Mexican state of Sonora an independent nation as well and confirmed himself president of both of the new nations of Sonora and Baja. Now Walker was the president of two new nations, but he could not get the United States to annex either one, or to even acknowledge his achievements. In fact, the United States was at that time involved in erstwhile and somewhat clandestine negotiations with Antonio López de Santa Anna, the president of Mexico, over the purchase of some of the very lands William Walker now claimed as his nations. This purchase of land would later become known as the Gadsden Purchase.

So Walker's invasion of northern Mexico collapsed as a result of diminishing supplies and the threat of Mexican retaliation. He and his followers dragged back across the U.S. border and faced charges of using military force to violate international neutrality laws. However, Walker was acquitted because of a public outcry of support, and he continued to write for California papers while he planned his next move. He soon began to build another military group of mercenaries and soldiers of fortune to accompany him on his next adventure in the name of Manifest Destiny. This time, he set his sights farther south, on the troubled nation of Nicaragua, which was the heart of the conflict between the United States and the United Kingdom.

Not only was Nicaragua the site of international contentions over canal treaties and big business, Nicaragua was also enmeshed in a violent civil war for control of its internal government. Walker and his soldiers departed for Nicaragua in the spring of 1855 and determined to win the entire country for the United States as a new slave state. When the filibusters arrived in Nicaragua, they joined themselves to a group of rebel insurgents and succeeded in capturing the capital city of Granada some months later. Almost exactly one year after his arrival in Central America, William Walker declared himself president of the nation of Nicaragua and presented it to the United States for annexation.[4]

However, the United States was not capable of acting on Walker's brash measures. The British would have certainly been incensed at the annexation of Nicaragua, and may have declared war on the United States over the issue. Furthermore, the slavery question was still so sharply debated in the U.S. Congress and in the streets in the United States that admitting Nicaragua as a slave state was not immediately even possible. So in the early spring of 1857, Nicaragua remained under the control of Walker, and the United States dared not do anything about it.[5]

Meanwhile, other governments in Central America resented the bold American who dared to conquer an entire nation, and began to build a Central American coalition against Walker. The United States decided it must act in order to avoid an even greater international incident than Walker had caused when he captured the nation in the first place. So U.S. troops were sent to Nicaragua to capture Walker and return him to the United States to stand trial again for violation of international neutrality laws. Again, following the trial he was acquitted, but Walker's days were numbered.

The U.S. government and courts considered Walker a flight risk and imposed an international travel ban on him. He was not permitted to leave the country. However, he believed that if he could somehow return to Nicaragua just one more time, he could set things right again. He tried to build another militia out of local roustabouts and mercenaries, but had great difficulty putting them to sea because of the restrictions on his traveling outside the country. He finally managed to sneak past vigilant authorities in 1860 on a pretext of traveling to Cuba by himself for nonaggressive purposes. He sent his army ahead and planned to reunite with his forces in Honduras where they would then invade Nicaragua from the north. But he was captured by the British Navy almost immediately after landing near Trujillo on the northern Honduran coast. The British were delighted to have taken Walker, but were also conscious of the fact that they could easily start an international incident if they kept him, so they turned him over to a local Honduran militia unit which promptly concluded the fiasco by shooting Walker to death in September of 1860.

Although William Walker is still remembered with vehemence in Nicaragua and Central America as a prime example of U.S. imperialism, he remains relatively unknown in the United States today. It is very likely that the United States has forgotten Walker because of the fact that almost immediately after his death in the autumn of 1860, the U.S. Civil War began the following spring and eventually, after much struggle, ended the slavery debates. Without the contentious issue of slavery, the United States was able to add new states to the Union with more ease than before the Civil War when a balance of free and slave states had to be maintained. The only permanent vestige of William Walker in U.S.–Latin American relations is the feeling in Central America that Walker represented the vanguard of U.S. imperialism which, while in its nascent form throughout Walker's adventures, became an ever-present dilemma for the Latin American nations by the end of the nineteenth century.

U.S. INTERVENTIONS IN LATIN AMERICA PRIOR TO 1898

In 1854, three U.S. ambassadors in Ostend, Belgium, developed a course of action designed to liberate Cuba from Spain and subsequently attach it to the United States. Their plan, eventually named the Ostend Manifesto, called for the purchase of the island of Cuba from Spain for $120 million. If the Spanish government were to refuse the offer, then the U.S. military would simply take Cuba from Spain. Ultimately the plan was never implemented because of its aggressive nature, combined with slavery tensions in the United States which mandated the justification of every new slave state.

But the Ostend Manifesto did portray American feelings during the middle of the nineteenth century regarding both Spain and Latin America. With regard to Spain, the United States believed it was only a matter of time before the decrepit Spanish Empire would be forced to abandon Cuba and Puerto Rico. With regard to Latin America, the notion of Manifest Destiny proclaimed—in some ears—that the United States had the right to expand wherever it desired in the hemisphere, regardless of the wishes of the Latin Americans. By the time the U.S. Civil War was over, these ideas of expansionism would be revisited, but the question of Cuba would not be resolved until the end of the century.

While the United States was occupied with the American Civil War between 1861 and 1865, the French decided to conquer and occupy Mexico. Napoleon III, the leader of France, solicited the help of an Austrian prince, Ferdinand Maximilian von Habsburg, who he installed as the new emperor of Mexico once the French military had occupied and subdued that nation. Mexico of course fought to free itself at the same time the North and the South fought the Civil War in the United States. After 1865, America told the French emphatically that their occupation of Mexico was a violation of the Monroe Doctrine. The French pulled out immediately and Mexico, under the leadership of President Benito Juárez, captured the Mexican emperor Maximilian von Habsburg and shot him.[6]

Between the end of the U.S. Civil War and 1898, the United States experienced enormous industrial and commercial growth. Some Americans became quite wealthy, and one of the principal results was that the United States temporarily neglected the Latin American nations more than they had done both before and after. But despite this temporary apathy, the United States managed to get involved in a few important incidents prior to the end of the century, particularly in the Caribbean, Chile, and Venezuela.[7]

In each of these cases, Latin Americans believed that the United States was intervening in situations that did not concern it, and the motives and expectations of the United States were viewed with more and more suspicion and hostility. However, from the American perspective, they believed they were obligated to get involved in Latin America in order to prevent European powers—particularly the British and French—from becoming too enmeshed in Latin American affairs, which could have disastrous repercussions such as the French occupation of Mexico.

The Caribbean Basin

Between 1847 and 1854, the Yucatan Caste War between Mexicans and Indians raged and caused much destabilization in Mexico's Yucatan Peninsula. At one point, the United States believed that one plausible solution to the violence would be to simply annex the Yucatan Peninsula. Eventually this alternative was rejected, but Britain began to wonder if the United States might not eventually desire to obtain most or all of Mexico. In the United States this was not ever really seriously considered for any length of time. But as hostilities in Yucatan quieted down, the United States did engage in much more serious discussions about the island of Cuba. Prior to the American Civil War, many proponents of slavery in the South had favored annexing Cuba as a slave state. These discussions were truncated instantly by the Civil War, and following the fighting, American interest in annexing Cuba diminished somewhat until the end of the century.[8]

Another Caribbean point of interest for expansionistic American statesmen was the Virgin Islands. Prior to William Seward's purchase of Alaska, he tried to convince the U.S. Congress to purchase several pieces of real estate in Latin America and elsewhere, including Panama, Hawaii, Midway, and the Virgin Islands. In 1867, when negotiations began, the Virgin Islands were controlled by the Dutch.[9]

Seward offered to pay more than $7 million for the purchase of the Virgin Islands. The Dutch agreed to the deal and it was sent to the U.S. Senate for ratification. But the Senate could not decide whether they truly wanted the Virgin Islands or whether they wanted to pay that much for them. As the Senate dragged its feet, President Andrew Johnson was impeached in the wake of the American Civil War, and the U.S. government decided to back out of the deal with the Dutch. The international community in Europe and Latin America disdained America's inaction because the United States had initiated the transaction in the first place, and then changed its mind.[10]

Another Caribbean episode prior to 1898 occurred in the Dominican Republic. In 1821 when the Dominican Republic declared its independence from Spain, the United States had refused to extend official diplomatic recognition to the nation because it was composed predominantly of black and mulatto ex-slaves. Then the same year, the Dominican Republic was conquered by Haiti, which shared the island with the Dominicans. Haiti maintained control of the Dominican Republic until 1844 when it finally managed to free itself from Haitian control. But problems in the Dominican Republic multiplied. By 1861, the Dominican Republic had declined so drastically economically and politically that it attempted a solution unprecedented in the history of colonialism in the western hemisphere: the Dominican Republic invited Spain to take it back as a colony. Spain was happy to oblige, but had not completely accomplished the reacquisition of the Dominican Republic by the end of the U.S. Civil War in 1865.[11]

When the United States realized that Spain was attempting to reacquire territory in the hemisphere, the U.S. Congress immediately granted the Dominican Republic official diplomatic recognition as a country in 1866. Spain, unwilling to cross swords with the United States, backed down momentarily and the U.S. government was left to discuss what should happen to the island nation.[12]

By the 1870s, the U.S. government continued to debate the possibilities of simply annexing the Dominican Republic and using the territory for sugar cultivation. But the final decision became bogged down in the inertia of inaction. Eventually, the U.S. Congress concluded that neither the Dominican Republic nor any other Latin American territory would be suitable for annexation into the United States because, as Lester Langley writes, these areas "represented an alien culture that could not be molded into a tropical Anglo-Saxon outpost."[13] So the Caribbean region was neglected by the United States for the moment as more pressing matters emerged on the South American continent.

Chile

In the nation of Chile, two important episodes during the years prior to 1898 became meaningful landmarks of American actions and South American reactions. The first was the War of the Pacific (1879–1884) and the second was the Chilean Civil War (1891). In both instances, the United States involved itself to a certain extent in Chilean affairs despite Chile's desires for U.S. detachment.[14]

By the early 1850s, Chile began to look for other natural resources to exploit and export in order to bolster its growing economy. On Chile's northern border lay the Atacama Desert, a 100-mile wide and 600-mile long region that is so dry and desolate that the average rainfall in the Atacama is .004 inches of rain per year. There are areas in the Atacama Desert that have had no rainfall in the past 400 years. Also, because of its high elevation along the Pacific slope of the Andes Mountains, around 2,500 feet, the average temperature of the Atacama Desert remains between 32 and 73 degrees Fahrenheit. In this desolate and inhospitable region, Chile found something of great worth, nitrates. Sodium nitrate had many uses including the production of nitro-glycerin and smokeless gunpowder. There was only one problem. The Atacama Desert in the early 1850s was part of the nation of Bolivia and as such was Bolivia's only outlet to the Pacific Ocean.

Because the nitrate fields in the Atacama Desert were in the Bolivian territory of Antofagasta, Chile was forced to pay concessions to Bolivia in order to mine nitrates on Bolivian soil. But Chile chafed at having to pay and argued that Bolivia did not have the technical wherewithal to mine the nitrates anyway. Furthermore, Chileans correctly believed that their naval and military might were greater than those of Bolivia, and began to contemplate a more aggressive solution to the dilemma.

While this situation was building to a head, leaders in Peru watched from north of Bolivia with great interest. Peru also owned some of the nitrate-rich regions of the Atacama Desert including the territories of Tacna, Arica, and Tarapacá. In order to prevent a potential conflict between Chile and Peru, the Chileans stipulated that Peru remain neutral in the event that Bolivia and Chile engaged in hostilities with each other. Chile's intent was to keep Peru out of any potential war over the ownership of the nitrate fields. Peru refused and expressed its intentions to support Bolivia if such a conflict arose.[15]

The War of the Pacific came soon enough. In 1879 Chile declared war on Bolivia and then on Peru as well. Within months, Peru's naval forces were defeated and the Peruvian and Bolivian militaries collapsed against the stronger and better equipped Chilean forces. The conditions of the fighting were vastly in Chile's favor. Chile seized not only the Bolivian territory of Antofagasta, but also the three Peruvian territories of Tacna, Arica, and Tarapacá. By 1881 Chilean forces invaded Lima, the capital city of Peru, and eventually the Peruvian and Bolivian governments were obliged to admit defeat.

By 1884 the treaties between Chile, Peru, and Bolivia had been ratified, and a tense peace returned to the region.[16] The most important result of the War of the Pacific was the fact that Bolivia lost its only coastline and outlet to the Pacific Ocean. Thereafter, Bolivia was completely landlocked and had to rely on river and land transportation for import and export traffic from the Pacific and Atlantic Oceans.

In terms of U.S.–Latin American relations, the War of the Pacific was not immensely important, but it did set a precedent of sorts for United States meddling in the affairs of South American nations. Officially, the United States did not get involved in any overtly militaristic manner. The United States could not claim that the Monroe Doctrine had been trampled in any way since no European power had been involved in the conflict. Furthermore, the War of the Pacific did not adversely affect South American trade with the United States because trade along the Pacific coast of South America did not fully mature until after the creation of the Panama Canal during the early years of the twentieth century. There was a negative result for the United States, but it was negligible. American ships carrying men and supplies to the California coast often put in at ports in Chile while enroute to California. The War of the Pacific may have disrupted or inconvenienced American travel along the coast of Chile, but this was a matter of mere irritation.

When the fighting was over in the early 1880s, the United States watched the three South American nations quarrel over how to divide up the concessions and ratify the treaties. The United States briefly entertained the notion of attempting to obtain some Peruvian territory, particularly some of the rich guano-nitrate islands off the Peruvian coast, but then gave up on the notion and advocated that Chile, Peru, and Bolivia solve their own problems.

Latin American diplomats and politicians criticized the United States for its inaction in the whole affair. For many Latin Americans, the United States had been in a position to aid the diplomatic conclusion of the War of the Pacific by acting as an ambassadorial intermediary. On the other hand, if the United States had stepped in and acted in a more intrusive manner, it is quite likely that Chile, Peru, and Bolivia would have accused the United States of meddling in their affairs. Instead, the United States began to exploit nitrate and copper resources in the area through negotiations with Peru and Chile, and these nations resented the United States for its growing economic power.[17] Nevertheless, while the War of the Pacific had more or less negligible results in terms of U.S.–Latin American relations, the 1891 Chilean Civil War was much more decisive in not only establishing the United States as an aggressive and intimidating northern neighbor, but also reinforcing Latin American distrust and resentment of the behemoth to the north.

The Chilean Civil War itself was a conflict of interests between a conservative faction of rebels and guerrilla fighters, and the president of Chile, José Balmaceda, supported by his liberal followers. The conservative revolutionaries believed that Balmaceda, who had been the president of Chile since 1886, was centralizing Chile's economic power structure too tightly around the capital city of Santiago in the center of the nation. Regions to the far north and south did not benefit as much from this policy and believed that President Balmaceda and his supporters were making irresponsible economic decisions that did not take into consideration Chile's enormously long geography.

The issue took on an international flavor when the Chilean government tried to raise taxes and tariffs on nitrate exports. The two nations that stood to lose the most from this revision in Chilean policy were the United States and Great Britain. The British observed the hostilities in 1891 with great interest. The United States did more than observe. The American Navy sent a brand new 4,000-ton cruiser, the USS *Baltimore*, to the Chilean coast to protect U.S. interests and citizens in the region. This was probably a mistake in and of itself because it looked like the United States was throwing its weight around. But had this been the end of the situation, things would have likely ended more positively. The United States had dedicated a naval cruiser and military personnel to the region, and once the U.S. ship was in place, American military commanders began to make a series of mistakes that infuriated the Chileans and led to a serious deterioration in U.S.–Chilean relations.[18]

The first mistake was over a Chilean ship called the *Itata*. President Balmaceda had arranged for the *Itata* to carry weapons and ammunition to his forces on the Chilean coast from contacts in San Francisco, California. But the ship made it only as far as San Diego before it was boarded and detained by American war ships. The commander of the *Itata* disobeyed orders, escaped the San Diego harbor, and sent the supplies on their way to Chile. The United States was so furious that they followed the *Itata* to port in Iquique, Chile, refused to let it unload the needed munitions, and forced it to sail all the way back to San Diego. Then, the United States determined that no laws had been violated, and permitted the *Itata* to sail for Chile once again. Chileans were livid at the audacity of the United States in meddling in Chilean affairs.

The United States also angered Chilean military personnel by interfering in their communications technology and telegraph lines, and then by mishandling information and appearing to actively support the Balmaceda government against the rebel faction. To Chileans, it appeared that the United States had not only come to Chile to interfere in their affairs, but had also taken sides and joined in the hostilities.

But perhaps the biggest mistake of all came in October of 1891 when over 100 sailors from the *USS Baltimore* were permitted to go ashore in Valparaiso. The sailors went to local bars, drank large quantities of alcohol, and then interacted with the local population. Several fights ensued in the bars and then in the streets. The evening's activities resulted in two dead U.S. sailors, around twenty wounded, and nearly forty incarcerations.[19]

The United States demanded that the imprisoned sailors be released and that Chile pay indemnities to the families of the dead and wounded men. Chile flatly refused and even threatened to declare war on the United States. Later, when Chile thought better of the situation, they apologized and did indeed send some monetary remunerations to the United States. The entire incident of U.S. involvement in the Chilean Civil War appeared to Latin Americans to be nothing but the great blunderings of the obtuse Americans who were perceived to be throwing their weight around in places where they were neither wanted nor needed. For the United States, the Chilean Civil War was an arena where the U.S. military could test the waters so to speak, and see what the United States could indeed accomplish in the hemisphere.

Venezuela

Finally, one more incident that helped shape U.S. foreign policy regarding Latin America prior to the 1898 Spanish American War bears mentioning here. Coinciding with the debacle and misunderstanding between the United States and Chile, the South American nation of Venezuela played a small part in defining the role of the United States in nineteenth-century hemispheric diplomacy. The problem originally started over the border between Venezuela and the British-controlled territory of British Guyana (modern-day Guyana) to the east. Around the middle of the nineteenth century, a border dispute between Venezuela and the United Kingdom had resulted in tense relations between the two nations that lasted until the end of the century. The British claimed that the territory of Guyana extended close to 100 miles east of the Orinoco River. On the other hand, the Venezuelans argued that they had the right to govern all the land between the Orinoco and Essequibo Rivers, which, if true, would have resulted in Venezuela controlling more than 50 percent of British Guyana.[20]

The United States became involved in the growing crisis when Venezuela intentionally brought the United States into the situation in the late 1870s by arguing that the British were in fact in violation of the Monroe Doctrine. This was a very curious turn of events in U.S.–Latin American relations. This episode is vitally important for two reasons. First of all, Venezuela, a sovereign nation in South America, acknowledged the efficacy and reach of the Monroe Doctrine by appealing to its precedent in an attempt to drive the British out of the area.[21]

Second, Venezuela recognized that the United States was the dominant power in the western hemisphere, and that Latin American nations could remain on friendly terms with the United States in order to avoid being taken advantage of by Britain and, potentially, by other European powers. Regarding this exchange, Schoultz argues that Venezuela formally and publicly acknowledged that "the United States was 'the most powerful and the oldest of the Republics of the new continent,' [therefore] it naturally was 'called on to lend to others its powerful moral support in disputes with European nations.'"[22]

So almost inadvertently, Venezuela became the voice for the rest of Latin America by appealing to the United States to help them out of their predicament with the British government. They publicly recognized that the United States was the dominant player in the hemisphere and that the U.S. Monroe Doctrine policy was potent enough to be appealed to in time of need. (Of course, on future occasions when the United States acted under the auspices of the Monroe Doctrine, Latin American nations were quick to criticize American imperialistic tendencies.)

The United States reacted by ordering Secretary of State Richard Olney to arbitrate the crisis between Britain and Venezuela. Olney's solution was to steamroll and bulldoze his way through both sides with a particularly nondiplomatic series of communications which managed to offend all parties involved. In part, Olney stated, "The safety and welfare of the United States are so concerned with the maintenance of the independence of every American state . . . as to justify and require the interposition of the United States whenever that independence is endangered."[23] He went on to mirror the language of the Monroe Doctrine by stating that the

United States simply would not tolerate

> that the political control of an American state shall be forcibly assumed by an European power.... Today the United States is practically sovereign on this continent, and its fiat is law upon the subjects to which it confines its interposition. Why?... It is because, in addition to all other grounds, its infinite resources combined with its isolated position render it master of the situation and practically invulnerable as against any or all other powers.[24]

This statement was part of a much longer communication between Secretary of State Olney and American Ambassador to Britain Thomas Bayard, which became known as the Olney Doctrine, and was the first substantial expansion of the Monroe Doctrine since its promulgation in 1823. Venezuela was more or less pleased that the United States had defended them in the border dispute. But the British response, as voiced by the British Prime Minister Robert Gascoyne-Cecil (who was also known as Lord Salisbury, and who functioned simultaneously as the British Foreign Secretary), was annoyed and tense. He disputed that,

> the disputed frontier of Venezuela has nothing to do with any of the questions dealt with by President Monroe. It is not a question of the colonization by a European power of any portion of America. It is not a question of the imposition upon the communities of South America of any system of government devised in Europe. It is simply the determination of the frontier of a British possession which belongs to the Throne of England long before the republic of Venezuela came into existence.[25]

However, despite these contentions, the British eventually backed down and agreed to the U.S. arbitration in the matter. By the turn of the twentieth century the issue was essentially resolved, both sides were content for the most part, and the British were awarded most of the territory that they had initially claimed as theirs.

Nevertheless, notwithstanding the British irritation over the position of the United States, two important things can be ascertained by British actions over the Venezuelan border dispute. First of all, Britain demonstrated, particularly in Lord Salisbury's statements, that they fully understood what the Monroe Doctrine said and what it did not say. Second, despite the fact that the British did not necessarily agree with or even like the precedent set by the Monroe Doctrine, they essentially acknowledged its traditional value in the western hemisphere by claiming that they were abiding by its precepts—or at least not breaking them! Now not only had a Latin American nation appealed to the Monroe Doctrine for protection against European aggression, but a significant European power had more or less acknowledged its willingness to abide by the Monroe Doctrine's tenets as well.

By the time of the Spanish American War in 1898, the United States had grown into a position of influence and power in the western hemisphere that vastly overshadowed its former claims of hemispheric authority over the preceding 100 years. It was with this attitude of power and control that the United States entered into the Spanish American War. The United States now felt more justified than ever in maintaining an active role in nearly every aspect of hemispheric diplomacy.

THE SPANISH AMERICAN WAR

In 1898 the islands of Cuba and Puerto Rico were still Spanish colonies. The only other Spanish colony of any significance in addition to these two Caribbean islands were the Philippine islands in the Pacific Ocean off the southeast coast of Asia. But despite Cuba's colonial status and ties to Spain, ever since the end of the U.S. Civil War in 1865 Cuba had become more and more important to American business interests. Cuba had always held the persuasive ability to allure and tempt American businessmen and entrepreneurs, and by the 1880s the United States had invested tens of millions of dollars in the Cuban economy in order to stimulate trade.

The principal commodity that was produced in Cuba and then sold to the United States was sugar. Like other Caribbean islands, Cuba relied on the cultivation and sale of sugar to bolster and in some cases dictate the economy of the island. And even though Cuba remained a Spanish colony, by 1894 most of the sugar produced in Cuba ended up in the United States.

Cubans eventually chafed at their colonial status. They remained politically dominated by Spain and economically dominated by the United States. They desired independence from both. Cuba believed that if somehow they could extricate themselves from Spanish hegemony, they could then retain all the profits that poured in from the United States in sugar revenues, and create a more positive existence for themselves. So in 1868 Cuba revolted against Spanish control, the result of which was a violent ten-year struggle for freedom, which was finally successfully quashed by Spanish military forces.[26]

But by 1895, under the direction and leadership of Cuban intellectual, statesman, and national icon José Martí, the Cubans began another revolution when Martí proclaimed Cuban independence in his famous *Manifesto de Montecristi*. Martí despised Spanish rule in Cuba and wanted more than anything for the Cuban peoples to be free. Martí also was wary of the growing influence of the United States on the island.[27]

The year 1895 was also a key year in the United States because it represented a shift in American attitudes toward Latin America. Americans began to fear that they were running out of room for expansion. The United States had enjoyed the unique situation of having virgin wilderness right on their western doorsteps for over 100 years. There had been little thought of running out of space, overpopulation, or diminishing natural resources prior to the turn of the twentieth century. But now that California was settled and the United States was connected via the Union-Pacific Railroad (which had been completed in 1869 with a golden spike at Promontory Point, Utah), many began to fear that the frontier days were ending.[28]

In 1896 William McKinley was elected president of the United States. His platform included various promises, and most of them were expansionistic. He represented that portion of the American population that favored continued expansion, not within the territorial United States *per se*, but increasingly outside it. He promised to purchase or otherwise gain control of the Hawaiian Islands, the Danish West Indies, and possibly Cuba as well. He further pledged to dig an American canal through Nicaragua and remove all European nations from the hemisphere on grounds of maintaining and bolstering American and Latin American security and well-being. So less than a decade before the turn of the twentieth century, there was a prevalent attitude in the United States of expansion, imperialism, and benevolent paternalism toward the territories that could be brought under the umbrella of U.S. protection.

Nevertheless, getting the American public to support the idea of going to war against Spain to liberate Cuba was not an easy sell. The U.S. general public was not completely convinced that a war was necessary, even though the Cubans were at that time locked in a struggle against Spain for their freedom; so President McKinley waited. Instead of sending troops to Cuba to fight in the conflict, McKinley opted to send a naval vessel there instead. The *USS Maine*—a second-class armored battleship that had been launched a decade earlier in 1889—was sent to Cuba in January of 1898 for the express purpose of safeguarding American citizens on the island of Cuba, and protecting U.S. investments in the sugarcane fields, and other industries. Many Americans feared, however, that the *USS Maine* had been sent to Cuba as a preliminary step to eventual military deployment on the island.

But whatever its purpose in Cuba, disaster struck the *USS Maine* on February 15, 1898, when it exploded in the harbor near the capital city of Havana. In the years since the detonation and destruction of the *USS Maine*, at least three likely scenarios have been put forward to explain the explosion of the ship and the subsequent deaths of 252 sailors who were aboard when the ship blew up and sank. The immediate belief in the United States, which was espoused by a large percentage of the population, was that the Spanish had sunk the ship. The most likely manner in which the Spanish could have exploded the Maine was through underwater mines in the Havana harbor. For many years this was the popularly held belief and the principal justification that brought the United States into the war against Spain in 1898.

However, the second theory that began to circulate, almost as soon as the ship sunk, was that the U.S. military, acting on orders from the government, could have exploded the ship intentionally in order to influence the American public to support a war against Spain in Cuba. Many cynical Americans believed that since President McKinley could not win sufficient public support for a war in Cuba, he orchestrated a scenario whereby it would appear that the Spanish had killed American sailors, thus creating an undeniable need for American retaliation. However, other Americans believed this scenario to be much too calloused and nefarious to be plausible.

The third explanation that eventually came to the surface was that it was quite likely that the boiler and machinery in the bowels of the ship had unexpectedly exploded, damaging the ship beyond repair and killing the American sailors aboard. In other words, it had been purely an accident. The modern consensus and interpretation seems to favor the third scenario, that the explosion was an unintentional catastrophe, and that neither the Spanish nor the Americans had anything to do with the disaster. But whatever the cause, it brought the American military into the conflict between Cuba and Spain, resulting in the Spanish American War of 1898.[29]

As early as 1895, future U.S. President Theodore Roosevelt had expressed his opinions on the matter in a letter to Massachusetts Senator Henry Cabot Lodge when he said, "Let the fight come if it must. I don't care whether our sea-coast cities are bombarded or not.... Personally I rather hope that the fight will come soon. The clamor of the peace faction has convinced me that this country needs a war."[30] After all, Roosevelt believed that a war could be good for the economy, and politicians could accomplish things while at war that they could not during peace times. Furthermore, by 1898, Roosevelt was the Assistant Secretary of the Navy in the McKinley Administration, and had political aspirations of his own which he implemented after returning from Cuba in 1898 at the conclusion of the Spanish American War.

In any event, the damage was done after the sinking of the *USS Maine*, and President McKinley began preparations for war with Spain. A tentative cease-fire was ordered by Spain in Cuba as the Cubans and Spanish wondered what the United States would do. The response came on April 1, 1898, when the United States invoked the terms of draft proposal written by Senator Henry Teller of Colorado (later known as the Teller Amendment) which did a couple of things. First of all, the Teller Amendment basically declared Cuba an independent nation and admonished the Spanish to withdraw from the hemisphere and accept Cuban independence, or face war with the United States. Spain refused, whereupon the U.S. Congress, through the terms of the Teller Amendment, demanded that Spain remove all personnel and weaponry from the island by April 22, 1898. Then the United States instituted a naval blockade of the island in an attempt to safely land U.S. troops and supplies, and prevent Spain from doing the same.

Spain ignored the Teller Amendment, but could not ignore the blockade which was an informal act of war. So on April 24 Spain declared war on the United States. The U.S. government then officially declared war on Spain on April 25. America had waited until Spain declared war so as not to appear overly aggressive. But when the U.S. Congress declared war on Spain, it made the declaration of war retroactive to April 21 anyway. Regarding American motives and interests in declaring war on Spain, Langley argues persuasively that

> American entry into this war was no miscalculation. The United States went to war against "heathen Spain" in 1898 because the public wanted it, because American business at last concluded that the loss of Spanish-American trade would be offset by expanding American economic interests in the fallen Spanish empire, because the American Navy appeared prepared to fight it, and because the president of the United States had an uncanny ability to shield his international strategic calculations. The United States went to war because it had long coveted Cuba for strategic and economic reasons, and for its strongly held conviction that the Cubans were so irrational that they could not be entrusted with power, and thus required tutelage.[31]

The actual fighting during the Spanish American War heavily favored the U.S. Navy and troops. The United States landed over 15,000 soldiers on the island including a regiment that came to be known as the Rough Riders under the command of Theodore Roosevelt and Leonard Wood.[32] Supported by untrained and ill-equipped Cuban militants, the U.S. soldiers swiftly cut through Spanish lines and caused much damage despite being outgunned and less well supplied in some instances.

While U.S. ground troops fought for control of the island of Cuba, the U.S. Navy also enjoyed several key successes in other areas. On May 1, 1898, a week after America declared war on Spain, a U.S. fleet destroyed the Spanish fleet at Manila in the Philippines in around six hours, and then took control of the Philippine Islands. Some wondered how the U.S. Navy was able to maneuver a fleet into position in the Pacific Ocean so quickly. In fact the U.S. Navy had been sailing for the Philippines for weeks prior to the official declaration of war just in case war broke out.

In the Caribbean the United States enjoyed more victories against Spain. The Spanish fleet was old and no match for the newer U.S. warships. On June 10, 1898, U.S. forces invaded Cuba, and on July 3, the entire Spanish fleet was destroyed in the Caribbean Sea after refusing an offer of truce. The Spanish chose to remain and die honorably rather than return to Spain humiliated by surrender. Roosevelt and his Rough Riders secured San Juan Hill in July, while other U.S. forces liberated the island of Puerto Rico. By August 12, a cease-fire was implemented, and two days later on August 14,

Spanish forces in Cuba and the Philippines surrendered. By December 10, 1898, the Spanish and U.S. governments signed the Treaty of Paris, ending the conflict, and a U.S. (not Cuban!) flag was raised over the city of Havana.

RESULTS OF THE WAR

For the Cubans, the results of the war were varied and conflicted. Finally after more than 400 years as a colony of Spain, Cuba was free. But the price Cubans paid for that freedom was dear. In addition to the loss of life (which amounted to more than 2,000 American deaths and around 9,000 Spanish and Cuban fatalities), most of the economic infrastructure of the island was destroyed. Tens of thousands of ranches and farms were obliterated. Hundreds of coffee plantations and sugar mills—the backbone of the Cuban economy—were razed. Cuba was economically weak and vulnerable to U.S. intervention. But Cubans hoped to offset the cost of the war by selling sugar and other items to the United States which had promised to help Cuba recover economically.

For the United States, the results of the war were much more impressive in terms of the territory acquired. At the end of the war, the United States gained direct territorial control over the islands of Puerto Rico, Guam, and the Philippines. The only remuneration granted to Spain on its losses was a payment of $20 million, which was earmarked as payment for the Philippine Islands. Now the United States of America had once again found an avenue for territorial expansion despite the fact that the Great American Frontier was more or less closed.[33]

Cuba was of course free from Spanish hegemony as a result of the war, and the United States remained true to another condition outlined in the Teller Amendment, that America would not annex the island of Cuba, or otherwise incorporate it directly into the United States. However, the United States did still maintain an impressive amount of control over Cuba's domestic and foreign affairs through a new piece of legislation called the Platt Amendment. In this document, Cuba's status was listed as a protectorate of the United States, and to the dismay and aversion of most Cubans, the U.S. government began to exercise more political and economic control over the island's affairs than ever before.

The Platt Amendment was a document that was literally attached to the new Cuban Constitution in 1901. Written by the U.S. Secretary of War, Elihu Root, and named for Senator Orville Platt of Connecticut, the Platt Amendment strictly limited Cuban political and economic activities and gave the United States enormous say in Cuban affairs. For example, Cuba was denied the authority to make treaties with foreign powers. Cuba was also limited in the amount of foreign debt it could accrue. The Platt Amendment guaranteed that the United States could maintain an active military presence on the island in order to keep the peace, maintain security and safety for American citizens and business owners, and defend the island militarily if necessary. Also, Cuba was expected to sell most if not all of its sugar to the United States. Eventually, most economic ventures on the island came under the umbrella of the Platt Amendment such as ranching, banking, mining, utilities, transportation, and so forth.[34]

At first Cubans were delighted to have their political freedom from Spain. Eventually however, they recognized the bittersweet truth that the Platt Amendment had turned them into a virtual economic colony of the United States. And as the relationship continued to sour, Cubans continued to seek for a solution to their perpetual dilemmas. That solution would not appear until 1959 in the person of Fidel Castro, and since then many Cubans have questioned the efficacy of Castro's new Cuba as well. But in the early years of the twentieth century, no one really foresaw the great schism that would eventually separate Cuba and the United States. In 1900, at the turn of a new century, the United States had emerged as an imperial world power, and the predominant force in the western hemisphere.

6

Gunboat Diplomacy, Panama, and the New World Policeman

Is America a weakling, to shrink from the work of the great world powers? No! The young giant of the West stands on a continent and clasps the crest of an ocean in either hand. Our nation, glorious in youth and strength, looks into the future with eager eyes and rejoices as a strong man to run a race.   – Theodore Roosevelt

The man who really counts in the world is the doer, not the mere critic—the man who actually does the work, even if rough and imperfectly, not the man who only talks or writes about how it ought to be done.   – Theodore Roosevelt

I took Panama and let Congress debate that while I went ahead and built the canal.   – Theodore Roosevelt

Following the end of the Spanish American War, the United States emerged as a powerful new player in international politics and diplomacy. For the United States the western hemisphere represented a brave new world of opportunities and economic ventures. With the mantra of benevolent paternalism to describe its relationship with the nations of Latin America, the United States forged boldly onward with its hemispheric policies. But the strategies and practices of the United States during the early years of the twentieth century earned it a tarnished reputation, accompanied by the growing fear and mistrust of almost every Latin American nation.

BRAVE NEW WORLD

The United States was now determined to enforce the Monroe Doctrine as vehemently as possible in order to keep European powers out of the hemisphere and protect the political and economic opportunities of Latin America for the benefit of the United States. One of the ways the United States determined to both protect and defend the hemisphere was to construct the largest and strongest navy in the world.[1]

Theodore Roosevelt was one of the most vocal supporters of building a more powerful U.S. Navy. Earlier in 1895 as the prospect of war with Spain had become a reality, Roosevelt had remarked that "It is very difficult for me not to wish a war with Spain, for such a war would result at once in getting a proper Navy."[2] Roosevelt returned to the United States following the Spanish American War as a hero. Prior to his involvement in the war, Roosevelt had served as the Assistant Secretary of the Navy, and his loyalties to the U.S. Navy continued into his own presidency.

Once back in the United States, Roosevelt returned to his growing political aspirations. In 1898 he campaigned for and was elected to the position of governor of the state of New York. He only had time to get settled in his new office when he was asked to run for the office of Vice President alongside the incumbent Republican President William McKinley. Then in a twist of fate, Roosevelt served even less time as Vice President than he had as Governor of New York. On September 14, 1901, Roosevelt became the youngest man to assume the office of president of the United States—he became the president following the assassination of President McKinley several days earlier. But not everyone was delighted to see Roosevelt in the Oval Office. Ohio Senator Marcus Hanna is reported to have said, "Now look! That damned cowboy is President of the United States."[3]

As president of the United States, Roosevelt wanted the U.S. Navy not only to be the most powerful naval force in the world, but also to be capable of defending the United States in both the Atlantic and Pacific Oceans—it had to be fast and highly mobile. By the end of 1907 the new fleet was almost complete. It eventually consisted of sixteen battleships, six destroyers, and six associated ships that performed various functions including a hospital ship and repair vessels. Between December 1907 and February 1909 the entire fleet sailed around the world in fourteen months as part of a publicity campaign aimed at demonstrating the power, speed, and mobility of the new U.S. Navy. And even though the Panama Canal would not be completed until 1914, Roosevelt's Great White Fleet demonstrated that the U.S. Navy now could command considerable control in both oceans.

Between 1901 when Roosevelt took office and 1914 when the United States formally completed construction of the Panama Canal, the United States exercised considerable authority over Latin American foreign policy and diplomacy. American decisions angered several nations and led to resentment and distrust, particularly over the manner in which Panama gained its independence from Colombia in 1903.

But the first real test of Roosevelt's foreign policy and Latin American agenda came a year earlier in 1902 in Venezuela. It had been only a few years since the United States had mediated the solution in Venezuela's border dispute with Britain. Now Venezuelans found themselves again involved in an international dilemma, this time with Germany and Britain. During the nineteenth century, Venezuela had borrowed thousands of dollars in foreign loans from European nations including Germany, Italy, and Britain. In 1902 when Venezuela announced that it could not pay back the debts, Germany and Britain took action.[4]

The German and British navies set up a blockade of the Venezuelan coast and announced that they were there to gain remuneration on their loans. For Roosevelt, it was intolerable that European nations could sail into the western hemisphere and act with impunity over something as tertiary (at least from his perspective) as international debt collection. So Roosevelt threatened a U.S. naval response if the antagonizing European powers did not disengage immediately.[5]

Latin American nations watched in dismay as the United States, Britain, and Germany debated the status and repayment of Venezuela's foreign debt. In frustration, the Argentine Minister of Foreign Affairs, Luis María Drago, issued a statement condemning outright the actions of the European powers, and to a lesser extent the arrogance of the United States of America. Drago intended his statement to be considered as an appendage or clarification to the Monroe Doctrine. He stated in part that in addition to the tenets of the Monroe Doctrine already outlined in 1823, an additional stipulation or clause should be added that would guarantee that no European nation could resort to military or naval force in order to collect a debt owned by a Latin American nation. Drago wrote,

> The acknowledgment of the debt, the payment of it in its entirety, can and must be made by the nation without diminution of its inherent rights as a sovereign entity, but the summary and immediate collection at a given moment, by means of force, would occasion nothing less than the ruin of the weakest nations, and the absorption of their governments, together with all the functions inherent in them, buy the mighty of the earth.... The collection of loans by military means implies territorial occupation to make them effective, and territorial occupation signifies the suppression or subordination of the governments of the countries on which it is imposed. Such a situation seems obviously at variance with the principles many times proclaimed by the nations of America, and particularly with the Monroe Doctrine, sustained and defended with so much zeal on all occasions by the United States.[6]

Drago's intention was that his statement would eventually become part of hemispheric tradition and precedent, much the same way that the original Monroe Doctrine had. Unfortunately, his statement (soon labeled the Drago Doctrine) was eventually superseded by a much bolder series of statements issued by President Theodore Roosevelt himself; these statements eventually became known as the Roosevelt Corollary to the Monroe Doctrine.[7]

THE FRENCH CANAL

While the Venezuela debt crisis was coming to a conclusion, the United States began to pursue more vigorously their intentions of constructing a canal somewhere in Central America.[8] The United States and Great Britain had engaged in tense discussions regarding a Central American canal off and on for the previous half-century. Discussions were held regarding the most likely place to construct a canal, and several locations were at least temporarily considered. The most likely were, from north to south, the Isthmus of Tehuantepeque in Mexico, the border between Honduras and Guatemala, the border between Nicaragua and Costa Rica, and finally the Isthmus of Panama. Almost immediately, the first two alternatives proved not to be options at all; neither Tehuantepeque nor the Honduras–Guatemala border were short enough for a canal, and the terrain in both locations was fairly mountainous. So that left Nicaragua and Panama as the only viable options.[9]

In 1846, the United States had signed the Bidlack–Mallarino Treaty with Colombia regarding the Colombian territory of Panama. The treaty stipulated that, among other things, the United States would have free and unimpeded right of transit across the Isthmus of Panama for at least the next twenty years; in other words, the United States would be free to move persons and goods across the isthmus from ocean to ocean free of most taxes or duties. The United States also pledged to guarantee that the Isthmus of Panama would remain under the protection of the nation of Colombia and that any canal, road, railroad, or other means of transportation constructed there would also remain free and neutral. To this end, the United States then constructed a railroad line across the isthmus in 1855 which greatly accelerated transportation from one ocean to the other.[10]

But the Bidlack–Mallarino Treaty between the United States and Colombia sparked the interest of Britain. The British did not want to be left out of the prospects of an interoceanic canal someplace in Central America. The United States and Britain subsequently negotiated the Clayton–Bulwer Treaty in 1850 regarding the potential canal route through Nicaragua. This document—created by the U.S. Secretary of State John M. Clayton and a British Governmental representative, Sir Henry Bulwer—guaranteed that neither the United States nor the British could construct a canal in Nicaragua unilaterally. Eventually, many disgruntled Americans believed that Bulwer had bested Clayton in the diplomatic language of the treaty because the provisions of the document were extended to include all the territory of Central America from the Isthmus of Panama to the Isthmus of Tehuantepeque, including the territory formerly under the provisions of the previous Bidlack–Mallarino Treaty.

With the British and the United States locked in a game of all or none in Central America, the French entered the arena in 1879 and negotiated their own deal with Colombia regarding the territory of Panama and the construction of a French canal. The French were confident of their ability to construct a canal in Panama because Ferdinand de Lesseps, the French engineer who had conceived and financed much of the construction of the Suez Canal in Egypt (completed in 1869), had agreed to go to Panama and duplicate his feat there as well.

For Colombia's part, they were willing to permit another country to construct a canal across Panama as long as the remuneration was sufficient. But the United States and United Kingdom were both aggravated at the apparent French impudence in entering the canal arena. The United States tried to argue that by the terms of the Bidlack–Mallarino Treaty the United States was the only country currently at liberty to construct a Panamanian canal (which was technically incorrect since the subsequent Clayton–Bulwer Treaty prevented the United States from doing so without the blessing and participation of the British). So the United States had to be content with arguing that the future French canal remain neutral so as not to violate the tenets of the Monroe Doctrine.

Problems emerged immediately with the French construction in Panama. De Lesseps desired to reproduce another sea-level canal in Panama like the one he had funded and promoted at Suez in Egypt. The fact was that a sea-level canal in Panama was utterly impossible. Because of differing ocean levels and tidal phases in the Atlantic and Pacific, a sea-level canal in Panama would have been difficult if not impossible to construct. But the French did not see these problems or their solutions until their project was already doomed by pecuniary scandals and economic insolvency. Early in 1889, just ten years after the French began construction on their canal, they withdrew from the venture completely, leaving many unemployed laborers, many unmanned machines, much of the Panamanian population frustrated, and much of the canal unfinished.[11]

As the French retreated, the United States stepped in and began negotiations again with Colombia for the right to complete the canal. But the United States was still restricted by the stipulations of the Clayton–Bulwer Treaty which guaranteed a joint canal venture between the United States and Britain. The only solution was for U.S. President William McKinley to renegotiate with the British over canal construction in Central America. Therefore it fell to McKinley's Secretary of State, John Hay, to parley with the

British Ambassador Lord Julian Pauncefote, and convince him to change the British position on a Central American canal. But before an accord could be agreed upon, President McKinley was assassinated and Theodore Roosevelt became president of the United States.

THE INDEPENDENCE OF PANAMA

After Roosevelt became the president of the United States in 1901, Secretary of State Hay continued his negotiations with Ambassador Pauncefote. After several months of discussion and debate, the two diplomats reached an agreement, the Hay–Pauncefote Treaty of 1901, which officially abrogated the previous Clayton–Bulwer Treaty and removed the British from canal negotiations. The British conceded that the United States could construct a canal in Central America as a unilateral project with no British participation. However, they mandated that any such canal must remain neutral to any and every country that wished to use it and could pay the price of passage. Finally, in an effort to maintain the neutrality of a Central American canal, the United States would be permitted to use military force to protect and reinforce the neutrality of the canal zone if necessary.[12]

So now that the British barrier was taken care of, the next challenge was deciding where to build the canal. Purely in geographic terms, Nicaragua would have been the more obvious choice for several reasons. First of all, it was nearly 500 miles closer to the continental United States than Panama. Second, the amount of work was estimated as significantly less than that of constructing a canal in Panama because the Nicaragua route would have made use of the San Juan River and Lake Nicaragua.

However, in the final decision, the United States returned to the Colombian territory of Panama for various reasons that they believed to be more compelling than any of the arguments for the Nicaraguan route. First of all the surrounding nations of Costa Rica, El Salvador, and Honduras all complained that an American canal through Nicaragua would infringe on their rights and security in the region. Second, the French had already done significant work in Panama which meant that the United States would not need to start from scratch there. Third, engineers estimated that a canal in Panama would be far superior to a Nicaraguan canal because it would be smaller in overall size, require less maintenance, cost less to construct and maintain in the long run, and permit ships to pass through in a shorter amount of time. Finally, the French agreed to sell the rights Colombia had granted them for their failed canal to the United States, and the United States had already laid the foundations with Columbia when they negotiated the Bidlack–Mallarino Canal Treaty back in 1846.[13]

So President Roosevelt sent Secretary of State Hay into new negotiations with the nation of Colombia and specifically with the Colombian Ambassador, Tomás Herrán. But Hay grew impatient with Herrán's deliberate negotiations and threatened to return to talks with Nicaragua instead if Herrán did not concede more quickly.

Therefore, on January 22, 1903, the Hay–Herrán Treaty was signed by both parties. The document stipulated that the United States would lease a 6-mile-wide strip of land across the Isthmus of Panama in the proposed canal zone, that the United States would pay Colombia an upfront sum of $10 million on the lease of this strip of land, and beginning in 1912, the United States would pay an annual supplementary payment of $250,000 to Colombia for continued lease of the canal zone.[14]

When Herrán returned to Colombia with the proposed treaty, the Colombian government refused to ratify the document that the U.S. Senate had already ratified. Colombian politicians argued that the 1903 Hay–Herrán Treaty was too one-sided in favor of U.S. interests in the area and compromised Colombian sovereignty in the canal zone. They suggested that the treaty might become more acceptable if the United States were to increase the dollar amount of the initial payment and the yearly subsidies.

President Roosevelt was incensed and began to explore other options. One of the individuals who had played an important role in the earlier French attempt to construct a canal in Panama was Ferdinand De Lesseps's Chief Engineer, Philippe Bunau-Varilla, who had been in charge of the construction before the French Canal Company went bankrupt in 1889. After the French abandoned the project, Bunau-Varilla had remained in Panama in an attempt to salvage what he could of the company's assets. Eventually Bunau-Varilla succeeded in selling the idea of building a canal in Panama instead of Nicaragua to the U.S. government and President Roosevelt.

But now that Colombia had balked at the terms of the failed 1903 Hay–Herrán Treaty, Bunau-Varilla also began to explore other options. The Panamanian territory had staged dozens of revolutions against the Colombian government ever since Colombia's independence from Spain in 1821. But these small rebellions had all been quickly quashed by the Colombian military. But now, Bunau-Varilla, Hay, and even Roosevelt began to seriously entertain notions of a free and independent Panama which was not governed or controlled by Colombia in any way. After all, if Panama were a free nation, it could negotiate and ratify its own treaty with the United States independent of Colombian meddling.

So Philippe Bunau-Varilla made it known among revolutionary circles in Panama that if they were to stage another revolution against Colombian control, they would very likely succeed. Bunau-Varilla also used his influence in Washington where he received vague assurances that the United States would be amenable to such an independence movement and would perhaps support it outright if conditions were favorable. Bunau-Varilla returned to Panama with the equivalent of an "independence kit" that would help the Panamanian revolutionaries along in their plans and insurrection. The package included "a flag, a declaration [of independence], military plans and a promise of $100,000" from the United States in aid.[15] With these assurances, Panamanian rebels set a date of November 3, 1903, for their uprising.

Colombia was not ignorant of the fact that Panamanians might try another insurrection. Columbian troops stationed in Panama were put on alert, but Colombia did not immediately send reinforcements. One of the interesting things about the geography of the Isthmus of Panama and its connection with Colombia was the fact that Colombia had the option of sending troops by ship through either the Atlantic Ocean or the Pacific Ocean. Either of these options would have supplied and fortified troops in Panama much faster than sending soldiers and equipment overland through the dense forests.[16]

As November approached, Colombia did try to position more soldiers in Panama via both oceans, but failed in both cases. On the Pacific side, Colombia ordered two ships to return from Panama to Colombia to transport troops back to Panama. But a coal shortage prevented these ships from completing these orders. On the Atlantic side the situation was much more interesting. To prevent Colombia from landing troops in Panama, the United States ordered the USS Nashville—a 1,300-ton gunboat commissioned in 1897—to anchor off the coast of the Panamanian city of Colón. The official hubris for the presence of the USS Nashville was to maintain the neutrality of the American-funded railroad that ran across the isthmus. But it also proved very conveniently capable of preventing Colombian troops from landing in Panama from the Atlantic Ocean side.[17]

Soon after the arrival of the USS Nashville, Colombian transports and gunboats arrived off the coast of Colón. There was a momentary confusion about what should happen, and the Colombians apparently entertained the notion of either firing on the U.S. gunboat, landing troops, or both. On the Pacific side near Panama City, Colombian ships fired shells at the city causing minor damage.[18]

But if the Colombian military had any thoughts of carrying out a full-scale invasion in Panama, those ideas were completely abandoned within a few days of the Panamanian declaration of independence on November 3. The U.S. Navy sent the USS Atlanta, USS Dixie, USS Maine,[19] USS Mayflower, and USS Prairie to the Atlantic side to join the Nashville. To the Pacific coast the U.S. Navy sent the USS Boston, USS Marblehead, USS Concord, and USS Wyoming. A total of ten U.S. gunboats had been dispatched to Panama to "observe" and maintain neutrality of the railroad as per the 1846 Bidlack–Mallarino Treaty. There is no question that Teddy Roosevelt created the nation of Panama with the support of the U.S. Navy so that he could build the Panama Canal. This form of aggressive negotiation earned the impressive moniker gunboat diplomacy.

By November 6, 1903, the United States of America became the first nation to extend official diplomatic recognition to the new nation of Panama. Colombia was incensed as was much of the rest of Latin America. And European nations were incredulous at the audacity of Theodore Roosevelt in pulling off such an impetuous flaunting of diplomacy. Philippe Bunau-Varilla became the new Panamanian ambassador to the United States, and he immediately began formal negotiations with Secretary of State John Hay over the status and conditions of an American canal in the new nation of Panama. The result of their negotiations was formalized in the Hay–Bunau-Varilla Treaty which was signed on November 17, 1903, and which historian Thomas Pearcy has called "the single most controversial (and hated) piece of legislation in the history of the Panamanian nation."[20]

The Hay–Bunau-Varilla Treaty resembled the earlier Hay–Herrán Treaty that had failed ratification in Colombia. However, the differences are worth noticing. First of all, instead of the United States receiving a 6-mile swath of territory across Panama, the United States now received a 10-mile-wide path across the isthmus, 5 miles to each side of the proposed canal. In return, Panama received the $10 million originally offered to Colombia, and the original annual subsidies of $250,000. The United States also reserved the right to defend the canal zone with military and naval force if necessary, and to maintain a visible presence in the cities of Colon and Panama City. All these terms were to be maintained between the United States and Panama in perpetuity.

For Colombia's part, the whole affair was particularly galling and they refused to recognize the new nation of Panama. Nevertheless, now that Panama had been created and the Hay–Bunau-Varilla Treaty had opened the way for an American canal, the United States lost little time sending men and supplies to the Panamanian jungle to complete the task the French had taken up almost twenty-five years before.[21]

THE ROOSEVELT COROLLARY TO THE MONROE DOCTRINE

While engineers proceeded to build the Panama Canal, President Roosevelt continued to enforce his "big stick" style of diplomacy with European and Latin American nations. Looking at the way the United States had handled Latin American situations in the past gave the Roosevelt administration a parameter and precedent to work from. But Theodore Roosevelt was unique, and eventually succeeded in redefining the scope and function of the Monroe Doctrine in ways that were more drastic than any of the previous modifications of the doctrine.

By the end of 1904 when the Dominican Republic defaulted on its loan payments to several foreign lender nations, Roosevelt took the opportunity to act in a forceful and decisive manner. The Dominican Republic owed over $30 million and announced that it could not continue to pay back the interest or the principal. Roosevelt feared that this situation might spark a military response from Europe similar to what had happened in Venezuela in 1902.[22]

Furthermore, the problem of debt collection would not go away anytime soon as far as Latin America was concerned. Following Latin American independence in the early decades of the nineteenth century, the former colonies found themselves responsible for their own economic welfare with little or no prior experience at fiscal self-sufficiency. As a result, almost every new Latin American nation went heavily into debt in the years immediately following independence. By the early years of the twentieth century, almost 100 years later, these nations were mired in reflex economies and market-driven export mentalities that had failed to generate economic stability. The result was defaulting on payments, and the liquidation or insolvency of entire national economies.

Roosevelt was familiar with the Drago Doctrine that had been proposed for the express purpose of limiting or eradicating European involvement in the western hemisphere with regard to debt collection. But Roosevelt had other notions about how to handle the situation. He spurned the Drago Doctrine and issued his own series of statements, which soon came to be known collectively as the Roosevelt Corollary to the Monroe Doctrine.[23]

Roosevelt believed that if European powers entered the hemisphere to collect debts that Latin American countries simply could not pay, these European nations would be very likely to turn from lender nations to occupying antagonists; in order to redeem the value of their loans, European powers might resort to covert or even overt control of portions of Latin American economies in order to facilitate debt remuneration. For Roosevelt this situation was simply unacceptable. It represented a potential breach of the Monroe Doctrine because it put European powers in a position to literally control the political and economic destiny of sovereign Latin American states. Furthermore, since 1898 the United States of America had grown more and more protective of its national security in the hemisphere. Additionally, now that the United States governed Puerto Rico and controlled much of the economic structure of Cuba through the Platt Amendment, the security of the Caribbean Sea became a much greater priority. Finally, the Panama Canal, when completed, might need to be defended from aggressive military violence. So with all these considerations, Roosevelt was utterly unwilling to gamble with the possibility that a European power might try to blockade or otherwise dominate the Dominican Republic over debt collection and thus contribute to the destabilization and lack of security of the entire Caribbean region.

Therefore, as early as his annual address to the United States Congress in 1901, Roosevelt began to unveil his evolving hemispheric policy. Between 1901 and 1906, Roosevelt—like President Monroe himself had done in issuing the original statements that became the Monroe Doctrine—used his State of the Union addresses to promulgate new U.S. policy in the hemisphere. In his December 3, 1901, State of the Union address, Roosevelt said,

> The Monroe Doctrine should be the cardinal feature of the foreign policy of all the nations of the two Americas, as it is of the United States. . . . The Monroe Doctrine is a declaration that there must be no territorial aggrandizement by any non-American power at the expense of any American power on American soil. . . . Through the Monroe Doctrine we hope to be able to safeguard . . . independence and secure . . . permanence for the lesser among the New World nations.[24]

The following year on December 2, 1902, he said, "The Monroe Doctrine should be treated as the cardinal feature of American foreign policy; but it would be worse than idle to assert it unless we intended to back it up, and it can be backed up only by a thoroughly good navy. A good navy is not a provocative of war. It is the surest guaranty of peace."[25]

These early statements, seen in historical context, set the foundations and groundwork for Roosevelt's ultimate management of the Monroe Doctrine which he officially announced in his fourth State of the Union address on December 6, 1904. The Monroe Doctrine, which had signified hands-off to Europe for nearly 100 years, was now also becoming the authority for a hands-on approach by the United States.

> If a nation shows that it knows how to act with reasonable efficiency and decency in social and political matters, if it keeps order and pays its obligations, it need fear no interference from the United States. Chronic wrongdoing, or an impotence which results in a general loosening of the ties of civilized society, may . . . ultimately require intervention by some civilized nation, and in the Western Hemisphere the adherence of the United States to the Monroe Doctrine may force the United States, however reluctantly, in flagrant cases of such wrongdoing or impotence, to the exercise of an international police power. . . . We would interfere with them only in the last resort, and then only if it became evident that their inability or unwillingness to do justice at home and abroad had violated the rights of the United States or had invited foreign aggression to the detriment of the entire body of American nations.[26]

Here Roosevelt appealed to the popular notion of the United States as a benevolent father figure watching over the well-being of a child.

A couple of months later, in February of 1905, Roosevelt gave a speech to the U.S. Senate where he stated his intentions with regard to U.S.–Latin American relations more clearly than he had yet done in his State of the Union addresses. With regard to debt crises in the hemisphere, Roosevelt was explicitly transparent. In part he said,

> When the question is one of a money claim, the only way which re-
> mains . . . to collect it is a blockade, or bombardment, or the seizure of the
> customhouses, and this means what is in effect a possession, even though
> only a temporary possession, of territory. The United States then becomes
> a party of interest, because under the Monroe Doctrine it cannot see any
> European power seize and permanently occupy the territory of one of these
> republics; *and yet such seizure of territory, disguised or undisguised, may
> eventually offer the only way in which the power in question can collect
> any debts, unless there is interference on the part of the United States.*[27]

By this time, Roosevelt's "big stick" attitude was attracting more negative attention in Latin America. His big stick was obviously the large navy
he continued to construct and support. But many believed he was not speaking softly at all. In his State of the Union address dated December 5, 1905,
Roosevelt responded to some of the negative repercussions of his previous
statements.

> We must recognize the fact that in some South American countries there
> has been much suspicion lest we should interpret the Monroe Doctrine as
> in some way inimical to their interests, and we must try to convince all the
> other nations of this continent once and for all that no just and orderly
> Government has anything to fear from us. . . . Moreover, we must make it
> evident that we do not intend to permit the Monroe Doctrine to be used by
> any nation on this Continent as a shield to protect it from the consequences
> of its own misdeeds against foreign nations.[28]

Damage control continued the following year as Roosevelt argued, "In
many parts of South America there has been much misunderstanding of
the attitude and purposes of the United States towards the other American
Republics. An idea had become prevalent that our assertion of the Monroe
Doctrine implied, or carried with it, an assumption of superiority, and of
a right to exercise some kind of protectorate over the countries to whose
territory that doctrine applies. Nothing could be farther from the truth."[29]

In effect, whereas the Monroe Doctrine had stated the policy of the
United States as hands-off to Europe as far as political or economic colonization went, the Roosevelt Corollary took this policy a step further. Now
Latin America was still hands-off to Europe, but it was also hands-on to
the United States. Not only could Europe not intervene in the affairs of
Latin America, but the United States now could and should intervene politically, economically, and militarily in Latin American affairs *wherever* and
whenever it was deemed vital to the safety and security of the United States
For nearly the next thirty years, the Monroe Doctrine and its Roosevelt

Corollary became the primary justification for U.S. military intervention in Latin America.

U.S. INTERVENTIONS IN LATIN AMERICA

The eventual result of Roosevelt's Corollary to the Monroe Doctrine was almost three decades of unimpeded U.S. military intrusions and incursions in the affairs of Latin American nations. This is not to say that the U.S. military had not sent troops into Latin American nations prior to 1901. Several U.S. presidents (principally James Buchanan, Andrew Johnson, Ulysses S. Grant, Grover Cleveland, and William McKinley) had used the U.S. military in various countries (such as Mexico, Nicaragua, Colombia/Panama, and Uruguay) for a multitude of purposes.

But beginning in 1901 and continuing until 1933, the United States drastically increased its use of military force in the hemisphere. Almost until the end of his term in 1909, Theodore Roosevelt sent the U.S. military into more Latin American nations than any other U.S. president before or since. Roosevelt intervened in Colombia three times, Panama twice after its independence in 1903, Honduras twice, the Dominican Republic twice, Cuba once, and Nicaragua once.[30] Roosevelt's heavy-handedness in Central America and the Caribbean between 1901 and 1908 caused many Latin American nations to distrust and dislike the United States more than at any other time in U.S.–Latin American relations.

And even though no other U.S. president would use the Monroe Doctrine and the Roosevelt Corollary to the same extent as Theodore Roosevelt (Woodrow Wilson came very close to matching Roosevelt's record between 1913 and 1920), Roosevelt set a precedent in U.S.-Latin American relations that the United States would not begin to retreat from until 1933 and the Good Neighbor Policy of Franklin D. Roosevelt.

Between 1901 and 1933, the United States sent military units repeatedly into Latin American countries. In fact, every major nation in Latin America and the Greater Antilles Caribbean Islands—twenty-five nations in total, not counting the smaller Caribbean Islands or the Bahamas—has had U.S. military forces on the ground at least once, except Jamaica, Belize, Ecuador, Guyana, Surinam, and French Guiana. However, it must be noted that Jamaica remained a British colony until 1962; Belize remained a British colony until 1981; Guyana remained a British colony until 1966; Surinam won its independence from the Netherlands in 1975; and French Guiana has not yet gained its independence from France. That leaves only Ecuador which won its independence from Spain in 1822, and was not subsequently subjected to a U.S. military intervention.

Theodore Roosevelt was succeeded in the Oval Office by William Howard Taft, also a Republican president, who largely continued to implement the Latin American policy that Roosevelt had laid down during his two terms in office. One of the things that President Taft implemented while in office was an economic initiative called Dollar Diplomacy. The idea was to use loans and banking to influence and control nations predominantly in Central America. In order to make Latin American countries less susceptible to European involvement, the United States floated loans and bought up debts in Haiti, Honduras, Nicaragua, and other areas.

In 1913 Taft was succeeded by Democrat Woodrow Wilson, and many U.S. citizens and politicians believed that perhaps the United States would back down from the heavy-handed "big stick" approach to Latin America that the previous Republican presidents Taft, Roosevelt and even McKinley had utilized. To that end, Wilson abandoned Taft's Dollar Diplomacy soon after taking office. But then to the dismay of many, Wilson sent troops into Latin America for the next seven years nearly as frequently as Roosevelt himself had done. In fact, the period between 1909 and 1918, presided over by Presidents William Howard Taft and Woodrow Wilson, has been dubbed the Nine Gray Years because of the nearly continuous U.S. military presence in Cuba, Haiti, Nicaragua, and elsewhere. And even though many in the United States and in Latin America believed that Democratic President Wilson would reverse the imperialistic trend of the Republican presidents that stretched clear back to William McKinley in 1898, Wilson actually sent troops into Latin American nations more times than any other president of the United States with the sole exception of Theodore Roosevelt himself.[31]

Meanwhile, World War I began in 1914 in the Balkans. Between 1914 and 1917, before the United States began to participate in the hostilities in Europe, President Wilson attempted to maintain the security of American shipping in the Caribbean and protect U.S. citizens in various Latin American countries from minor revolutions by sending Marines into Mexico, the Dominican Republic, Haiti, Nicaragua, Panama, and Cuba. Finally, in 1919, following the end of World War I, Wilson sent additional troops into Honduras and Guatemala as well.

Intervention in Mexico

One of Woodrow Wilson's major concerns during the years of his presidency was the diplomatic relationship between the United States and Mexico. But he struggled to maintain positive relations with Mexico, and ended up sending troops into that country on several occasions between 1914 and 1917 which very nearly took the two nations to the brink of another Mexican American war.

The first episode involved only a small American military force that was sent to the Mexican state of Sonora in 1913 to protect American citizens from a minor Mexican uprising. Later in April of 1914, a few U.S. sailors were arrested and forcibly removed from an American ship anchored in the harbor near Tampico. They were eventually released and returned to their vessel with the apologies of the Mexican government. However, several days later, American sailors were ordered by President Wilson to land in the Mexican city of Veracruz and occupy the city to prevent a German weapons shipment from unloading. The outcome for Mexico was bleak as the U.S. troops outgunned Mexican defenders. The eventual result was the overthrow of the Mexican president-dictator, General Victoriano Huerta, and Mexican dislike for American imperialism skyrocketed.[32]

This series of events eventually culminated in raising the ire of Francisco "Pancho" Villa—a general in the Mexican Revolutionary Army, and a hopeful for the Mexican presidency—who sent nearly 500 men across the Mexican border into the U.S. town of Columbus, New Mexico, in 1916, where they terrorized the local citizens and killed some of them. For much of the following year, nearly 12,000 American troops under the direction of General John J. Pershing searched in vain for Villa on the Mexican side of the border.[33]

One final episode of note between the United States and Mexico during World War I was the incident of the Zimmermann Telegram. In January of 1917, British intelligence successfully acquired and decoded a telegram sent from Germany to Mexico. The Germans proposed a truce between Mexico and Germany in the very likely event that the United States should declare war on Germany. In return for Mexican support against the United States, the German government pledged to help Mexico regain the territory it lost to the United States seventy years earlier as a result of the Mexican War. Mexico did not respond to Germany's offer but instead remained neutral, and by World War II two decades later, Mexico and the United States had, for the most part, smoothed over most of their differences.[34]

Intervention in Nicaragua

Perhaps one of the most well-remembered and long-term interventions in a Latin American nation occurred in the small Central American nation of Nicaragua in the early decades of the twentieth century. Over the previous century, U.S. troops had been sent into Nicaragua over and over: in 1853 by Franklin Pierce; 1867 by Andrew Johnson; 1894 and 1896 by Grover Cleveland; 1898 and 1899 by William McKinley; 1907 by Theodore Roosevelt; 1910 and 1912 by William Howard Taft; and 1926 by Calvin Coolidge.[35]

By the early 1930s the situation in Nicaragua came to a head in violent and, for the United States, frustrating ways. Augusto César Sandino was born in May of 1895 to a Nicaraguan coffee plantation owner and an Indian mother. When Sandino was around twenty-five years old, he was forced to flee Nicaragua to avoid murder charges. He traveled through Honduras, Guatemala, and Mexico taking odd jobs and speaking to revolutionaries.

He soon began to organize in his own mind the foundations of revolution and social organization that he would eventually form into his own political ideology of Sandinismo.[36]

In 1926 when Sandino returned to Nicaragua, he found the country severely fragmented ideologically. He formed a small guerrilla movement and quickly developed and honed the charisma and talent for public speaking that would attract people to him for the rest of his life. He then aimed his aggression and ideological revolutionaries against the conservative political faction running the country, and also against Nicaraguan General José María Moncada who had political aspirations. The conflict became so charged that Nicaragua soon plunged into a violent civil war. Sandino took his followers into the mountains and jungles of Nicaragua where they became one of the first modern examples of guerrilla combatants. Neill Macaulay states, "Sandino lacked the political sophistication of the leaders of the post–World War II liberation movements, but in guerrilla tactics, he could have been their teacher."[37] Indeed, many of the Latin American revolutionary leaders of the latter half of the twentieth century, such as Fidel Castro, Che Guevara, Jacobo Arbenz, and others, took lessons and inspiration from Sandino's campaigns in the Nicaraguan mountains.

In order to restore peace and order to Nicaragua, President Calvin Coolidge sent U.S. Marines into Nicaragua in 1926 where they remained more or less until 1933 when they were brought home by Franklin D. Roosevelt. When General Moncada permitted U.S. troops to occupy Nicaragua in order to end the civil war, Sandino redirected his enmity from the conservative elements in Nicaraguan society to the imperialistic North Americans who were now meddling in Nicaraguan affairs.

Sandino and his small army ranged over thousands of miles of forest and hills in northwestern Nicaragua, evading Nicaraguan military forces and U.S. Marines alike. Even with their advanced technology, weaponry, and the highest number of U.S. soldiers deployed in a Latin American country to date, the Americans still could not capture Sandino.[38]

In 1932, a liberal named Juan Bautista Sacasa was elected president of Nicaragua. After overseeing the election, the U.S. Marines withdrew from the country in 1933 to allow Sacasa and his military advisor, General Anastasio Somoza, to run Nicaragua. Now that the United States had left Nicaragua, Sandino retired to his lands in the north and persuaded his men to stand down as well. Around a year later, however, Sacasa feared that a new Sandinista revolution would topple his government. So Sandino was lured into a secret meeting where he was captured by General Somoza's men and executed.

Many believed that Sandinismo had died with Sandino himself. But as other revolutionaries inside and outside Nicaragua continued to take up Sandino's ideologies and guerrilla tactics, Sandinismo continued to provide an outlet for frustrated rural agriculturalists into the 1980s and beyond when the United States would once again, under President Ronald Reagan, send troops into Nicaragua (see Chapter 9).

CONCLUSIONS

The first three decades of the twentieth century were bleak in terms of U.S.–Latin American relations. Between 1898 and 1933 the U.S. military intervened in Latin American nations on more occasions than they had in the previous 100 years, and more frequently than they would in the subsequent 70 years. Many American citizens and statesmen began to realize that military intervention did not work very well, and was quite expensive to sustain over lengthy periods of time.

Some began to desire a change from this very aggressive epoch in hemispheric diplomacy, and some reexamined the maturing relationship between the Latin American nations and the United States. In the early 1920s, some of the foundations that would eventually grow into the Good Neighbor Policy were laid. But hemispheric good relations were still a long time coming.[39]

7

The Great Depression, the Good Neighbor Policy, and World War II

In these days of difficulty, we Americans everywhere must and shall choose the path of social justice . . . the path of faith, the path of hope, and the path of love toward our fellow man.
— Franklin D. Roosevelt

True Individual freedom cannot exist without economic security and independence. People who are hungry and out of a job are the stuff of which dictatorships are made.
— Franklin D. Roosevelt

If civilization is to survive, we must cultivate the science of human relationships— the ability of all peoples, of all kinds, to live together, in the same world at peace.
— Franklin D. Roosevelt

THE CLARK MEMORANDUM ON THE MONROE DOCTRINE

In 1921, Warren G. Harding became president of the United States. After two decades of almost nonstop U.S. intervention in many Latin American nations, Harding began to contemplate a change in policy toward Latin America. But before he could change anything of lasting importance, he died of a heart attack less than two years into his term of office. He was replaced by his vice president, Calvin Coolidge, who finished the two remaining years and then won another full term. Coolidge continued in the same vein as Harding had begun with regard to softening relations between the United States and Latin America. It was not difficult to see that the primary reason for the increase in U.S. interventionism in Latin America had come from justifications rooted in the Roosevelt Corollary to the Monroe Doctrine. It was also not difficult to realize that this general policy had led to a significant deterioration in the relations between the United States and the Latin American countries.

So President Coolidge asked the Undersecretary of State, J. Reuben Clark Jr., to review both the Monroe Doctrine and the statements that comprised the Roosevelt Corollary in order to determine the validity and necessity of such an addendum to the original doctrine. The result was yet another significant clarification of the scope and limits of the original Monroe Doctrine. In December of 1928, Clark presented his findings to the Secretary of State, Henry L. Stimson. This document has since become known as the Clark Memorandum on the Monroe Doctrine, and represents the last major reinterpretation of the doctrine and its implications for U.S.–Latin American relations.

In short, Undersecretary of State Clark argued that the Roosevelt Corollary was irredeemably redundant and should be detached from the original doctrine. Clark clarified the purpose of the Monroe Doctrine, stating that Latin American nations should be "beneficiaries" of the doctrine, not "victims." The redundancy was explicitly clarified in Clark's arguments; the "self-preservation" of the United States—something that Roosevelt had used as a justification for intervention under the guise of the Monroe Doctrine—was in fact a sovereign right of the United States and every other nation, with or without any such doctrine or statement to that effect. He argued, "It is evident . . . that the Monroe Doctrine is not an equivalent for 'self-preservation'; and therefore the Monroe Doctrine need not, indeed should not, be invoked in order to cover situations challenging our self-preservation. . . . These other situations may be handled, and more wisely so, as matters affecting the national security and self-preservation of the United States as a great power."[1]

Clark concluded that the "so-called Roosevelt Corollary" was not "justified by the terms of the Monroe Doctrine" and should be abandoned as official American foreign policy. Regarding the doctrine itself, he clarified once and for all that it had

> nothing to do with the relationship between the United States and other American nations, except where other American nations shall become involved with European governments in arrangements which threaten the security of the United States, and even in such cases, the Doctrine runs against the European country, not the American nation, and the United States would primarily deal thereunder with the European country and not with the American nation concerned.[2]

So a quarter-century after its inception, the Roosevelt Corollary to the Monroe Doctrine began to fade from American foreign policy. Latin American nations had experienced almost three decades of unimpeded U.S. military intervention and the results were far from positive. Mistrust and criticism of the behemoth to the north were at an all-time high. Toward the end of his term as president, Calvin Coolidge remarked that it would be better if the United States could offer not hostility and fear, but generosity to all the nations of the earth. Coolidge refused to run for another term, and the republican nomination went to Herbert Hoover who had served in the cabinets of both Coolidge and Harding.

After his inauguration in 1929, Hoover appeared prepared to continue along the same path as his predecessors with regard to a soothing of U.S.–Latin American relations. The idea was simple: instead of using the U.S. military to force Latin American countries to behave in certain ways, the United States could rely on other methods and means to persuade and encourage Latin American countries that were less malignant, such as political and diplomatic deliberations, and also economic motivations in the form of markets, goods, and trade incentives. However, when the stock market crashed in October of 1929, Hoover was compelled to focus almost all of his attention on domestic issues, and once again, Latin America fell to a very low position on his list of U.S. priorities.

ECONOMICS AND THE GREAT DEPRESSION

One of the most important economic tendencies in Latin American history has been dependence on other nations for fiscal survival. While the nations of Latin America still existed as colonies of Spain and Portugal, these mother countries enacted strict economic policies that regulated trade and commerce in the colonies, and stipulated the frequency, quality, and geography of all hemispheric and global trade in which they were involved.

Following the wars for independence in the early 1800s, as a general rule the nations of Latin America had underdeveloped economies and weak trade prospects. This is not to say they had no prospective trading partners, for the United States and Great Britain were among the first and most eager to trade with Latin America. But these economic relationships were excessively one-sided, and where Latin America had existed as political colonies of Iberia prior to the nineteenth century, they became the economic colonies of Britain and the United States following their transition to nationhood. The results have generally been consistent throughout the region—unequal distribution of wealth between the rich and the poor, and an unhealthy dependence on the United States and Europe for financial solvency.

Scholars have labeled this trend several times. One of the more traditional labels is that of colonialism, or in this case, neocolonialism. In other words, the nations of Latin America traded their political independence from Iberia for financial domination by the more economically stable powers of the western world.

Another term for this condition that has been applied to much of the third world, including Latin America, is imperialism. Nevertheless, by the time Herbert Hoover was elected president of the United States in 1928, imperialism was not as popular as it had been during the preceding 200 years. And the United States was usually quick to defend its economic position in Latin America as something much less malignant, something much more paternal.

The third label for economic involvement in Latin America is diffusionism. The diffusionist theorists have argued that the spreading of moneys, values, and technology from the United States and Europe to the nations of Latin America was much more positive than negative and that the profits of modernization that gradually began to appear in Latin American nations would greatly benefit the people in the long run.

But whichever terminology one subscribes to, the economic development of Latin America between 1820 and 1920 was more negative than positive. Latin American nations suffered under the limitations of reflex economies that were designed to bring cash into the national economy in exchange for "cash crop" resources that were developed to the exclusion of most other industries. In other words, Latin American nations tended to focus their economic growth around the production and sale of commodities such as sugar, coffee, tobacco, bananas, rubber, cochineal, henequen, guano, copper, and so forth, all of which brought in a certain amount of profit, but none of which helped the country industrialize and expand into a fully developed market economy.

Part of the problem was that even though Latin American countries were producing all of these resources, no single country produced more than a handful of them, and some based their national economy on only one or two! There are two major problems with this kind of national economic development. First of all, each one of the items listed above was subject to price fluctuations in the world market. So when the market for a particular commodity became saturated, prices dropped, which meant that all the time and investment that had gone into producing that item could not yield a high enough return to the nation that produced it and depended on the revenue from sales of that commodity.

Second, none of the products listed above were capable of unilaterally feeding, clothing, or otherwise supporting the inhabitants of the nation that produced them. For example, in 1927 and 1928 when Brazil produced bumper crops of coffee, the world coffee market became quickly saturated and prices began to plummet. Coffee that had sold for 15 cents per pound quickly dropped to around 5 cents on the pound or less. In 1930 in the city of São Paulo alone millions of tons of coffee sat in warehouses instead of being shipped to consumer nations. And the worst part of the whole thing was that Brazil could not simply distribute the coffee to Brazilians and tell them to live off of the coffee until next year.[3] The same held true for countries that produced bananas or sugar or dye or rubber. When the markets were flooded, Latin American economies collapsed.

This reflex economy phenomenon is one of the reasons why the Great Depression had such a devastating effect on not only the United States and Europe, but on Asia, Africa, and Latin America as well. And even though the United States had relatively good intentions in trying to mitigate some of the damage it had caused in the past by overusing its military in Latin American nations, the Great Depression—which lasted from 1929 to roughly 1941—dissolved nearly all ideas of progressive Latin American foreign policy and forced U.S. politicians to focus on the domestic issues in the United States that resulted from the crash. Latin American nations were left to fend for themselves and try to deal with the deteriorating economic conditions on their own.

UFCO and the Economic Relationship between the United States and Latin America

One of the principal examples of economic and commercial ties between the United States and Latin America during the early years of the twentieth century—both before and after the Great Depression—was the United Fruit Company, or UFCO. The early history of UFCO centers predominantly on the production, shipping, and sale of bananas and other tropical items from key ports in Latin America to a few select cities in the United States. Prior to the 1850s, bananas were exceptionally rare in the United States because it was practically impossible to transport the ripe fruit from Central America back to the United States before it spoiled. But during the 1860s and 1870s, a few American shipping and fishing companies began to bring an occasional bunch of bananas back to harbors on the eastern seaboard of the United States where they were sold to curious customers.[4]

By the turn of the twentieth century, there were around 100 different small companies in the United States that had been formed for the sole purpose of shipping bananas and other tropical fruits from Central America and the Caribbean back to markets in the United States. One of the predominant entrepreneurs in early fruit exports was an American businessman named Minor Keith who owned three very profitable companies: The Tropical Trading and Transportation Company, International Railways of Central America, and The United Fruit Steamship Company. With these three entities, Keith became a leading importer of bananas into U.S. ports. But there were other competitors as well. The Boston Fruit Company and the Cuyamel Fruit Company (owned by Sam Zemurray) both began shipping fruit to the United States as well.[5]

In 1899, the Boston Fruit Company merged with Minor Keith's three companies to form the massive conglomerate UFCO. Then in 1930, Sam Zemurray merged his Cuyamel Fruit Company with UFCO and created an export corporation so large that Central Americans and Caribbeans began to call it *El Pulpo*, or the octopus. In time, UFCO became such a powerful monopoly in the region that its annual income was greater than the entire national revenues of most of its Latin American host countries.[6]

Standard operating procedure for UFCO in Central America and the Caribbean was to buy up enormous tracts of land and then use some of that land for the cultivation of bananas. Scholars have estimated that UFCO actually owned around twenty times more land than it cultivated simply to keep other prime pieces of land out of the hands of its competitors. By the mid-1930s, UFCO operated plantations in Belize, Colombia, Costa Rica, Cuba, Ecuador, Guatemala, Honduras, Jamaica, Mexico, Nicaragua, Panama, and the Dominican Republic, and owned more than 3.5 million square acres of land.[7]

The manpower needed to maintain such a massive operation was enormous, and UFCO offered amenities and services for its employees such as housing, education, religious services, health care, and company stores or commissaries where basic goods could be obtained. But conditions were anything but pleasant on banana plantations. Dormitories were small, cramped, and dirty; education was often unfeasible because of the difficulty of bringing teachers to plantations; religious services were sporadic at best; commissary items were more often than not expensive or very difficult to obtain; and health care often did not exist at all.

But UFCO's problems did not end with the condition of its workers. UFCO businessmen and lawyers became well known for their aggressive tactics in acquiring land and dictating conditions to politicians in the host countries. Rail lines were laid, but usually only between plantations and ports, not to major cities in host countries. Bribery and intimidation were used to gain tax breaks and other concessions from local politicians. Illegal immigration provided cheap labor from Caribbean islands like Jamaica, instead of paying local laborers in host countries like Belize and Honduras.

In the 1920s, the manager of an UFCO plantation in Honduras wrote to a company lawyer, "we must produce a disembowelment of the incipient economy of [Honduras] in order to increase and help our aims. We have to prolong its tragic, tormented and revolutionary life."[8] And in 1951, Sam Zemurray himself (dubbed "the Banana Man"), the then CEO of UFCO, was quoted as follows in *Life Magazine*, "All we cared about were dividends. I feel guilty about some of the things we did."[9] Finally, UFCO played some major roles in political upheavals in Central America, most predominantly the 1954 coup that ousted President Jacobo Arbenz from power in Guatemala (see Chapter 8).

In the long run, UFCO was responsible for some positive effects on host countries in Central America and the Caribbean. UFCO brought increased revenue to many nations, technological development, and employed thousands of laborers. And UFCO was involved with more than simply the production and distribution of tropical fruit. They were occupied with advances in transportation technology and even provided services such as mail delivery for some areas. But notwithstanding the few positive outcomes for Latin American host countries, UFCO came to represent the under-handed, imperialistic tactics of the Americans to the north, and even though UFCO did not rely on military power for active intervention, the economic and political control it wielded over some regions was a significant source of frustration for Central American and Caribbean nations.

THE GOOD NEIGHBOR POLICY

Herbert Hoover was elected president of the United States in 1928. One of the first things he did after taking office in 1929 was to set out on a goodwill tour of Latin America that was scheduled to last for around two months. Like his immediate predecessors, Hoover was convinced that the United States needed to change its posture toward Latin America, both militarily and economically, or the two would never achieve any measure of solidarity. And military incursions into Latin American nations—such as the troops that were on the ground in Haiti and Nicaragua when Hoover took office—would have to cease.[10]

Hoover had some background in the new style of international good-neighborliness from his governmental service prior to becoming president of the United States. He had served as the Secretary of Commerce from 1921 to 1928 under the Harding and Coolidge administrations where he attempted to direct U.S. policy increasingly away from military solutions to perceived Latin American problems, and more toward economic and business solutions. He believed that economic resolutions would, in the long run, be more financially profitable for the United States, and would be perceived as less aggressive by the Latin Americans. But Herbert Hoover's neighborly aspirations were cut short when the stock market crashed in October of 1929.

After four years in office, Hoover was replaced by Franklin D. Roosevelt in 1933. And even though the United States and the world still felt the effects of the Great Depression as intensely as ever, FDR believed the time had come to refocus on creating greater hemispheric solidarity and perhaps economic stability. As early as his first inaugural address on March 4, 1933, FDR stated, "In the field of world policy, I would dedicate this nation to the policy of the good neighbor—the neighbor who resolutely respects himself and, because he does so, respects the rights of others—the neighbor who respects his obligations and respects the sanctity of his agreements in and with a world of neighbors."[11]

At first some Americans and most Latin Americans were skeptical and fully expected Roosevelt to behave as a reincarnation of his cousin Theodore

Roosevelt whose heavy-handed approach to Latin America was still remembered with resentment. But FDR soon began to make good on his promise to be a good neighbor to the other states of the hemisphere.

One of the first significant changes to result from Roosevelt's Good Neighbor Policy was the abrogation of the Platt Amendment that the Cubans despised. In 1934, Roosevelt was instrumental in having the Platt Amendment—which had dictated U.S.–Cuban relations since 1901—repealed by a new treaty called simply Treaty between the United States of America and Cuba. Article I of the treaty stated that the Platt Amendment would "cease to be in force, and is abrogated, from the date on which the present Treaty goes into effect."[12] Article III laid the groundwork for the United States' continued use of Guantanamo as a naval base and coaling station for American ships on the island. The agreement went into full diplomatic effect on June 9, 1934, and signaled the beginning of a new era in U.S.–Latin American relations.

With the abrogation of the Platt Amendment, Cubans had a greater degree of political freedom than they had enjoyed for hundreds of years. The United States had not completely abandoned Cuba, however, and maintained close military and economic ties to the island, its sugar, and its growing potential as a tourist location for wealthy Americans.

The United States followed this diplomatic astonishment with similar actions in 1936. During that year, the United States redefined its relationship with Panama in the Hull-Alfaro Treaty by assuring the Panamanians that the United States would not use its military to enforce its position in the country, except if necessary in the canal zone, and increased the annual payment for the American presence in the canal zone from $250,000 to $430,000.[13] Also in 1936 the United States removed Marines from Haiti where they had been stationed since being sent there by President Woodrow Wilson back in 1915.

The Good Neighbor Policy and Mexico

But the major challenge to the Good Neighbor Policy, which would test the true intentions of the United States in enforcing this new strategy of nonintervention, came in 1938 when the United States and Mexico again dealt with crisis. In 1938 Mexican President Lázaro Cárdenas began implementing some left-wing reforms in his country aimed at strengthening the economy and improving conditions for poor Mexican laborers and farmers. Cárdenas presided over a massive agrarian reform wherein he redistributed millions of acres of land to hundreds of thousands of Mexican peasants.[14]

But Cárdenas's redistribution of Mexican land was accomplished so quickly and dramatically that Mexico soon began to experience severe negative economic consequences. Much of the hacienda land that Cárdenas gave to poor peasant farmers had previously been used to cultivate lucrative

Mexican cash crops such as sugar, coffee, tobacco, cotton, and henequen, all items that had been harvested and exported to U.S. and European markets. Now that peasant farmers were using these lands to grow corn and beans, Mexico experienced a severe loss of revenue, and Cárdenas began to lose the support of some politicians and citizens alike.[15]

But Cárdenas was not finished with national Mexican economic reform. Since the turn of the twentieth century, Mexico had relied increasingly on oil revenues. Under the leadership of former Mexican president and dictator Porfirio Díaz (who ruled from 1876 to 1911), Mexico had encouraged foreign investment and funding in several Mexican industries including electricity and oil. This meant that Mexico had admitted thousands of foreign laborers from the United States and Europe, and some corporations in Europe and the United States had purchased the rights of ownership and operation over certain Mexican resources. One of the result was a massive production of oil that made Mexico one of the most important oil-producing nations in the world by the 1920s. A significant portion of this Mexican oil found its way north into the United States. However, it also meant that Mexicans who were employed by such companies were paid very little.

In order to offset decreasing profits due to his agrarian reforms, President Cárdenas ordered the investigation of several foreign oil companies operating in Mexico including the U.S.-owned Standard Oil and the British-owned Shell Oil Company. Cárdenas's investigation revealed that Mexican workers employed by foreign oil corporations received terrible wages and lived and worked in extremely adverse conditions. When Cárdenas suggested that the oil companies deal with these conditions, he was rebuffed. The Mexican Congress got involved by approving legislation that called for better compensation for Mexican laborers, including better living conditions, higher salaries, and greater benefits. Again the oil companies refused and the case went to the Mexican Supreme Court which upheld the decision of the Mexican Congress.

When the oil corporations refused again, Cárdenas was ready for his next move. He argued that the oil companies were in direct violation of their contracts with the government of Mexico. So on March 18, 1938, Lázaro Cárdenas expropriated all of the lands, tools, and equipment of the oil companies on Mexican soil, and nationalized the oil fields themselves. In other words, Cárdenas kicked the foreign oil companies out and returned Mexican oil reserves to Mexican proprietary control.[16] The reaction in Mexico was staggering. Instantly Mexicans believed that Cárdenas was the greatest leader in modern Mexican history. Parades and celebrations erupted across the country. Finally Mexico had stood up to foreign hegemonic powers, especially the United States, and won! Make no mistake, Mexicans and Latin Americans were not fooled about the ability of the United States to intervene aggressively with its military; the important point was that

President Roosevelt chose not to intervene militarily despite his ability to do so. Apparently the United States was serious about the Good Neighbor Policy!

The reactions in the United States were cooler. Because of past tendencies in the United States—since before the Big Stick policies of Theodore Roosevelt at the turn of the century—many advocated sending the military into Mexico to protect U.S. economic interests and investments there. Some even labeled the Cárdenas government a socialist regime. But Franklin D. Roosevelt was determined to uphold the Good Neighbor Policy, and instead of falling back on an aggressive military solution, he simply asked the Mexican government to pay for the equipment that had been confiscated from U.S. oil companies. Initially the United States requested a payment of several hundred million dollars. Cárdenas riposted with an offer of $10 million (the same amount that the United States paid Mexico in 1853 in the Gadsden Purchase).

The remuneration was eventually worked out to around $25 million, and Cárdenas supervised the creation of a new oil company in 1938 named Petróleos Mexicanos (or Pemex). But even though Mexico soon began to export its own oil, several negative repercussions rocked the Mexican petroleum business for the rest of the decade. First of all, both Britain and the United States temporarily boycotted Mexican oil. Additionally, foreign investors were now more reticent about pouring money into the Mexican economy because of the possibility that their investments might be nationalized as well. Britain was particularly bitter and boycotted other Mexican goods as well as oil, and briefly ended diplomatic relations with Mexico.

But overall, the Good Neighbor Policy achieved some positive results in the short-term that led to greater trust and solidarity between the United States and Latin American nations. The U.S. government was convinced that the earlier policies of Theodore Roosevelt, who had positioned the United States as the New World Policeman, were doomed to fail for several reasons. Most of the time military interventions had not worked out as well as the United States had hoped because they were expensive financially, they were expensive in terms of military personnel, and they were ultimately unable to provide widespread oversight throughout the hemisphere because there were just too many countries that qualified for American oversight under this sort of paradigm.[17] So FDR made compelling arguments for spending more time and energy focusing on Latin American economies and building stronger trade relations with Latin American nations, instead of sending Marines to Latin America whenever they were in need of discipline.

WORLD WAR II

As a result of the United States' Good Neighbor Policy of the 1930s, some of the tensions and resentment that had built up in Latin American countries over the previous 100 years began to relax. As the United States opted not to use military force, Latin Americans began to feel a greater potential for hemispheric cohesion, and perhaps, in the near future, the possibility of some vestige of hemispheric equality as well. These sentiments of hesitant fraternity led to greater trust and cooperation between the United States and most of the Central and South American nations, which was essential as the global community pushed inexorably into World War II.

In 1938 the United States began to put some pressure on Latin American countries to scale back their ties to Axis countries because of the potential threat they posed for continued world peace. Fighting had already escalated in Asia as early as 1931 with the Mukden Incident, which led to hostilities between Japan and China, and eventually culminated in the Second Sino-Japanese War, which broke out in 1937, and did not end until the end of World War II in 1945. Furthermore, the United States was apprehensive that in the event that the major powers of Europe also went to war, it would be essential that the western hemisphere appear united and strong.

But not all of the countries of Latin America were convinced that they should completely sever their economic and political relationships with Germany or Italy. By the 1930s, many South American countries, including the three key nations in the Southern Cone—Argentina, Chile, and Brazil— had strong and maturing economic connections with both Germany and Italy. In addition, the concepts of fascism, developed by Benito Mussolini and modified into Nazism by Adolf Hitler, had a certain appeal to Latin American political leaders who saw fascism and its militant form of nationalism as economically stimulating, politically strengthening, and nationally unifying.

When Adolf Hitler sent his Blitzkrieg forces into Poland on September 1, 1939, the British, French, and eventually Russians all declared war on Germany. By 1940, Hitler's European control including the countries of Denmark, Norway, the Netherlands, Belgium, and France. In the western hemisphere, the United States began to realize that the situation could be much more serious than previously anticipated. Because both France and the Netherlands had controlled territory in the western hemisphere prior to their conquests by Hitler, FDR declared that despite the conquest of both France and the Netherlands in Europe, their territorial possessions across the Atlantic Ocean would not be permitted to fall under Axis control.

The territories in question included most predominantly the South American colonies of French Guyana and Dutch Suriname, but also involved some small islands in the Caribbean Sea. By expressing apprehension over Axis designs on territory in the hemisphere, the United States seems to have been concerned about territorial aggression on a more significant level as well. At the time, Great Britain governed several significant colonies in Central and South America including the Falkland Islands, British Honduras (Belize), and Guyana, not to mention the Caribbean island Jamaica.

In September of 1939, the United States declared its neutrality in the growing European and Asian conflict. But increasingly, the United States became more and more apprehensive about Axis designs on regions outside of the European and Asian theatres of the war. So President Roosevelt also announced the Pan-American Security Zone which was designed to keep the hostilities out of the hemisphere.

But in Latin America, mixed emotions prevailed about the continuing conflict, economic relations with the Axis, and the intentions of the United States. Finally, the United States became concerned that Germany might attempt aggressive clandestine forays into Latin American territories as a way of strengthening their position in the war. These concerns spanned every contingency from full-scale invasions to attempts at sabotage and terrorism, and to secret communication and transportation facilities that were alleged to exist in various locations in the Caribbean and throughout South America.

So the United States and several Latin American nations strengthened their own economic attachments. Since commercial activities with former European markets were now less secure or nonexistent because of the war, Latin American economies needed new markets for their goods. The United States began to purchase even more merchandise and raw materials from Latin American producers than they had before the war. But fortifying the economic relationship between the United States and Latin American nations was not enough.

The United States also attempted to influence the political movements in several countries through both the use of official ambassadors and advisors and through the less official use of anti-Axis propaganda designed to eliminate much of the trust that had been constructed between the nations of Latin America and Germany and Italy. But it would not be until the Japanese attack on Hawaii that these attempts at hemispheric solidarity would be put to the greatest test. Some Latin American nations supported the United States instantly following Pearl Harbor. Others were more taciturn to do so, and a few refused to get involved altogether, or waited until the final months of the war to be drawn in.[18]

Pearl Harbor and the Declarations of War

When the Japanese attacked Pearl Harbor in Hawaii at 8:00 a.m. on December 7, 1941, they simultaneously declared war on not only the United States, but also the United Kingdom, Australia, New Zealand, Canada, India, and South Africa. The U.S. Congress in turn declared war on Japan the next day on December 8. The effect of this attack on the United States had profound repercussions throughout Latin America.

Particularly interesting was the response in Central America and the Caribbean. On December 8, 1941, the same day that the United States declared war on Japan, eight nations in Central America and the Caribbean all immediately declared war on Japan as well—Costa Rica, Cuba, El Salvador, Guatemala, Haiti, Honduras, Nicaragua, and The Dominican Republic. But far more fascinating was Panama's response: the Panamanian government actually declared war on Japan *before* the United States, on December 7, 1941, the same day as the attack on Pearl Harbor. Then, when Germany and Italy declared war on the United States on December 11, 1941, again the response from Central America and the Caribbean was astonishing. Again, eight nations declared war on Germany and Italy on December 11, 12, and 13, including Costa Rica, El Salvador, Guatemala, Haiti, Honduras, Nicaragua, Panama, and the Dominican Republic.[19]

Why did these nations of Central America and the Caribbean Basin all voluntarily involve themselves in World War II so quickly? There are three general responses to this question. Perhaps the first reason was the fact that the United States had built stronger economic and commercial ties with the nations of the Caribbean and Central America than with nearly all other countries in Latin America.[20]

A second reason revolves around the new position taken by the United States that being good neighbors meant no more overt military interventions in Latin American countries. And the United States had previously interfered in the affairs of Central American and Caribbean nations much more frequently than in South American nations during the previous 100 years. This show of solidarity following Pearl Harbor did not necessarily mean that all had been instantly forgiven in the decade following Roosevelt's inauguration, but he had removed U.S. troops from several countries in the Caribbean and Central America, not to mention the fact that the United States did not invade Mexico in the aftermath of the oil expropriations. So Latin American nations north of the equator were willing to take the Good Neighbor Policy at face value for the time being, and support the United States after Pearl Harbor.

Finally, the nations of Central America and the Caribbean are among the smallest in the entire hemisphere in terms of geographic size, population, military strength, and economic capacity. Central American and Caribbean countries likely allied themselves quickly with the United States and the Allies so that they could have greater assurances of protection in the event of Axis aggression from either the Atlantic Ocean or the Pacific Ocean.

Mexico declared war on Japan, Germany, and Italy on May 22, 1942. The nations of South America were slower to follow suit in declaring war on the Axis Powers. The only other Latin American country to declare war in 1942 was Brazil, which finally committed to the conflict by declaring war on Germany and Italy on August 22. Other South American governments were less sure about lining up behind the British and Americans. In April of 1943 Bolivia declared war on all the Axis Powers, and Chile broke off all diplomatic relations with Japan, Germany, and Italy as early as January of 1943.

At the end of 1944 and during the early months of 1945, many of the remaining countries of Latin America finally decided to enter the war, although by this date their declarations of war against the Axis Powers were somewhat more political than anything else. In February of 1945, four countries declared war—Ecuador declared war on Japan, and Paraguay, Uruguay, and Venezuela all declared war on all the Axis Powers.

Then on March 27, 1945, Argentina finally declared war on the Axis Powers. Argentina had been particularly conflicted about this decision. Significant portions of the Argentine population were first-generation Germans and Italians who had not yet given up their first languages. Many of them felt greater kinship with their countrymen in Europe, and felt attachment and loyalty to Mussolini and Hitler. So only when it seemed certain that Italy and Germany were doomed to defeat did the Argentine government concede and declare war. Within less than a month, Chile followed suit on April 11, 1945, by declaring war on Japan. Then the German surrender came on May 7, and the hostilities in the European theatre of World War II came to a conclusion. Nearly a month after Germany's surrender, Brazil finally declared war on Japan on June 6, 1945, and then Japan surrendered on August 14, 1945, after the Japanese cities of Hiroshima and Nagasaki were leveled by nuclear blasts on August 6 and 9 respectively. World War II was finally over.

It is interesting to note that several areas in Latin America did not get involved in the war at all. These include Guyana, Surinam, French Guiana, Belize, Jamaica, and Puerto Rico. But a quick glance at this list is sufficient to discern why these areas were not involved. Every single one of the names listed were colonies of other countries at the time of the war, including Puerto Rico which was (and still is) a protectorate, or commonwealth of the United States. Of the six names listed, only one other region, besides Puerto Rico, is still under the guidance of a foreign power; this is French Guiana, which is now considered an overseas Department of France.

Two other South American nations also avoided direct declarations of war during World War II. Neither Colombia nor Peru officially entered the conflict on the side of the Allies. Colombia broke off diplomatic relations with Germany and Italy in December of 1941 after the bombing of Pearl Harbor, and then in November of 1943 Colombia declared belligerency status against Germany but never officially declared war. Likewise Peru declared belligerency status against both Germany and Japan in February of 1945 when several other South American nations joined the war, but like Colombia, never officially declared war on the Axis Powers.

Latin American Involvement in World War II

Even though almost every nation in the hemisphere declared war on some or all of the Axis Powers, very few actually entered combat during

World War II. Most of the wartime contributions of Latin American nations were either economic or political in nature in support of the U.S. war effort. Nevertheless, several Latin American countries suffered direct or indirect attacks by Axis military units. German U-boats in the Caribbean destroyed hundreds of ships belonging to various nations in the hemisphere. Likewise, the United States and United Kingdom used land in the Caribbean and in Central America for landing strips, and docks for ships.[21]

Brazil and Mexico were the most influential Latin American nations in the entire conflict. Both provided economic and military resources to the United States, and permitted the United States to station troops and equipment in their countries. And Brazil and Mexico were the only countries in all of Latin America that dedicated troops to actual combat during World War II.

Brazil sent an infantry division to Italy in July of 1944, which eventually exceeded 25,000 men. Frank McCann described Brazil's contributions in this way:

> Brazil took an active part in World War II as a supplier of strategic raw materials, as the site of important air and naval bases, as a skillful supporter of the United States in pan-American conferences, as a contributor of naval units, a combat fighter squadron and a 25,000 strong infantry division. It lost 1,889 soldiers and sailors, 31 merchant vessels, 3 warships, and 22 fighter aircraft. It came out of the war with modernized armed forces, thanks to its receipt of 70% of all United States Lend-Lease equipment sent to Latin America.[22]

Similarly, Mexico also eventually sent troops into combat during the war. Aircraft sent to Mexico under the Lend-Lease program culminated in the bolstering of a significant Mexican Air Force. Around 300 Mexican pilots of the 201st Squadron were trained and sent to the Asian theatre where they participated in bombing raids on Taiwan and the Philippine Islands in 1945.[23] And although Mexico did not commit ground troops directly to the war, around 15,000 Mexicans who lived near the U.S. border were recruited into the U.S. Army. Mexican casualties during World War II are difficult to reconstruct, but Alan Knight estimates that as many as 10 percent (or 1,500) of Mexicans recruited into the U.S. Army died in combat.[24]

The Aftermath of World War II in the Western Hemisphere

World War II had the effect of unifying most of the hemisphere. Perhaps the most telling example is that of Mexico and the United States, both of whom were almost reluctantly surprised to find themselves allied on the same side of a war.

Following World War II, the United States and Latin America entered a period of cooperation, cordial associations, and mutual goodwill unlike anything in the history of U.S.–Latin American relations to that point. Indeed many historians regard the years during and immediately following World War II as the zenith of diplomatic relations in the western hemisphere. Much of the good relations were the direct result of the war itself because all of a sudden there was a common enemy that threatened the entire hemisphere, and served to unite the United States and Latin American nations on the same side. For most Latin American countries the United States was suddenly not the bad guy, but an energetic and powerful ally that had hemispheric peace and prosperity as its principal objectives.

In the wake of hemispheric solidarity, the United States and twenty Latin American nations sent delegates to Bogotá, Colombia, in 1948 to attend the Ninth International Conference of American States. At the conference, the nations of the hemisphere created the Organization of American States (OAS) to function as a western hemispheric version of the United Nations. The creation of the OAS signaled the potential for a new era of cooperation and mutual collaboration in the Americas.

Unfortunately, U.S.–Latin American relations would never again be as mutual as it had been between 1939 and 1945. After the war was over and things began to return to normality, disillusionment and frustration returned. Some Latin American governments argued that the United States had only been interested in Latin America because of its ability to contribute *materiel* to the war effort; that in effect the United States had contrived amity with the Latin Americans as a ploy for gaining its ulterior motives through manipulating them to its own benefit during the war.

And even more importantly, with the conclusion of World War II, the globe was plunged into another, perhaps more sinister, conflict, the Cold War, between the two new superpowers, the United States and the Soviet Union. And the United States became so concerned with the global spread of communism that it dedicated most of its postwar economy and foreign policy to the rebuilding of both Germany and Japan so that they would not become susceptible to communist infiltration from either the Soviet Union or, after 1949, the People's Republic of China. Unfortunately, the concern that U.S. leaders felt over the worldwide spread of communism led to a new disregard and neglect of Latin America which quickly felt betrayed by the United States.

The Cold War, the Cuban Revolution, and the Cuban Missile Crisis

When we speak of the people we do not mean the comfortable ones, the conservative elements of the nation, who welcome any regime of oppression, any dictatorship, any despotism, prostrating themselves before the master of the moment. When we speak of struggle, the people means the vast unredeemed masses to whom all make promises and whom all deceive; we mean the people who yearn for a better, more dignified and more just nation.   – Fidel Castro

If there ever was in the history of humanity an enemy who was truly universal, an enemy whose acts and moves trouble the entire world, threaten the entire world, attack the entire world in any way or another, that real and really universal enemy is precisely Yankee imperialism.   – Fidel Castro

Condemn me, it does not matter, history will absolve me.   – Fidel Castro

In the months and years following the end of World War II, the globe saw the evolution of two superpowers that each wielded nuclear weapons, and together plunged the world into an ideological conflict of capitalism versus communism and democracy versus totalitarianism. The Cold War had profound effects on U.S.–Latin American relations in several ways. First and foremost, U.S.–Latin American relations were directly influenced because the United States was one of these superpowers and its relationship with the nations of Latin America continued to evolve along with its status in the international community.

Secondly, many nations in Latin America began to view the Soviet Union and socialism as a plausible alternative to the heavy-handed tactics of the United States in the western hemisphere. And even though it is true that immediately following World War II, the United States and the countries of Latin America enjoyed better and more cooperative relations than at any other time in their diplomatic histories, it did not take long for tensions and frustrations to resurface which sent Latin Americans looking for alternatives. And in the polarized environment of the Cold War, alternatives to the United States all tended to focus on the Soviet Union.

Some of these anxieties centered on financial commitments made by the United States both during and after the war. During World War II, the United States had made extensive use of the lands and resources of many Latin American countries. Many countries in Central and South America had the understanding that after the war was over, the United States would use its economic and political strength to help them recover and put their own economies back together again. Unfortunately, the United States saw the potential proliferation of communism throughout the world as a greater threat to the peace and prosperity of the globe than economic conditions in Latin American nations. So while the United States dedicated money and personnel to rebuilding European and Asian countries, some areas of Latin America, such as Peru, Guatemala, and Cuba, to name only a few, turned increasingly to the left-wing ideals and principles of socialism.

THE TRUMAN DOCTRINE AND THE MARSHALL PLAN

After World War II, the only major member of the Allies that had not been devastated economically, politically, or militarily by the fighting was the United States. Because so many of the nations of Europe and Asia were severely damaged by the fighting that took place inside their borders, the United States believed that these areas were especially susceptible to the spread of communism that was propagated by the Soviet Union. So in 1947, after communist revolutions occurred in several locations in Europe including Greece, Turkey, and Yugoslavia, President Harry S. Truman issued a statement that has since come to be known as the Truman Doctrine. On March 12, 1947, President Truman spoke in the U.S. Congress wherein he stated,

> The seeds of totalitarian regimes are nurtured by misery and want. They spread and grow in the evil soil of poverty and strife. They reach their full growth when the hope of a people for a better life has died. We must keep that hope alive. The free peoples of the world look to us for support in maintaining their freedoms. If we falter in our leadership, we may endanger the peace of the world—and we shall surely endanger the welfare of our own nation.[1]

President Truman argued that any country in the world that was threatened by communist expansion could expect aid from the United States in the form of funding and military support. In June of 1947, United States Secretary of State George C. Marshall delivered an address at Harvard University which has since become known as the Marshall Plan. In subsequent statements and documents, the Marshall Plan proposed the sending of around $13 billion to Europe to aid in rebuilding from the destruction of the war.

For the United States, this aid money was simply a good investment that would help promote security, capitalism, and democracy in Europe and Asia. But from the Soviet perspective of Josef Stalin, the Marshall Plan was nothing more than a diplomatic bribing of nations into siding with the United States against the Soviet Union.

Between 1948 and 1952, fifteen European countries received money from the United States under the provisions of the Marshall Plan. Meanwhile, Latin American nations became more and more frustrated that very little money from the United States was sent to their suffering economies during the same time period. They quickly began to understand that both the Truman Doctrine and the Marshall Plan, which pledged aid to countries suffering from economic and political instability, did not apply to them.

THE COLD WAR IN LATIN AMERICA

By the time U.S. policymakers began to take a closer look at what was occurring in Latin America during the years following the war, they were astonished to discover popular movements in rural Latin American communities and among Latin American politicians alike that looked like communism. However, it is important to remember that by the end of the 1940s, and throughout the 1950s, the United States went through a difficult period known in U.S. history as the Red Scare. Several global events triggered feelings of tension and mild paranoia among American citizens and statesmen alike. Other less high-profile events in Latin American countries in subsequent years were likewise labeled communism, and in some of these cases, communist expansion was indeed occurring. But in many other instances, what the U.S. government labeled "communism" in Latin America was in fact only social, political, and economic reform that was ideologically to the left of conservative American values and interests in the wake of the emerging Cold War.

So late in the 1950s when U.S. politicians refocused their attention on Latin America, they believed they saw popular left-wing movements and ideologies in various stages of planning and implementation. Most of these movements in Latin America were born of the frustrations of postwar relations with the United States, coupled with terrible economic conditions and political ineptitude. But the United States, in its heightened state of awareness and fear over the search for worldwide communist expansion, saw many popular social movements as proof of communist infiltration in the countries of Latin America.

In Peru, a political party called the American Popular Revolutionary Alliance (APRA) was beginning to earn a lot of attention among the rural and poor populations of that country. The party had been founded earlier in the 1920s by Víctor Raúl Haya de la Torre who had been considered dangerous enough by the right-wing Peruvian government that he was exiled to Mexico in 1923. When he returned from exile to run in the Peruvian presidential elections of 1930, he was apprehended and thrown into prison. The government of Peru then outlawed APRA and labeled the Apristas communists.[2]

In 1933 the president of Peru was assassinated by an APRA-based terrorist, and the right-wing government of Peru turned increasingly to the military for support against the Apristas and communist infiltration. During the years of World War II APRA had remained an illegal political party, but had continued to exist underground. Following the war, Haya de la Torre was again exiled—this time to Colombia—and APRA revolutionaries staged several minor revolutions and protests throughout the country. In 1954 Haya de la Torre returned to Peru again but was kept under the vigilant watch of the military. In 1962 when it appeared that Haya de la Torre had gained enough votes to carry the most recent presidential election, the military stepped in and annulled the elections to prevent him from taking office.

The United States observed Peru's struggle with the left-wing Apristas with great interest. But just as statesmen in the United States began to wonder if in fact the conditions of poverty in Latin America—coupled with European migration into specific Latin American nations—did indeed make Latin Americans more susceptible to communist propaganda, the Korean War broke out and kept the attention and the money of the United States focused away from the western hemisphere. When United States finally began to understand that the Central American nation of Guatemala was moving forward with sophisticated left-wing agendas, the time had come for more than interested observation, it was time to act.

THE CIA COUP IN GUATEMALA

In 1945, Juan José Arévalo, a former university professor who had previously been exiled to Argentina for his radical ideas, was elected president of Guatemala. As the leader of Guatemala, Arévalo managed to attract the interest of the United States in several different ways, none of them positive. First of all, he succeeded a conservative, right-wing, military general in the president's office, and was noticeably farther to the left ideologically. Second, Arévalo began to enact social changes that appeared more socialist than the United States was entirely comfortable with. For example, he began to enact legislation aimed at strengthening labor unions, and he talked of granting farmland to peasant farmers. The United States became concerned that Arévalo might in fact be a communist because he styled his brand of government "spiritual socialism," which no one in the U.S. government at the time could or would distinguish from communism anyway.[3]

Arévalo's plans for land redistribution and agrarian reform in the rural areas of Guatemala met with extreme resistance by the large landowners of Guatemala, and United Fruit Company (UFCO) was particularly wary because it owned over a million square acres of land in Guatemala and employed over 40,000 people there. UFCO was arguably the most powerful foreign entity in the entire country of Guatemala with its huge land holdings, hundreds of miles of rail, control of telephone and telegraph lines, and management of port cities. UFCO had also invested tens of millions of dollars in its production of bananas and other tropical fruit in Guatemala. So when President Arévalo prepared to confiscate some of UFCO's lands, the multinational American corporation prepared to fight back.[4]

But in 1951, before he could fully implement a serious attempt at agrarian reform in Guatemala, President Arévalo's term in office came to an end and he was replaced by newly elected Jacobo Arbenz, a colonel in the Guatemalan military, and therefore supposedly a conservative right-wing politician. The U.S. government and UFCO were momentarily delighted at the prospect of an old-fashioned military strongman in control of Guatemala, a statesman who would support U.S. policy in the region. But these disillusionments quickly turned to alarm when Arbenz not only did not back away from many of the reforms of the previous administration, but instead embraced and continued to carry many of them out. Subsequent investigations revealed that his wife María Vilanova de Arbenz and several of his close friends and associates were official members of the Guatemalan Communist Party. In fact, José Manuel Fortuny, one of the principal founders of the party, was one of Arbenz's closest personal friends, and wrote many of Arbenz's political speeches. Arbenz reciprocated in 1951 by legalizing the party and recognizing it as an official political party in Guatemalan politics.

In 1952, Arbenz issued Decree 900 which nationalized around 200,000 square acres of fallow land in Guatemala which he then redistributed to poor peasant farmers. Most of the land was expropriated from UFCO. Because of the Good Neighbor Policy of the previous decade, along with the improved relations that immediately followed World War II, Arbenz likely believed that the United States would react to his nationalization of UFCO lands in a manner similar to their previous reactions following the nationalization of U.S. oilfields in Mexico by President Lázaro Cárdenas; that is, that they would demand a payment and then walk away from the situation. So no one was that surprised when UFCO demanded payment for the expropriated acres of land. The Guatemalan government offered $600,000 on the basis of the value of the land previously declared by UFCO in legal and tax documents. But UFCO demanded close to $15 million, claiming that the land had appreciated in value since its purchase. When the Arbenz government refused, UFCO began to pull strings in the U.S. government to regain their lost land.[5]

Several authors have discussed the interesting connections between UFCO and the U.S. government. President Dwight D. Eisenhower, and several members of his cabinet had either direct or indirect ties to UFCO. For example, the president of UFCO, Thomas Cabot, was the brother of John M. Cabot, Eisenhower's Assistant Secretary of State for Inter-American Affairs, and Ambassador to Colombia. John Foster Dulles, Eisenhower's Secretary of State, was a UFCO company lawyer, and his brother Allan Dulles—who was also a UFCO lawyer—was the current CIA director.[6]

Early in 1954 the CIA began preparing forces in Honduras and Nicaragua for an invasion of Guatemala. Furtive radio broadcasts and leaflets dropped by aircraft in Guatemala spread negative propaganda about the Arbenz regime. When the invasion finally came in the summer of 1954, Guatemala put up very little resistance. Arbenz agreed to go into exile in Cuba, and the Guatemalan government was turned over to Colonel Carlos Castillo Armas, a Guatemalan exile in Honduras who participated with the CIA in toppling Arbenz. In terms of Arbenz and his untimely removal from office, Piero Gleijeses has argued,

> Jacobo Arbenz provided Guatemala with the best government it has ever had. He embarked on the first comprehensive development plan in the history of Guatemala . . . and he presided over the most successful agrarian reform in the history of Central America. Within eighteen months . . . five hundred thousand peasants had received land without disrupting the country's economy. . . . By the end of Arbenz's term, hundreds of thousands of peasants would have been solidly established on land granted them by Decree 900. . . . But the Pax Americana prevailed. Nowhere in Central America or the Caribbean has U.S. intervention been so decisive and so baneful in shaping the future of a country.[7]

The aftermath of the Guatemalan coup was devastating in terms of U.S.–Latin American relations. Latin American's worst fears of U.S. intervention were resurfacing in a new and ruthless manner. In the following years, the United States restated its intentions to uphold the Good Neighbor Policy by not participating in military interventions in Latin American nations. But Latin America had witnessed the ability of the United States to influence the politics of Guatemala through secret CIA operations, all the while claiming that the U.S. military had not been involved at all.

And the Guatemalan coup demonstrated the broader spectrum of the influence the Cold War had on U.S.–Latin American relations. It now became clear that right-wing military dictatorships were much better equipped to handle the stresses of fighting communist infiltration while simultaneously maintaining strong economic and political ties to the United States. Military dictators were able to use methods and means of stamping out left-wing revolutions that democratically elected and supported civilian presidents could never hold or wield.

But even while the Guatemalan crisis was drawing to a close, at the same time, another Latin American nation—just 90 miles south of the United States—was plunged into a struggle for identity and self-determinism that would eventually take the entire world to the brink of nuclear annihilation. That nation was Cuba.

FIDEL CASTRO AND THE CUBAN REVOLUTION

The Cuban Revolution of 1959 is one of the most important episodes in U.S.–Latin American relations. The roots of Fidel Castro's 1959 revolution run deep in Cuban history; Fidel Castro said that his revolution to reclaim the dignity and freedom of the Cuban people redressed wrongs that spanned centuries, including the Platt Amendment, the Spanish–American War, and the Spanish conquest of Cuba.

The immediate roots of the Cuban Revolution and Fidel Castro's rise to power go back at least to 1933 and the *coup d'état* that brought Fulgencio Batista to power in Cuba. On September 3, 1933, some enlisted soldiers in the Cuban military, including Sergeant Batista, approached their officers with demands for better conditions and higher pay. When they were rebuffed they took control of the military base and within two days, with the help of protesting student groups, toppled the government of Cuba. Between 1933 and 1940, several individuals held the position of President of Cuba, but most were puppets of Fulgencio Batista who had received a massive rank advancement (from Sergeant to General), and was then appointed Army Chief of Staff of the entire Cuban military. Behind the scenes, Batista ruled Cuba for most of the decade until becoming president himself in 1940.

By the end of his first term as president of Cuba in 1944, many saw Batista as a progressive and benevolent leader. When his term in office was completed, he retired to Florida in the United States and turned Cuba over to others. But by 1952, Fulgencio Batista had grown tired of his retirement in the United States and desired to return to power in Cuba. Cuban law forbade Batista from a second term in office, so Batista returned to Cuba, staged a second coup, and seized control of the Cuban government on March 10, 1952.

This time, Batista's government was much less formal and much more authoritarian. He threw out the old 1940 constitution, quieted the media, closed schools, and eventually dissolved the Cuban Congress, all in his attempt to wield absolute power in Cuba. Batista's heavy-handed tactics, combined with his close ties with U.S. commerce, left a bad taste in the mouths of many Cubans, particularly active university students and young professionals who had aspirations for future positions in the Cuban government. One such individual was Fidel Castro.

Fidel Castro was born on August 13, 1926, in Birán, Cuba. By 1945 Castro graduated from his secondary schooling and entered law school at the University of Havana. Over the next several years, Castro became heavily involved in student movements that promoted Cuban nationalism and anti-U.S. sentiments.[8]

By 1952, Castro had earned a law degree and determined to run for a seat in the Cuban Congress where he would be able to carry out his ideas on reform and restructuring of both Cuban politics and economics. But the 1952 coup that was carried out by Batista convinced Castro that diplomatic and political solutions to Cuba's problems could never solve anything, and the only way to reform Cuba was through violence.

A year later, on July 26, 1953, Fidel Castro and his followers led an attack on the Moncada Army Barracks in eastern Cuba. Castro's plan was simple: he and around 150 followers would storm the military compound and take control while most of the soldiers were away at local bars. Unfortunately, Castro's small army encountered close to 1,000 Cuban soldiers in the Moncada Barracks, and Castro's forces were rapidly devastated. Within less than a week, Castro and some of his surviving comrades were captured and imprisoned to await trial.

In September at his trial, Fidel Castro acted as his own defense attorney and defended his actions in the broader context of Cuban nationalism. He appealed to earlier writings of Cuban icon José Martí, and his speeches while on trial became some of the first official literature of the Cuban Revolution. His final remarks remain legendary to this day. Knowing that he faced a significant prison sentence for his actions, Castro insolently articulated the following: "I know that prison will be hard, harder than it has been for anyone, filled with threats, with callous and cruel barbarity, but I do not fear it, just as I do not fear the fury of the despicable tyrant that tore out the lives of seventy of my brothers. Condemn me, it does not matter, history will absolve me."[9] He was sentenced to a fifteen-year prison term on the Isle of Pines along the southwest coast of Cuba.

While in prison, Castro used his time to study. Among the many titles he devoured during his incarceration was *Mein Kampf* by Adolf Hitler. His understanding of *Mein Kampf* seems to have affected the later stages of his Cuban Revolution. At one point he argued that whereas Hitler had created a scapegoat out of the Jews of Europe, he, Castro, would likewise create a scapegoat out of the United States of America to fuel his own revolution. With these notions firmly in place in his mind, when he was released from prison prematurely in 1955 (in a general amnesty declared by the dictator

Batista) he went into exile in Mexico where he began to prepare a full-scale invasion of Cuba and the continuation of his revolution.

While in Mexico, Castro met another Latin American revolutionary named Ernesto Rafael "Che" Guevara who had traveled through Latin America as a would-be activist and revolutionary. Che had actually been living in Guatemala when President Jacobo Arbenz was toppled from power. He was able to contribute his knowledge of Latin American insurgency, along with his charisma, to Castro's movement to reclaim Cuba from the hands of Batista and Yankee imperialism.

The second most important date in the ongoing Cuban Revolution is December 2, 1956; this was the date of Fidel Castro's return to Cuba, along with his brother Raúl, Che Guevara, and eighty loyal guerrilla fighters. They set out from Mexico in a small boat called the *Granma* which nearly sank *en route*. When Castro and his followers landed on the southeast coast of Cuba, they were attacked by Batista's men and only twelve survived to flee into the Sierra Maestra mountains. Over the next two years, Castro's forces would grow dramatically. Local villages and poor farmers aided Castro and his guerrillas and soon Batista's forces were unable to gain any ground against Castro's stronger and more zealous followers.

And an American reporter working for the *New York Times* named Herbert Matthews traveled to Cuba in an attempt to speak with Castro face to face. On February 17, 1957, Matthews trekked into the Sierra Maestra Mountains to meet with Castro who had agreed to the meeting. As a result of Matthews's interview with Castro, the world began to understand the full force of Castro's movement in the mountains of Cuba. Castro became somewhat of a folk hero because of Matthews's reporting, and support for his movement inside Cuba swelled.[10]

By November 1958, Batista's forces were crumbling under Castro's revolution, and the Cuban military was experiencing massive defection to Castro's guerrilla fighters. When Che Guevara's army defeated Batista's forces at the Battle of Santa Clara, Batista realized he was finished. He fled to the Dominican Republic on the last day of the year. The very next day, on January 1, 1959, Castro's forces entered the city of Havana to the cheering of thousands of euphoric Cubans. A week later, when Fidel Castro addressed Cuba as their new leader and liberator, several white doves flew out of the crowd below him, and to everyone's surprise, one of the doves landed on Castro's shoulder where it remained for much of the rest of his speech. That was enough for almost everyone; Fidel Castro had become the savior of the Cuban people.

Reforms came quickly to Cuba as Castro made good on most of his promises. But as in Guatemala less than a decade earlier, when Castro did nationalize land owned by foreign corporations, much of the land that he seized belonged to the UFCO. Furthermore, Castro soon opened formal diplomatic relations with the Soviet Union early in 1960. Cuba began to sell hundreds of thousands of tons of sugar to the Soviet Union, and the Russians in return extended to the Cubans low-interest loans and began to ship oil to Cuba at low prices.[11]

In the wake of Castro's revolution, the United States increasingly reduced its importation of Cuban sugar; after all, now that Hawaii had been an official U.S. state since 1959, Cuban sugar was not as necessary. Castro responded by expropriating American oil companies and refineries in Cuba, and by nationalizing American property including sugar mills, hotels, casinos, companies of various kinds, and food and chemical processing plants.

At this point the United States officially cut off all diplomatic relations with Castro's Cuba in January of 1961, and the Eisenhower administration began to contemplate the implementation of more aggressive solutions to Castro's control of Cuba, and his apparent shift to the left. But by the time a solution was ready for implementation, President Eisenhower had left the White House and John F. Kennedy was left to call the shots of a Cuban invasion that had been planned by the previous administration, which would be known as the Bay of Pigs fiasco.[12]

THE BAY OF PIGS

On April 17, 1961, following bombing by U.S. aircraft over the previous two days, less than 1,500 quasi-military troops initiated an invasion of the island of Cuba from the southern *Bahía de Cochinos* (Bay of Pigs). Most of them were Cuban refugees and exiles who had been trained briefly by the CIA in Guatemala and elsewhere, and then were subsequently sent out to reclaim Cuba from the hands of Castro and his regime. They were told that they would have air support from the United States, and their goal was the immediate toppling of Castro's government.[13]

Unfortunately, the landing of these troops turned into a massacre. Their invasion was compromised, they were trapped on Girón Beach, and within less than three days, nearly 100 were killed and almost 1,200 were captured as prisoners of war. Furthermore, because most of them were former Cuban nationals or exiles, the Castro regime charged them with treason. Since the Bay of Pigs invasion, writers and historians have repeatedly called the entire incident a fiasco and a tragedy. It was humiliating for the new Kennedy administration, it spawned more clandestine operations such as the CIA's Operation Mongoose, and it ultimately had dire consequences for U.S.–Cuban relations because shortly after the invasion, Castro proclaimed his status as a socialist-communist, thus paving the way for Russian nuclear missiles in Cuba.

Castro had claimed he was a communist as early as the fall of 1960, but no one in Russia was prepared to take him very seriously until after the Bay of Pigs. For U.S.–Latin American relations, the Bay of Pigs invasion marked the official end of the Good Neighbor Policy of nonintervention by the U.S. military, and Latin American nations harshly criticized the Kennedy administration for its blundering approach to Castro's Cuba.

OPERATION MONGOOSE

Operation Mongoose has been the subject of much speculation and debate over the past four decades. In the aftermath of the debacle at the Bay of Pigs, the Kennedy administration decided to remove Castro from power in a less visible manner. As early as November of 1961 Operation Mongoose went into effect. Under the direction of the President's brother Robert Kennedy, the Pentagon and the CIA devised several intricate and elaborate schemes for removing Castro from power and possibly assassinating him. Most of the plots that were debated and developed for implementation against Fidel Castro never came to fruition; some were so outlandish that they did not survive the initial planning stages. Nevertheless, the CIA became involved to varying degrees in a spy-versus-spy mentality of secret and creative ways to remove the Cuban dictator and make it look like an accident that could not be traced back to the United States.

Resources allotted to Operation Mongoose were substantial. In fact, when Operation Mongoose was operating at full capacity, it was the largest clandestine American operation in the history of the CIA. Around 400 CIA officers were assigned to Mongoose and the annual budget approached $50 million.[14] Some of the plots that were devised and planned by the CIA included, but were not limited to, explosive sea shells, explosive cigars, poisoned cigars, poisoned ice cream, poisoned fountain pens, chemically treated wet suits to give Castro skin problems, and other products designed to make his beard fall out. Plans were also discussed to poison his drinks, have someone shoot him with a rifle (a curiously simply plot), contaminate Cuban sugar, and hire the Mafia to carry out a hit on Castro.[15]

These attempts to discredit or eliminate Castro represent the frustrations that the Kennedy administration felt due to the fact that Castro had come to power in a Latin American nation, less than 100 miles south of the United States, and brought with him an apparent tolerance for socialism, and intentions of flaunting U.S. Cold War policy by courting the favor of the Soviet Union. But Castro had not been interested in communism very much at all during his rise to power in Cuba. In fact, as late as April of 1959, while visiting the United States following his rise to power in Cuba, Castro told the National Press Club, "We are against all kinds of dictators.... That is why we are against Communism."[16] But following the aggressive moves by the Kennedy administration, first with the Bay of Pigs and subsequently through the covert Operation Mongoose, Castro was, at least in his own mind, forced to seek protection from an increasingly aggressive United States.

THE CUBAN MISSILE CRISIS

The idea to put medium- and long-range nuclear missiles in Cuba was of course implemented by Nikita S. Khrushchev in 1962. But there is some evidence that the idea may have been placed in Khrushchev's mind some months earlier during meetings with Che Guevara. As Aleksandr and Naftali write,

> On November 7, [1960,] Che celebrated the anniversary of the Russian revolution as an honored guest atop Lenin and Stalin's mausoleum. As he watched row upon row of shiny missiles pass in front of him, he was thinking of ways to formalize the Soviet nuclear deterrent, to prevent future invasion scares [in Cuba]. Sometime during the visit, Che is said to have probed Khrushchev about the possibility of stationing Soviet missiles in Cuba. If Che did raise this matter it did not produce any Presidium decision in 1960. . . . Nevertheless, this was probably the germ for the decision that would emerge in 1962.[17]

Khrushchev himself argued that his rational for placing nuclear weapons on the island were purely defensive, that they were to prevent the United States from further plans to invade the island or topple Castro from power. From Khrushchev's perspective, the Kennedy administration, through the Bay of Pigs and Operation Mongoose, had expressed its hostile intent toward Castro's regime. And because of Castro's shift toward communism, Khrushchev likely felt obligated to defend the island from any subsequent aggressions by the United States, which seemed imminent at the time.

In May of 1962 Khrushchev and the Soviet Defense Council approved Operation Anadyr, which called for the installation of nuclear missiles at various locations across the island of Cuba. Later during September, the Soviets deployed several different kinds of military personnel and weaponry to Cuba including tanks, fighters, anti-aircraft guns, rifles, ammunition, and around 42,000 troops, pilots, and technicians. In terms of defensive weapons, the Russians sent to Cuba patrol boats, bombers, and several batteries of defensive missile systems such as cruise missiles, surface-to-air missiles, and Luna missiles. Finally, in terms of nuclear capabilities, the Soviet Union installed on Cuba several launch sites for both medium-range ballistic missiles (MRBM) and intermediate-range ballistic missiles (IRBM). In terms of the actual nuclear warheads themselves, various scholars have estimated that probably no more than twenty nuclear warheads were transported to Cuba from the Soviet Union.[18]

The United States had been using U-2 aircraft since 1955 to spy on Soviet activities and nuclear buildup in the Soviet Union. The U-2 aircraft could fly at incredibly high altitudes—70,000 to 90,000 feet—and at incredibly high speeds—over 500 miles per hour. U-2 aircraft used state-of-the-art technology to observe and photograph installations and movements on the ground. On October 14, 1962, a U-2 aircraft piloted by Richard Heyser flew over western Cuba and took several photographs. When the plane returned to California and the film was processed and analyzed, it appeared that the Russians had placed at least two medium-range ballistic missile sites at San Cristóbal in western Cuba. There was also evidence of several surface-to-air missile (SAM) sites under development which was perplexing. President Kennedy was informed of the intelligence on the morning of October 16, and the Cuban Missile Crisis was underway.

Kennedy was presented with both diplomatic and military solutions to the Cuban Missile Crisis. But Kennedy chose neither option at first. Instead, he opted for a less aggressive blockade of the island of Cuba. On the night of October 22, 1962, John F. Kennedy went on live radio and television in the United States to announce that the United States had discovered Russian nuclear missiles in Cuba, that the Russians had openly and directly lied about their nuclear buildup on the island, and that the United States would not tolerate the presence of nuclear weapons in Cuba. Kennedy said,

> Each of these missiles, in short, is capable of striking Washington, D.C., the Panama Canal, Cape Canaveral, Mexico City, or any other city in the Southeastern part of the United States, in Central America, or in the Caribbean area.... Additional sites... appear to be designed for intermediate range ballistic missiles—capable of traveling twice as far—and thus capable of striking most of the major cities in the Western Hemisphere, ranging as far north as Hudson's Bay, Canada, and as far south as Lima, Peru.[19]

President Kennedy then outlined his plan of action that included a naval blockade of the Cuban island, continued U-2 surveillance, and meetings at the United Nations. Finally, it was during this televised speech that President Kennedy pronounced those famous words that have become the hallmark of the Cuban Missile Crisis, "It shall be the policy of this nation to regard any nuclear missile launched from Cuba against any nation in the Western Hemisphere as an attack by the Soviet Union on the United States, requiring a full retaliatory response upon the Soviet Union."[20]

The blockade of Cuba went into effect at 2:00 p.m. on October 24, 1962; the blockade zone was established at 500 miles around the coast of Cuba. However, a naval blockade was considered by many to be illegal at the time.[21] This is why the Kennedy administration did not use the term blockade at all. Instead they called it a quarantine of the island. Second, it did nothing to remove the weapons and nuclear missiles already operational on the island. However, what it did do was give Khrushchev time to reconsider his actions and the consequences of his brinkmanship tactics. The tactic seemed to work, and Khrushchev sent Kennedy several letters over the next few days. In one response, Khrushchev stated,

> If you have not lost command of yourself ... then, Mr. President, you and I should not now pull on the ends of the rope in which you have tied a knot of war, because the harder you and I pull, the tighter the knot will become. And a time may come when this knot is tied so tight that the person who tied it is no longer capable of untying it, and then the knot will have to be cut. What that would mean I need not explain to you, because you yourself understand perfectly what dread forces our two countries possess.[22]

On the same day that Khrushchev sent these words (later known as the knot letter) to Kennedy, Fidel Castro sent a letter to Khrushchev in Moscow. It was the content of this letter that seriously persuaded Khrushchev that Castro might be a mad man. In Castro's correspondence to Khrushchev, he wrote,

> At this time I want to convey to you briefly my personal opinion. If the ... imperialists invade Cuba ... the danger that that aggressive policy poses for humanity is so great that following that event the Soviet Union must never allow the circumstances in which the imperialists could launch the first nuclear strike against it. I tell you this because I believe that the imperialists' aggressiveness is extremely dangerous and if they actually carry out the brutal act of invading Cuba ... that would be the moment to eliminate such danger forever through an act of clear legitimate defense, however harsh and terrible the solution would be, for there is no other.[23]

Castro has since tried to mitigate the impact of this statement, but at the time, Khrushchev was horrified to realize that Castro seemed to be advocating a nuclear first strike against the United States.

Khrushchev knew that he either had to end the crisis or prepare to engage in a nuclear holocaust. The Soviet vessels in the Caribbean were ordered to turn back, and on October 28, Khrushchev publicly announced Russia's intention to remove all offensive nuclear weapons from Cuba.[24] Perhaps the understatement of the entire crisis was a declaration uttered by the Secretary of State Dean Rusk to National Security Advisor McGeorge Bundy. Upon hearing of the Russians' intentions to withdraw from the quarantine line and remove the missiles, Rusk replied, "We're eyeball to eyeball and I think the other guy just blinked."[25]

Both Khrushchev and Kennedy were relieved that an escalation had been avoided. But Castro was enraged and refused to allow UN weapons inspectors on the island to verify the removal of the missiles. He was bitter that he had been left out of the final negotiations, and began to feel a real disillusionment over Soviet support for his Cuban revolution.

CONCLUSIONS

The Cold War affected U.S.–Latin American relations in drastic ways. When the United States became so preoccupied about the worldwide proliferation of communism, Latin American military dictators were encouraged, endorsed, and funded by the United States in their bids for power because of their abilities to fight left-wing insurgency inside their own countries. But the Cuban Missile Crisis—which some consider to be the apex of the entire Cold War—actually had very little to do with U.S.–Latin American relations. President Kennedy said several times that his actions were designed to defend not only the United States, but the entire hemisphere against Soviet aggression. Kennedy argued that not only American cities were vulnerable to nuclear attack from Cuba, but also cities throughout Central and South America as far south as Peru and northern Brazil. And during the crisis, Kennedy's actions were supported by most of the leaders of Latin American nations. But the crisis itself was mostly a dialogue between President Kennedy and Premier Khrushchev. And even though Fidel Castro spoke often and loudly during the crisis, neither the Americans nor the Russians paid much attention to him.

But following the Cuban Missile Crisis, U.S.–Latin American relations entered a new era of right-wing anxiety over the growing communist threat. After all, Cuba had become a communist nation and Soviet satellite, less than 100 miles south of the U.S. border. Could this happen to other Latin American nations? The implications were staggering. In 1959, in addition to Fidel Castro, there were only four or five other leaders of Latin American nations that could be labeled dictators, loosely or otherwise. But between 1962 and 1966, ten different Latin American governments were toppled by military coups that brought right-wing dictators to power throughout Central America, South America, and the Caribbean. Most were reactionary, and none were very democratic at all. But they were supported by the U.S. government because they were anticommunist and they used their influence and funding to fight the spread of socialist insurgencies inside their nations.[26]

9

The End of Nonintervention and the End of the Cold War

I don't see why we need to stand by and watch a country go communist due to the irresponsibility of its people. The issues are much too important for the Chilean voters to be left to decide for themselves.　　　　　 – Henry A. Kissinger

Central America's problems directly affect the security and the well-being of our own people. And Central America is much closer to the United States than many of the world trouble spots that concern us. El Salvador is nearer to Texas than Texas is to Massachusetts, Nicaragua is just as close to Miami as Miami is to Washington.
　　　　　 – Ronald Reagan

After John F. Kennedy was assassinated on November 22, 1963, Lyndon B. Johnson became the president of the United States and would remain in the White House until 1969. The Vietnam War was raging at the time, and the world was still reeling from the Cuban Missile Crisis. In Latin America, Fidel Castro continued to export revolution through the poverty-stricken regions of the hemisphere, and right-wing Latin American dictators attempted to drive all vestiges of communism from their borders.

Prior to his death, President Kennedy had instituted the hemispheric Alliance for Progress in 1961 which continued to play a part of Lyndon Johnson's Latin American policy. The Alliance for Progress was a new economic proposal that was supposed to regulate and encourage relations between Latin American countries and the United States. Unlike Dollar Diplomacy, the Alliance for Progress focused on capital incentives to prevent left-wing revolutions. But many in Latin America saw the Alliance for Progress as a watered-down version of the Marshall Plan that came too late to Latin America. The program was later disbanded by President Nixon in the early 1970s.[1]

After the threat of the missile crisis, Johnson decided that economic investments and tax incentives in Latin America were not strong enough to keep worldwide communism out of the hemisphere. President Johnson was determined that another situation like Cuba would never happen again in the Americas, and therefore a stronger course of action than the Good Neighbor Policy was required to maintain peace and prosperity in Latin America.

As a result, he sent U.S. troops into Latin American nations in the old style of armed intervention more times than any president since Woodrow Wilson. The most visible military intervention under Johnson was the committing of over 20,000 troops to the Dominican Republic in 1965. Historian Gaddis Smith argues that "were it not for Vietnam, Lyndon Johnson's foreign policy might be remembered primarily for his approach to Latin American issues."[2]

THE END OF GOOD NEIGHBORS AND A RETURN TO MILITARY INTERVENTION

During the last months of 1963 and into 1964, President Johnson became more and more concerned about socialism in Latin American countries, and particularly in the large South American country of Brazil. The president of Brazil, João Goulart, had come to power in 1961 and was decidedly left-wing. Goulart's reforms in Brazil resembled the earlier left-wing practices of Lázaro Cárdenas in Mexico, Jacobo Arbenz in Guatemala, and Fidel Castro in Cuba, all of which ended up negatively affecting the United States and hemispheric relations. So as President Goulart moved closer and closer to the Soviet Union commercially and politically, the United States became more and more uncomfortable with Brazil's decline into socialism. In 1964 the Johnson administration prepared the U.S. military to enter Brazil and topple the Goulart regime in order to prevent communism from taking over the largest nation in Latin America. But before President Johnson could act decisively, Goulart was ousted by an internal Brazilian coup led by right-wing military generals.

When Goulart was replaced by military dictators, Brazil's danger had apparently passed. However, in the United States, President Johnson found his plans for a massive Brazilian intervention interrupted. Smith writes that Johnson's plans for Brazil had included aircraft, naval vessels—some of which had already been deployed or were in the process of being sent south to Brazil—and thousands of troops. The proposed invasion had been so massive that had it been carried out, it could have turned into "the largest

[American military intervention] in the history of the western hemisphere."[3] So when conditions in the Dominican Republic swiftly deteriorated into civil war, President Johnson was ready to quickly dedicate troops to the Caribbean instead of Brazil.

Intervention in the Dominican Republic

Previously in May of 1961, the dictator of the Dominican Republic, Rafael Trujillo, had been shot to death by his own military bodyguards. Trujillo had ruled the Dominican Republic since 1930 as one of the most corrupt and violent dictators in Latin American history. His death sparked a struggle for control of the Dominican Republic which saw several different individuals or groups trying to run the country unsuccessfully, and eventually culminated in a bloody civil war that began in April of 1965. On one side of the conflict were the military leaders who desperately wanted to regain control of the Dominican Republic and prevent it from declining into utter anarchy and bedlam. On the other side were the left-wing popular leaders and students who desired political and economic changes and saw no other way of achieving them.[4]

It soon became apparent to Johnson's advisors that if the situation in the Dominican Republic were ignored, there was a high likelihood that the military faction would not be able to regain control of the country, and a new government could be established upon the foundations of socialism. It was even possible that with sufficient backing by the Soviet Union, another Cuba could emerge in the Caribbean Sea. Lyndon Johnson could not tolerate such an eventuality.

So on April 28, 1965, President Johnson ordered 405 Marines to go ashore in the Dominican Republic. Latin American nations were furious and demanded that Johnson recall the troops immediately. President Johnson explained that the Marines were there to secure U.S. interests and investments on the island, and to protect the lives of U.S. citizens in the Dominican Republic from the destruction of the civil war. But when Latin American statesmen did not buy this explanation, the Johnson administration argued that the U.S. military would remain in the Dominican Republic until the threat of communist revolution had passed and a democratically elected government had been instated. The number of American troops in the Dominican Republic would eventually approach 23,000 men.[5]

In the United States, public opinion of Johnson's use of troops in the Dominican Republic was generally positive. American citizens were by and large convinced at that time that worldwide communist proliferation was a serious dilemma. However, sentiments throughout Latin America regarding the American intervention in the Dominican Republic were much more negative. Public demonstrations by angered citizens, along with official proclamations by heads of state, all demonstrated Latin America's resentment of

Johnson's decision. For Latin Americans, Johnson's use of force set a new precedent that foreboded a return to the days of Theodore Roosevelt and the use of the big stick, a return of the hemispheric policeman, and the demise of the good neighbor.

After sporadic violence and sniping in the Dominican Republic by both sides during the summer of 1965, the possibility of finding a solution that could meet the needs of all sides was finally discovered. In September, a provisional government was created which would preside over new presidential elections, scheduled for sometime the following year. U.S. troops remained in the Dominican Republic to ensure a peaceful transition between the provisional government and the newly elected one. The election occurred on June 1, 1966. The two principal candidates were Juan Bosch, one of the individuals who had seized power after the assassination of Trujillo back in 1961, and Joaquín Balaguer, who enjoyed the blessing of the United States. Balaguer won the election and remained in power in the Dominican Republic until 1978.

Balaguer immediately made changes that favored the Dominican Republic's continued relationship with the United States. He doubled the annual sugar quota, made it illegal for laborers to stage strikes, replaced the leadership of the Dominican National Police, and exiled various military leaders under the guise of sending them away from the Dominican Republic as "military attachés, or to pursue professional educations." Eventually, Balaguer asked the United States to remove the troops from the Dominican Republic to signify that peace and prosperity had returned to the eastern half of the island. Correspondingly, American troops were recalled from the Dominican Republic in September of 1966.[6]

For the rest of Johnson's tenure in office, he focused most of his attention and foreign policy decisions on the Vietnam War, and Latin American relations with the United States remained more or less static. But the threat of communism in the hemisphere was not over, and by the time Johnson left office in 1969, one of the most stable and economically prosperous nations in all of Latin America was, in the eyes of some U.S. statesmen, on the verge of toppling into a communist government which the people were unable or unwilling to recognize. This nation was Chile.

RICHARD NIXON AND DETERIORATING RELATIONS

In 1969 Richard Nixon became the president of the United States. He had previously served as the vice president under Dwight D. Eisenhower. As the vice president, Nixon had been sent to visit several Latin American nations earlier in 1958, prior to the Cuban Revolution and the missile crisis. Lars Schoultz narrates the events of Nixon's tumultuous visit and calls his 1958 diplomatic mission to Latin America "one of the most significant brief episodes in the history of U.S.–Latin American relations."[7]

In 1958 Nixon had traveled to Uruguay, Argentina, Paraguay, Bolivia, Peru, Colombia, and Venezuela, where he was scheduled to engage in various meetings with dignitaries and participate in public relations events. As the tour progressed from the southern Latin American nations up through the Altiplano of Bolivia and Peru, the crowds that came to look at, listen to, or otherwise interact with Vice President Nixon became more and more aggressive. By the time Nixon's entourage reached Venezuela, the groups had turned explicitly violent.

On May 13, 1958, in Caracas, Nixon's motorcade had been intercepted by a mob of angry protesters who proceeded to smash the windows out of the cars and then for almost 15 minutes, they marched past the cars that contained the vice president and his wife and spat upon them. The situation became so desperate that U.S. troops were sent to rescue Nixon and his group, but before they arrived, "Nixon's driver ... gunned his befinned Cadillac over the highway's median and raced down the wrong side of the road to the [U.S.] embassy residence, where the Vice President stayed until he left for a hero's welcome at Washington's National Airport."[8]

The events of Nixon's short expedition to Latin America in 1958 had both short- and long-term repercussions in U.S.–Latin American relations. Schoultz records that when Nixon returned to the United States, he was greeted not only by President Eisenhower, but also by around 40,000 federal employees who had been given the day off to meet the vice president at the airport. As the Nixon's returned to the White House, another 85,000 people stood alongside the road cheering and holding placards that said, among other things, "Don't let Those Commies Get You Down, Dick."[9] Many in the U.S. government and outside it were completely convinced that Nixon's treatment in Latin America was organized and perpetuated by communists.

Later in 1969, when Nixon became the president of the United States, he had not forgotten his treatment by the "communists" of Latin America nearly a decade earlier. And so when the government of Chile appeared to be on the brink of collapsing under a communist infiltration in 1970, the Nixon administration acted decisively. In 1970, the people in Chile were growing frustrated with Chilean President Eduardo Frei's inability to provide for their needs, and they increasingly began to support a socialist named Salvador Allende who was preparing to run for the presidency of Chile. And American support for Eduardo Frei in Chile only increased Chilean disdain for American hegemony in the hemisphere.[10]

THE CIA COUP IN CHILE, "A SLOW-MOTION MORTIFICATION WITHOUT END"

The Chilean presidential election of 1970 was bitterly fought and produced results that were initially inconclusive because none of the candidates achieved a majority of the popular votes—Salvador Allende received

36.2 percent of the votes cast; Jorge Alessandri received 34.9 percent; and Radomiro Tomic received the remaining 27.8 percent. So the legislative branch of the Chilean government chose Salvador Allende as the new president of Chile because despite the fact that he had not achieved a majority, he still had received more popular votes than the other candidates. The United States was greatly disturbed by the fact that Allende had legitimately become the president of Chile.[11]

In 1970 Nixon's National Security Advisor was Henry A. Kissinger. When the Nixon administration learned that the Chilean people were likely to elect Allende as the Chilean president, Kissinger made the now famous statement, "I don't see why we need to stand by and watch a country go communist due to the irresponsibility of its people. The issues are much too important for the Chilean voters to be left to decide for themselves." The situation was summed up to President Nixon in another, perhaps less erudite way by a visiting businessman who argued, "with Castro in Cuba, [and Allende in Chile] you will have in Latin America a red sandwich. And eventually, it will all be red."[12]

The prospect of a communist state in South America was frightening to the Nixon administration. Chile was one of the largest and more economically stable countries in Latin America at the time. Politically, Chile had avoided many of the brutal and violent upheavals that its neighbors in Central and South America had endured over the past century and a half. And dealing with socialism in Chile was entirely different from the situation in Cuba or the Dominican Republic. In both of these instances, the country in question had been a Caribbean island (or part of an island in the case of the Dominican Republic). Placing a quarantine or embargo around Cuba was a relatively simply procedure compared to doing the same thing to a country the size of Chile which had a pacific coastline that stretched nearly 3,000 miles! And sending Marines into the Dominican Republic was not the same thing as carrying out a full-scale invasion of Chile which was fifteen times larger than the Dominican Republic, and had twice as many people.[13]

So the United States had spent around $500 million to support the campaigns of Alessandri and Tomic against Allende. When Allende ended up winning the election anyway, an American corporation in Chile—the International Telephone and Telegraph Company (ITT)—tried to have the vote overturned in the Chilean Congress. When this plan failed, ITT and the CIA became involved in other clandestine maneuvers designed to cause enough destabilization in Chile that the Chilean military would feel justified in stepping in and ousting Allende on their own.[14]

The United States also provided large sums of money to Allende's foes in Chile in an effort to prevent the country from fully embracing communism. Opposition groups purchased newspapers and radio stations in an attempt to spread anti-Allende propaganda. Finally, the Chilean military received money and equipment from the United States in an effort that seemed designed to build up the strength and determination of the Chilean military in opposing the Allende regime. Perhaps the final straw for the Nixon administration was the fact that the Allende administration received around a half billion dollars of aid, loans, and credit from the Soviet Union and the People's Republic of China.[15]

But in the end, Allende was unable to support the international pressure mounting against him, combined with the frustrations of the Chilean population who wanted better economic and social conditions. On September 11, 1973, the leader of the Chilean military, General Augusto Pinochet, used the Chilean Army and Air Force to capture Allende. The events of the coup remain cloudy, but at some point during the day, Salvador Allende died. There are two surviving arguments. Some continue to claim that he was murdered in or on the grounds of the national palace by Pinochet's men. On the other hand, Pinochet's forces declared that Salvador Allende committed suicide with a machine gun that was a gift to him from none other than Fidel Castro.[16]

In the aftermath of the coup, General Pinochet assumed power in Chile, dissolved the constitution and the congress, and then imposed a reign of terror on the people of Chile that included strict curfews, media censorship, torture, and terrorizing suspected socialists. Scholars estimate that more than 2,500 Chilean citizens were either exterminated or "disappeared" by the Pinochet government, while thousands more were tortured and incarcerated for left-wing political activism. Nevertheless, the Nixon administration was so pleased with the result of the coup that in October of 1973, the United States floated a loan to Chile in the amount of $24 million, which was more money than the United States had given to Chile during the entire Allende administration.[17]

Was the United States unilaterally responsible for the collapse of the Allende administration in Chile? Both Langley and Sater argue that while American involvement in Chile's affairs in the early 1970s played a key role in the ultimate collapse of the regime, stating that the United States should bear the sole responsibility ignores years of domestic and social frustrations from among the Chilean population, not to mention the Chilean military that had ousted leaders prior to 1973. The United States bears some of the responsibility for removing Allende, but that same responsibility should not be completely taken off the shoulders of the Chileans themselves. Ultimately, the Chilean coup was a troubled time that produced troubled results. Lars Schoultz called the situation in Chile a "slow-motion mortification without end."[18]

JIMMY CARTER AND HUMAN RIGHTS IN LATIN AMERICA

Following Richard Nixon's resignation on August 9, 1974, in the wake of the Watergate scandal, Gerald Ford became the president of the United

States. He granted Nixon a full pardon almost exactly one month later. Following Ford's brief time in the White House, in 1976 the people of the Untied States elected Jimmy Carter as the 39th president of the United States.

Jimmy Carter's influence on U.S.–Latin American relations has been both criticized and praised in the United States and in the nations of Latin America. One of the most important pillars of the Carter administration, with regard to foreign policy and Latin American relations, was his disdain for human rights violations. Whereas former presidents in the United States had supported or at least turned a blind eye upon the methods and actions of ultraconservative, military-style leaders in Latin America, the Carter administration supported the position that the manner in which such right-wing regimes enforced their policies was so violent and demeaning to the citizens of their nations that such regimes would no longer be supported politically or economically by the U.S. government.[19]

Many Republicans and conservatives in the U.S. government were uncomfortable with Carter's unwillingness to continue funding right-wing regimes based on their human rights violations. Carter defended his policy by arguing that the Cold War was, for all intents and purposes, over. In 1977 Carter stated, "We are now free of that inordinate fear of communism which once led us to embrace any dictator" who would stand against socialism. Many did not agree with his assessment, but the test came in the Central American nation of Nicaragua which had been ruled by the Somoza family for over four decades.[20]

Previous U.S. presidents had looked the other way with regard to the negative aspects of the Somoza dynasty in Nicaragua. But in 1977 Carter cut U.S. military and economic aid to Nicaragua because of its deplorable record of human rights violations. As a result of the withdrawal of U.S. aid, by the end of 1978, Nicaragua had grown so unstable that the Carter administration feared a socialist revolution in Nicaragua in the vacuum of Somoza's collapsing government. So the Carter administration encouraged Somoza to go into exile and permit new elections in Nicaragua. On July 17, 1979, Anastasio Somoza resigned and went into exile in Florida in the United States.[21]

Even though Jimmy Carter tried to focus U.S. foreign diplomacy away from the specter of communism by increasing awareness of human rights violations, and even though he did not resort to armed military intervention in a Latin American country, his critics still continue to accuse him of ousting Somoza from power in Nicaragua by rescinding the U.S. aid that had actually kept Somoza and his dynasty in power for four decades. However, Jimmy Carter is remembered more for his role in the renegotiation of the Panama Canal Treaty than for his inadvertent removal of Somoza from power in Nicaragua. In fact, many scholars consider the renegotiation of the Panama Canal Treaty in 1977 as the single most important episode in U.S.–Latin American relations (positive or negative) during Carter's four years in the White House.[22]

During the 1970s, the leader of Panama was General Omar Torrijos, a military dictator who had ruled Panama since a successful coup in 1968 when he ousted popularly elected president Arnulfo Arias. Once in power, Torrijos consolidated his hold of Panama and then pressed the United States for a renegotiation of the hated Hay–Bunau-Varilla Treaty, which had been signed on November 17, 1903, and which had established the relationship between the United States and Panama in the Canal Zone. Panama had chafed at the conditions of the treaty ever since its ratification in 1903.[23] So once in power, Torrijos used his influence as the leader of Panama to urge the United States into renegotiations that earned him favor in the eyes of Panamanians; he gambled that the United States would do business with him because of his ability to fight left-wing insurgency in Panama, and to use his military to secure the ever-important Canal Zone.

After Carter came to the presidency, he soon decided that the time had come to give the Panama Canal to Panama. Negotiations between the two governments focused on the continued security and neutrality of the Panama Canal, and the economics of the transfer. In the autumn of 1977, two separate treaties were drafted that did different things. The Neutrality Treaty guaranteed that in the future, any threat to the neutrality or operation of the Panama Canal could be dealt with by the U.S. government and military. The associated Panama Canal Treaty was the document that transferred control of the Panama Canal from the United States to Panama, effective no later than January 1, 2000.

On September 7, 1977, Jimmy Carter and Omar Torrijos signed the documents—which have since come to be known as the Torrijos–Carter Treaty—and sent them to their respective governments for ratification. General Torrijos ordered a general plebiscite to be held in October of 1977 wherein the Panamanian people approved the treaties. But convincing the American public and the U.S. Senate was not as easy. The treaties were eventually ratified by the Senate in the spring of 1978, but not without serious contention and debate. Many senators strenuously objected to Carter's proposal and made various statements of rejection and consternation that could basically be summed up by the words of Samuel Ichiye Hayakawa, a senator from California, when he simply stated, "We stole it fair and square."[24]

Ronald Reagan, who had been the governor of California until 1975, and who would become the Republican presidential nominee in 1980, said at the time, "the world would see it as . . . a case where Uncle Sam put his tail between his legs and crept away rather than face trouble." On another occasion, Reagan argued, "When it comes to the Canal, we built it, we paid for it, it's ours, and we should tell Torrijos and company that we're going to keep it." But enough other senators saw the gesture as a positive episode in U.S.-Latin American relations, and the treaties were both ratified by votes of 68 to 32.[25]

Why did President Carter "give away" the Panama Canal? Smith offers the following explanation: "By thus shucking off a relic of an unhappy, imperial past, Carter believed the United States would regain some of the moral purity lost in the era of Vietnam and dubious covert actions by the CIA. Peaceful concessions would prevent violence and bloodshed and keep the canal from being sabotaged. And, the President hoped, all of Latin America would take notice and look warmly on the United States for the first time in generations."[26] But there were other considerations as well. By the 1970s, the U.S. Navy had vessels deployed in both the Atlantic and Pacific Oceans, and the larger aircraft carriers were too large to fit through the canal locks anyway. So the expediency of having a fast path between the oceans in the early decades of the twentieth century was now of lesser importance because of both the size of some Navy vessels, and also the fact that ships were permanently deployed in both oceans anyway.

The remaining years of the Carter administration were less eventful with regard to U.S.–Latin American relations. He increasingly lost favor in several nations in South America, and he attempted some diplomacy with Fidel Castro in Cuba which was eventually aborted. In 1980, less than a year before Ronald Reagan replaced Carter in the White House, Castro lifted the ban that restricted Cubans from traveling to the United States. This action resulted in over 100,000 Cubans attempting to emigrate to the United States by fleeing Cuba from the town of Mariel. Castro then opened his prisons and insane asylums and "encouraged" the former inmates of both to go to the United States as well.

Ultimately, Jimmy Carter appeared to be a less effective leader in U.S.–Latin American relations for many of the same reasons he was considered, by many Americans, to be an ineffective president. Langley sums up attitudes about Carter by stating "Latin American governments came to regard Carter as yet another American leader who promised much and delivered too little.... What Latin America wanted in the 1970s was the benefits of a modern economic order without the strains it often places on the social order. This ideal was beyond the ability of Carter or any American leader to bring about." However, despite Carter's inability to "blend morality and power into an effective foreign policy" while in office, during the decade of the 1980s and early 1990s when Ronald Reagan and George Bush ran the White House, Latin American governments and citizens came to more fully appreciate Jimmy Carter, and granted him the post-presidential designation of being one of the "most admired modern U.S. Presidents," in the history of U.S.–Latin American relations.[27]

RONALD REAGAN AND THE COLD WAR IN CENTRAL AMERICA

By the time Ronald Reagan became the president of the United States, the situation in Central America had deteriorated significantly. By the late 1970s and early 1980s, Central America appeared to be on the verge of widespread turmoil and anarchy in several locations. For some, the problem was obviously the worldwide proliferation of communism. For others, Jimmy Carter was to blame for his softer approach to left-wing socialists.

El Salvador was involved in an extremely violent civil war that the Reagan administration labeled a struggle against communism. The El Salvadoran Civil War began in 1980 as a struggle between a democratically elected government and the left-wing rural guerrilla insurgency. It was during the El Salvadoran Civil War that one of the more brutal tragedies of the later half of the century occurred—the El Mozote Massacre where more than 900 El Salvadoran peasants were slaughtered in a single day.

In Nicaragua and Guatemala, the violence paralleled that of El Salvador. Following the ousting of dictator Anastasio Somoza from Nicaragua in 1979, opposition forces led by Daniel Ortega called themselves the Sandinista National Liberation Front—or Sandinistas for short—and formed a new government that Reagan also considered to be an outright socialist regime. Similarly, following the removal of Jacobo Arbenz from power in Guatemala by the CIA back in 1954, Guatemala had been so destabilized economically and politically that it had plunged into a massive civil war that lasted nearly four decades and was responsible for the deaths of over 100,000 Guatemalans.

Honduras remained relatively quiet during the 1970s and 1980s following a minor conflict with El Salvador in 1969 called the Soccer War. Because of its central location in Central America, Honduras was used by both El Salvador and Nicaragua as a relatively safe base of operations against insurgency groups fighting in both countries; likewise Panama occasionally served as a training ground for counter-insurgency forces, or Contras, fighting the Sandinistas in Nicaragua. Interestingly, the only Central American nation not devastated by chaos and violence during the 1970s and 1980s was Costa Rica, which abolished its army in 1949 and has remained relatively peaceful and prosperous ever since.

So Reagan modified the relationship between the United States and Latin America by turning his back on Carter's emphasis on human rights violations, and instead returning a more aggressive position on communist proliferation in Central America. In an effort to combat the spread of communism throughout Latin America, Reagan began to reconstruct the relations between the United States and several countries in Latin America that had deteriorated under the Carter administration. Finally, to drive home to the U.S. Congress and the American people the seriousness of the situation in Latin America, Reagan delivered televised speeches wherein he explained his motivations and defended his actions.

In July of 1983, at the International Longshoremen's Association in Florida, Reagan laid the foundations for his policies by commenting on the way the previous administration handled the Central American situation. Reagan said, "We all know that Central America suffers from decades of poverty, social deprivation, and political instability. And because these problems weren't dealt with positively [under the Carter administration], they're now being exploited by the enemies of freedom." Reagan continued by discussing the Sandinista government in Nicaragua, the money the United States had sent to help the people there (around $118 million by 1983), and then excoriating the Sandinista leaders in Nicaragua, calling them promise-breakers, and stating that it was "time that all of us in the Americas worked together to hold Nicaragua accountable."[28] He then turned his attention to El Salvador. "There's a vital link between what's happening in Nicaragua and what's happening in El Salvador. And the link is very simple: The dictators of Nicaragua are actively trying to destroy the budding democracy in neighboring El Salvador."[29]

Using these kinds of examples, combined with his abilities as an orator that earned him the moniker "the Great Communicator," President Reagan rallied much support from the U.S. Congress and the American people. Then he went into Nicaragua fighting communism with a vengeance. He sent millions of dollars to El Salvador, Guatemala, Honduras, and Panama to encourage them to resist socialism within their borders.

Reagan also instituted the Caribbean Basin Initiative (CBI) in 1983 which was a program designed to provide aid—in the form of investments, tariff reduction, and loans—to nations in Central America and the Caribbean, all in an effort to help them fight off communist insurgency inside their own borders. Cuba, Nicaragua, and Grenada were excluded from receiving any of the aid because of their relations with socialist governments. But while Reagan proceeded to shore up Central American defenses against communist insurgency, trouble at the other end of the hemisphere threatened to damage the reputation the United States had struggled to build since the proclamation of the Monroe Doctrine back in 1823.[30]

THE FALKLAND ISLANDS WAR

While Ronald Reagan was dealing with these issues in Central America, Argentina and Great Britain moved toward an equally important confrontation. During the spring of 1982, Great Britain and Argentina went to war over the status of the Falkland Islands (known as the *Islas Malvinas* in Argentina). Back in December of 1981, Argentinean General Leopoldo Galtieri had ousted the president of Argentina, Roberto Viola. Once in power, Galtieri desired to increase feelings of Argentine nationalism and support for his regime, so he resorted to military solutions such as antagonizing Chile over border issues, threatening to send troops to Nicaragua to help Reagan's forces fight the communists, and attempting to regain sovereignty over the Falkland Islands which had been governed by Great Britain since 1833.[31]

The initial Argentine invasion of the Falkland Islands was carried out on April 2, 1982. The token British military forces stationed there were taken completely by surprise and driven from the islands. Immediately, Argentine troops and equipment reinforced the islands, and Argentineans cheered their government's stand against the imperialism of Great Britain. Many hoped that the British government might simply let the islands go—the population of the islands numbered less than 2,000 persons, most of whom were sheep herders—and in fact, the British government had debated discarding the islands in the past.

And as David Rock notes, General Galtieri believed that a British response was, in his own words, "absolutely improbable," and furthermore, he believed that in the event that the British did object, the Reagan administration would likely defend Argentina from British aggression because of Galtieri's encouragement of Reagan's Central American policy, and because of the influence of the Monroe Doctrine that prohibited aggression by European powers against the countries of the western hemisphere.[32]

But British response came in a much quicker and stronger manner than anyone expected. Over the next two weeks, while Argentina continued to reinforce its position on the islands, the British military prepared an invasion that included aerial bombardments, amphibious landings of troops, and a trick they learned from the United States two decades earlier during the Cuban Missile Crisis: they imposed a blockade around the Falkland Islands to prevent Argentina from further reinforcing the area. Of course, blockades were still problematic in terms of legality under international law. President Kennedy had circumvented this dilemma in 1962 by calling his blockade a quarantine. In 1982, Prime Minister Margaret Thatcher did much the same thing by calling her blockade an "exclusion zone."[33]

British forces quickly defeated the Argentine military and retook portions of Falkland territory by the end of April, but sporadic fighting continued into the middle of June when Argentina finally surrendered. From start to finish, the Falkland Islands War lasted just over two months, caused the deaths of less than 2,000 individuals (most of them Argentineans), and cost around $2 billion.

In terms of U.S.–Latin American relations, the Falkland Islands War was decidedly more negative than positive. Right at the time that President Reagan was calling for hemispheric solidarity in contending with international communism, he alienated Argentina by siding with British Prime Minister Margaret Thatcher against the Argentine government. In fact, one of the reasons that a diplomatic solution between Argentina and Britain ultimately failed to materialize was the fact that President Reagan had argued that Argentina's actions in seizing the islands had been both illegal and an international disgrace. To this end, Reagan actually moved against Argentina by offering support to the British military in the form of *materiel* and intelligence, and by imposing economic sanctions against the nation of Argentina.[34]

And there was another area of U.S.–Latin American relations that suffered as a result of the war. Many people, both then and now, have wondered about the *non-sequitur* logic of U.S. policy regarding the Falkland Islands. After all, did not British aggression in retaking the islands constitute a breach of the principles of the Monroe Doctrine? In fact, Smith points out that some seventeen Latin American nations not only condemned Britain's actions in the Falkland Islands, but also called on all OAS member states, including the United States, to provide whatever aid they could to Argentina to defend against British aggression.[35] Ultimately, the whole situation represents a paradox of U.S. interests that had existed outside the parameters of the Monroe Doctrine ever since 1833, and one which, over 150 years later in 1982, President Reagan was not prepared to back away from.

On the other hand, support from Latin American nations for Argentina was swift and nearly universal in spite of U.S. actions. David Rock records that Venezuela offered oil, Peru offered aircraft replacements, and in a surprising move, Nicaragua offered to send Sandinista troops to Argentina, even though only months before, Argentina had offered to send troops to Nicaragua to aid the United States by fighting the Sandinistas![36]

In the aftermath, Argentine President Galtieri bitterly accused the United States of supporting British imperial hegemony in the hemisphere and called the United States "the enemy of Argentina and its people." However, the people of Argentina became increasingly upset that the Galtieri regime had tried to use the Falkland Islands War as a publicity stunt aimed at reinforcing its own power. Ultimately, Galtieri was ousted from office in a military *coup d'état* during his first year by the Argentine military, and following the conclusion of the conflict, the hemisphere returned to Reagan's predominant preoccupation, the Cold War in Central America. And less than a year after the situation in the Falkland Islands ended, Reagan turned his attention to a small Caribbean island much closer to home.[37]

THE U.S. INVASION OF GRENADA

Grenada is a small island in the Caribbean Sea just north of Trinidad and Tobago. It is 133 square miles in size and in 1983 had a population of less than 100,000 people. It won its independence from Great Britain in 1974, and although Queen Elizabeth II of England has been Grenada's executive head of state since 1952, Grenada has been governed by a resident prime minister since its independence.

In the early 1980s, Grenada was under the leadership of Maurice Bishop. In 1983, just prior to the actual U.S. invasion, Bishop was ousted and shot by left-wing members of his own government who then moved forward with plans to construct a massive airport and landing strip, with the aid of Cuban and Soviet technicians, which could then be used to transport large amounts of Soviet goods and personnel to Caribbean, Central, and South American locations.

U.S. information on the Grenada situation was incomplete at the time, but several hundred American citizens lived on the island where they attended medical school, and their lives and property became a priority for the Reagan administration. Alarms were also raised about the possibility that the Soviets might be plotting to place nuclear missiles in Grenada to compensate for their failure to do so in Cuba two decades earlier.[38]

So on October 25, 1983, President Reagan sent Marines to topple the government of Grenada. Soldiers from other Caribbean islands—Jamaica, Dominica, Barbados, St. Vincent, and St. Lucia—were also present in the conflict that lasted around three days, but their presence was mostly ceremonial and meant to convey a sense of regional solidarity against communism in Grenada and the Caribbean Basin.

After several days of fighting, the Marines took control of the island. Eighteen Marines, twenty-nine Cubans, and forty-five Grenadians were killed in the conflict, while those injured numbered in the hundreds. Foreign military and technical personnel found in Grenada included individuals from several communist countries including Cuba, Russia, North Korea, Bulgaria, and East Germany. Additionally, there were even a few Libyans on the island.[39]

In terms of U.S.–Latin American relations, the Grenada invasion was deemed by most Latin American nations to have been necessary to prevent another Cuba from occurring. Great Britain was not as pleased, however, and Prime Minister Thatcher, who had been satisfied to accept U.S. support a year earlier over the Falkland Islands incident, excoriated President Reagan for invading a member nation of the British Commonwealth. But Reagan made several statements defending his actions and then returned to his primary objective, which was removing communism from Nicaragua. But the Reagan administration's Nicaraguan policies were approaching catastrophe faster than anyone knew or suspected at the time.

THE IRAN–CONTRA SCANDAL

Following Reagan's hardliner approaches to the Falkland Islands and Grenada, the United States, Latin America, and the world expected that Nicaragua would be next on Reagan's list.[40] In Nicaragua throughout the 1980s, the Sandinista government, under the leadership of Daniel Ortega, continued to accept aid from Fidel Castro. But those Nicaraguans who remained loyal to the previous Somoza dynasty, and others who followed Reagan's line of thinking about left-wing socialism, called themselves the Contras and continued to fight against the Sandinista government.

Reagan tried to send monetary aid to the Contras in Nicaragua and Honduras, but the U.S. government was not as convinced as Reagan was, and in 1983 the Congress imposed a ceiling of $24 million on Reagan's spending in Nicaragua. As if that were not enough, by 1985 Honduras became less enamored with the situation, denied that the Contras were using Honduras as a base of operations north of Nicaragua, and then confiscated several million dollars sent to aid the Contras in their fight against the Sandinistas. The Reagan administration had reached a stalemate in Nicaragua that required broader measures.[41]

Money seemed to be the primary factor in aiding the Contras against the Sandinistas, but the United States was also pouring millions of dollars into El Salvador to promote their emerging democracy. So when funds became unavailable or were denied by the Congress, the Reagan administration resorted to more creative methods of acquiring money for Nicaragua. Lt. Colonel Oliver North, a National Security Council aide, participated in fund-raising efforts aimed at wealthy, conservative Americans. When these efforts also came up short, North was directed to obtain funding through other channels.

Regarding President Reagan's involvement in the Iran–Contra Scandal that broke late in 1986, Smith writes, "Historians may never be able to determine the degree of President Reagan's personal knowledge of how policy was implemented, but his overall encouragement is beyond question."[42] The Iran–Contra Scandal had several layers of involvement. First of all, in order to acquire funding to support Contra activities in Nicaragua, certain members of the Reagan administration authorized the sale of offensive military weapons—primarily surface-to-air and antitank missiles—to the government of the Ayatollah Khomeini in Iran. In exchange, the Iranian government was supposed to use its influence to secure the release of American hostages being held in Lebanon by Hezbollah. The money from these transactions was then earmarked for the Contras in Nicaragua to help them topple the Sandinista regime. It was only a matter of time before this odd triangle of furtive and illicit diplomacy collapsed and implicated individuals in the Reagan White House.

When the story leaked to the American people—from sources both inside the United States, in Nicaragua, and in the Middle East—there was an instant outcry against members of the Reagan administration. The American public remembered all too well the Watergate Scandal a decade earlier, and all of a sudden, communism in Nicaragua was relegated to a much less important position in the eyes of many Americans and Latin Americans. As information on the scandal hit the press in 1986 and 1987, several individuals were fed to the press; Schoultz lists the "body count" that materialized in the wake of the scandal: National Security Advisor Robert McFarlane, National Security Advisor John Poindexter, Secretary of Defense Caspar Weinberger, National Security Council aide Oliver North, Assistant Secretary of State

Elliott Abrams, and several others were convicted of various crimes including perjury, destruction of documents, and obstruction of justice.[43]

In terms of U.S.–Latin American relations, the Iran–Contra Scandal essentially marked the conclusion of Ronald Reagan's Latin American policy. Reagan backed off from his mission to oust the Sandinistas from power in Nicaragua, and finished his second term of office when he was replaced by his own vice president, George H. W. Bush, who was elected in 1989. And as the decade of the 1980s came to a close, U.S.–Latin American relations were on increasingly unstable ground.

THE HUNT FOR NORIEGA

At the end of 1989, the new Bush administration made the final armed intervention of the decade in a Latin American country, this time in Panama. As a result of this intervention, the military leader of Panama, General Manuel Noriega, would be eventually removed from power; not by covert CIA manipulations behind the scenes, but by U.S. Marines.[44]

Noriega was the military dictator of Panama between 1983 and 1989. Despite the fact that Manuel Noriega ruled Panama as a military dictator during those years, he was never elected and never served as president of Panama. Between 1993 and 1998, Panama had at least five different presidents, and two other acting or provisional presidents. In most cases, however, the presidents of Panama during the Noriega years were puppets of his military regime and had little real authority or power.

Noriega was a known drug trafficker and had ties to some of Central America's and Colombia's worst criminals and drug lords. He was also on the payroll of the CIA for several years prior to his removal from power; the CIA had used Noriega's Panama as a staging ground from which to carry on the conflict against the Sandinistas in Nicaragua. Smith notes that Noriega permitted the Contras to use Panama for training purposes, and even offered to assassinate Sandinista government officials for the United States. In short, Noriega represented the policy of the former Reagan administration to support right-wing, conservative military dictators, in spite of their deplorable human rights records, because of their willingness to support America's anticommunism position.[45]

But in 1986 after reports of extreme corruption, drug smuggling, and numerous assassinations, the United States became wary of its relationship with Noriega. By the late 1980s when the Reagan White House tried to remove Noriega from power by having him arrested on murder, conspiracy, and drug-related charges, Noriega consolidated his hold on Panama and refused offers to go into exile in Europe. The United States resorted to economic sanctions against Panama, but Noriega refused to budge. Reagan then had several indictments filed against Noriega in Florida courts and tried to restrict monetary aid to the country. In 1988 the Reagan administration went so far as to order the president of Panama, Eric Arturo Delvalle, to fire Noriega, which he did. But Noriega refused to leave and belligerently replaced President Delvalle with Manuel Solís Palma who served as acting president of Panama until September of 1989.[46]

So under the Bush administration, the United States prepared to take more decisive measures. In May of 1989 during the Panamanian presidential elections, Noriega's plans to fix the votes backfired, resulting in the beating of "two opposition candidates . . . into a bloody pulp in front of television cameras" and Noriega's canceling of the elections. As Richard Nixon had done years earlier in Chile, the Bush administration funneled several million dollars to the presidential campaigns of the anti-Noriega candidates. When it became clear that Noriega's candidate could not legally win the election, he confiscated ballot boxes, annulled the election, and proclaimed that Francisco Rodríguez would act as the provisional president until new elections could be held.[47]

In October of 1989 some of Noriega's own military personnel staged a coup, captured Noriega, and attempted to turn him over to U.S. forces, Panama. But through some fluke of good fortune, Noriega managed to escape before the United States could take him into custody. By mid-December Noriega announced that Panama and the United States were in a "state of war," and on December 16, a U.S. Marine stationed in Panama was pursued and murdered by Noriega's men. It was at this point that President Bush decided to remove Noriega from power by force.[48]

Operation Just Cause began on the night of December 20, 1989, when over 20,000 U.S. Marines invaded Panama intent on capturing General Noriega. After several unsuccessful attempts to track down the dictator, he was finally located in the Panamanian embassy of the Vatican. Since U.S. troops could not enter the Vatican embassy to incarcerate him, they surrounded the complex and attempted to coerce him to give himself up. Finally on January 3, 1990, after being strongly encouraged to capitulate several times by the Vatican embassy, Noriega surrendered and was extradited to the United States where he stood trial on charges of drug trafficking. In the autumn of 1992, Noriega was convicted and sentenced to spend forty years in prison.[49]

President Bush's use of military force to remove Noriega from power—and the subsequent creation of a new Panamanian government by recognizing Guillermo David Endara as the legitimate president of Panama—represented a new era in American foreign policy. For the first time, and in an exceptionally visible manner, the United States had used its military to remove another leader from power in Latin America when no external threat or menace was present. In other words, President Bush had not defended the hemisphere against European aggression under the guise of the Monroe Doctrine, or used the threat of communist proliferation to take action, but instead he had used the U.S. military to remove a hostile and problematic

Latin American dictator from power because it was in the best interests of the United States to do so. Latin American nations found themselves between the proverbial rock and hard place: they were torn between what they saw as the necessity of removing Noriega from power, and the reality of yet another U.S. military intervention in a Latin American country that set a disturbing new precedent.[50]

Public opinion in Panama and the United States was positive, although one Los Angeles reporter summed up the invasion in this way: "I don't see that devastating a small country's economy, then mounting a 25,000-man invasion which kills more than 300 people and wounds hundreds more, to seize a disreputable but unimportant military adventurer over whom American courts have disputed jurisdiction, should be considered a success."[51]

CONCLUSIONS

The return to aggressive military intervention by Lyndon Johnson in the 1960s opened the floodgates for several other episodes of intercession in the hemisphere that involved the reintroduction of overt force by the U.S. military, the covert toppling of governments by the military and CIA, and corruption and scandal in Latin American nations and in the United States. As a result of these new episodes of U.S. military intervention in the hemisphere, the relationship between the United States and Latin American countries was damaged by broken promises and conflicting agendas. But as the 1980s came to a close and the Cold War began to reach a conclusion, the United States and Latin America were obligated to find a new paradigm to guide their troubled relationship as they approached the end of the twentieth entury.

10

Crossing the Threshold of a New Century

Latin America neither wants, nor has any reason, to be a pawn without a will of its own; nor is it merely wishful thinking that its quest for independence and originality should become a Western aspiration. . . . The immeasurable violence and pain of our history are the result of age-old inequities and untold bitterness, and not a conspiracy plotted three thousand leagues from our home. . . . It is not yet too late to engage in the creation of the opposite utopia. A new and sweeping utopia of life, where no one will be able to decide for others how they die, where love will prove true and happiness be possible, and where the races condemned to one hundred years of solitude will have, at last and forever, a second opportunity on earth.

– Gabriel García Márquez

Those who ignore Latin America do not fully understand America itself. . . . To the nations of Latin America I say: As long as you are on the road toward liberty, you will not be alone. As long as you are moving toward freedom, you will have a steady friend in the United States of America.   – George W. Bush

Bill Clinton became the 42nd president of the United States in 1993. Clinton represented a return to domestic issues following the demise of the Soviet Union and the end of the Cold War. It had been twelve years since the United States had elected a Democrat president, and many Americans were still displeased with the memory of Carter's one term in office. But with the demise of the Cold War, the United States now found itself the lone remaining superpower in the world's political and economic arenas. The implications were profound in terms of American foreign policy. And U.S.–Latin American relations changed as a result of the end of the Cold War as well. And even though some Americans were wary of having a Democrat back in the White House, Latin Americans generally had higher hopes for better relations with the United States under Bill Clinton than they had endured during the previous twelve years.

As President, Clinton focused most of his attention on domestic reforms such as health care, welfare, and education. But he also continued to interact with Latin American governments, although in a much quieter and less prolific manner than his predecessors had done. Clinton's Latin American policy centered predominantly on the North American Free Trade Agreement (NAFTA) and on Haiti, two important issues that represent both the potential for positive progress in U.S.–Latin American relations, and at the same time the unpleasant memories and policies of the past.[1]

NAFTA

During the 1980s, Mexico enjoyed considerably more control over its own economy than it had in many years. Unfortunately, the oil bubble that carried Mexico through the 1980s finally burst and when the Mexican economy began to drown under the weight of foreign debt and corrupt leadership, an all-too familiar solution presented itself in the form of a trade relationship between Mexico and the other two governments of North America.

The NAFTA agreement went into effect on January 1, 1994. But the groundwork that laid the foundations for NAFTA was born in the previous Bush administration, and conceived by the Reagan administration before that. In 1989 the United States and Canada had enacted the Free Trade Agreement (FTA) between their two countries to lower tariffs and duties on many items ranging from food and clothing to cars and computers. The president of Mexico at the time, Carlos Salinas de Gortari, believed that such an economic agreement could also benefit Mexico. And although Mexico and Canada did not have wide-ranging trade relations with each other, they both traded extensively with the United States.

So during the autumn of 1992 all three nations worked on the negotiations of the agreement, and later, on December 17, 1992, the leaders of all three nations, President Carlos Salinas de Gortari, President George H. W. Bush, and the Right Honourable Prime Minister M. Brian Mulroney of Canada, all signed the NAFTA proposal. After passing through the congressional bodies of all three nations, NAFTA was officially signed into law at the end of 1993 and was scheduled to begin operations the following year in 1994.[2]

Today, with barely a decade of statistics and numbers to analyze, many scholars from multiple disciplines have proven that it is equally easy to argue for or against the effects of NAFTA on the countries of North America. But in terms of the economy of Mexico, it appears that NAFTA is yet another chapter in the legacy of Mexican economic disequilibrium, of foreign capital investment and cash flow, and of economic paternalism and the potential for fiscal exploitation by stronger foreign powers.[3]

By the end of his term, supporters of NAFTA sharply criticized Bill Clinton over his hesitations not only to implement NAFTA, but also his inability to expand NAFTA to incorporate the nations of Central America, the Caribbean, and perhaps even the South American nation of Chile. In fact, in 1994 Clinton boasted that by the end of his first term Chile would join NAFTA. Nevertheless, by 1998 not only had Chile not been incorporated in NAFTA, but chances of this expansion coming to fruition appeared quite dismal.[4]

HAITI

Another concern of the Clinton administration was the frustrating situation in Haiti. Haiti has the reputation of being among the poorest nations on earth, and certainly the most abject in the western hemisphere. More than 80 percent of all Haitians live in squalor and paucity, and the growth percentage of the Haitian GDP has been in the negative for decades. During the closing months of 1990, Haitians had been permitted to vote in the first just presidential election in their national history. They elected Jean-Bertrand Aristide who was a vocal spokesman for poor Haitians. Unfortunately, not everyone in Haiti appreciated his grassroots approach to politics in Haiti. Seven months into his term as president, Aristide was ousted from power by the Haitian military in a *coup d'état* backed by wealthy landowners; Aristide went into exile in Venezuela.[5]

One of the repercussions of the 1991 Haitian coup was a mass exodus of poor Haitians from Haiti; individuals who refused to remain in Haiti under military rule tried to get out. Thousands of desperate Haitians attempted to flee to the United States on just about any item that would float. President George H. W. Bush had ordered the U.S. Coast Guard to send the Haitian refugees back to Haiti, an act that earned him the criticism of Bill Clinton who was campaigning for the presidency himself. However, less than a year later, President Clinton announced his similar intention to use the U.S. Coast Guard to prevent Haitian refugees from leaving Haiti on "unsound boats." When he was criticized for going back on his word, he countered that this policy would only be temporary because he was going to help President Aristide return to power in Haiti.[6]

In order to restore peace to the small Caribbean country, Clinton ordered U.S. troops to Haiti to assist in Aristide's return to power. Unfortunately, when U.S. troops arrived in October of 1993, the Haitian military would not permit them to come ashore, and the troops were recalled instead of engaging in hostilities with the Haitian soldiers. This embarrassing episode for Clinton evolved into a similar event the following year when the United States, supported by U.N. troops, again made preparations to restore Aristide to power through a military intervention. But last-minute negotiations by former President Jimmy Carter convinced the military dictatorship in Haiti to step down and allow Aristide to return to power in Haiti without violence.

This apparent success was not without its near misses however, for the Clinton administration had ordered 20,000 U.S. soldiers to the island where they occupied the nation, and although no hostilities ensued, Latin American governments were not very tolerant of U.S. troops stationed on Haitian soil. In the end, President Aristide returned to Haiti on October 15, 1994, and Latin Americans were generally relieved. However, by the end of 1996, both Bill Clinton and Jean-Bertrand Aristide had completed their terms of office, and Haiti was no better off than before.[7] Clinton went on to win a second term while Aristide plotted his return to power in Haiti.

Did Clinton's actions in Haiti constitute an intervention? Certainly U.S. troops were used, albeit in a different way, as an incentive for the Haitian military to step aside. And certainly one government was toppled and another reinstated. But here lies the difference. Clinton had not supported or installed a military regime under the pretext of covert or overt U.S. military retaliation, but instead he had convinced an illegitimate military government to step down and permit the legitimately elected leader to resume his term of office in Haiti. The tables had turned indeed. Unfortunately the controversy of Jean-Bertrand Aristide was not over.

CLINTON'S LEGACY

Other areas of Clinton's Latin American policy were more or less a mixed bag. He proved unable to deal with Central American problems that remained like ghosts from the 1970s and 1980s. He withheld economic aid, obfuscated the role of the CIA in the Guatemalan civil war, and tried to divert attention away from investigations into atrocities committed in El Salvador. However, Clinton succeeded in preventing the president of Guatemala, Jorge Díaz Serrano, from declaring himself a military dictator in 1993, and then in 1994 Clinton permitted several thousand Cuban refugees to enter the United States legally.[8]

Finally, in 1994 the leaders of over thirty nations in the western hemisphere came to Miami, Florida, where President Clinton presided over the First Summit of the Americas. Clinton claimed that as the world approached the twenty-first century, the United States and Latin America were also approaching a new level in their relationship. Unfortunately, by 1998 and the Second Summit of the Americas which was held in Chile, many believed that President Clinton had more or less abandoned Latin America.[9]

Some have argued that the Clinton administration simply got lucky because it did not have to contend with so many of the serious issues in Latin America that the previous Republican presidents had dealt with. Others counter that so many of the problems faced by the United States and Latin America over the previous decade had actually been the result of having Republicans in the White House in the first place. But whatever his legacy in terms of U.S.–Latin American relations, Latin Americans overall appreciated his proclivity to not get involved in their affairs. But this approbation from Latin American statesmen was not enough to keep a Democrat in the White House after 2001, and Clinton's legacy in terms of U.S.–Latin American relations seems to be, overall, one of inaction rather than strength and leadership.

9-11

In the autumn of 2000, as George W. Bush campaigned for the upcoming presidential election in November, he gave several speeches across the country outlining what he promised to accomplish if elected president. In August of that year, while in campaigning in Florida, Bush argued,

> Those who ignore Latin America do not fully understand America itself. And those who ignore our hemisphere do fully understand American interests. This country was right to be concerned about a country like Kosovo— but there are more refugees of conflict in Colombia. America is right to be concerned about Kuwait—but more of our oil comes from Venezuela. America is right to welcome trade with China—but we export as much to Brazil. Our future cannot be separated from the future of Latin America.[10]

Bush then went on to loosely outline his proposed diplomatic plans for U.S.–Latin American relations. He said, "I look forward to working closely with the nations of this hemisphere but recognize that they cannot be bullied into progress. We will treat all Americans—North, Central and South—with dignity. I will improve our bilateral relations and work with the Organization of American States to confront the problems of our hemisphere. My administration will strengthen the architecture of democracy in Latin America—the institutions that make democracy real and successful."[11]

However, following George W. Bush's election, the terrorist attacks on the United States in September of 2001 massively influenced Bush's foreign policy and ultimately shifted Bush's focus away from Latin America. Immediately following the terrorist attacks in New York City and Washington, D.C., the leadership of the OAS (Organization of American States) stated that the countries and leaders of Latin America not only supported the United States and denounced the terrorist groups, but they also claimed that when the terrorists attacked the United States, they attacked all the

American states in the western hemisphere as well. Unhappily, these feelings of hemispheric solidarity quickly evaporated, and subsequent relations between the Bush administration and Latin American governments have been less than positive as the focus of American foreign policy has magnified the Middle East to the exclusion of many other areas of the world.[12]

Coletta Youngers described the decline in U.S.–Latin American relations following the 9-11 terrorist attacks as a malaise born of "the never-ending and escalating economic crisis, deep-rooted corruption, and the inability of democracy to truly take root" throughout Latin America. She lamented that hemispheric relations have generally deteriorated since 9-11 through policies such as the close observation of Arab communities in Latin American nations, and the never-ending war on drugs. In fact, not long after the 9-11 attacks, U.S. Attorney General John Ashcroft stated, "Terrorism and Drugs go together.... They thrive in the same conditions, support each other and feed off of each other," thus implying that in Latin America—and specifically in Colombia—the War on Terror and the War on Drugs have become one and the same thing.[13]

President George W. Bush's determination to aggressively attack terrorist organizations in Afghanistan and topple the regime of Saddam Hussein in Iraq drew criticism from several Latin American leaders who feared the economic and political backlash of such actions. Economically, soaring gas prices have affected most nations in the hemisphere, prompting the Bush administration to propose increasing oil imports into the United States from both Mexico and Venezuela, both of which have been wary of permitting the United States too much influence over their oil exports, and ultimately creating tensions between all three.[14]

Politically, the future looks just as troubling. The War on Terror, while distinctly different from the Cold War, seems to be having a familiar effect on U.S.–Latin American relations. During the Cold War, the U.S. government encouraged and supported military regimes throughout Latin America as the primary method of combating the spread of communism in the hemisphere. A familiar paradigm seems to be at work in U.S.–Latin American relations in the wake of the 9-11 terrorist attacks. The U.S. government has returned to "encouraging Latin American militaries to take on greater roles in the internal affairs of their own countries" in an effort to keep terrorism out of the hemisphere, and to prevent terror sympathizers—such as the "Narcoterrorists"—from carrying out acts of aggression and violence throughout the hemisphere.[15]

On perhaps a brighter side, Assistant Secretary for Western Hemisphere Affairs, Ambassador Otto Reich, made the following assessment more than a year after the terrorist attacks:

> The U.S. sells more to Latin America and the Caribbean than to the European Union; Trade with our NAFTA partners is greater than our

trade with the EU and Japan combined; We sell more to the Southern Cone [Argentina, Paraguay, Uruguay, and Chile], than to China; and Latin America and the Caribbean comprise our fastest-growing export market.... President Bush believes in the future of the Americas, and our policy reflects his confidence and his vision.[16]

Unfortunately, many areas of Latin America continue to struggle with democracy and economic stability and the United States has been less helpful than in the past as Latin America seems to be relegated to a position of benign neglect far down the list of U.S. priorities. And many Latin American leaders fear the broader implications of George W. Bush's doctrine of preemption. What will be the long-term results of such precedents in terms of U.S.–Latin American relations? Many Latin American governments fear a return to the aggressive interventionist policies of many U.S. presidents during the early decades of the twentieth century.

VENEZUELA

The Bush administration also appeared to struggle over the rapidly deteriorating conditions in Venezuela. Between April 9–12, 2002, an internal military coup removed President Hugo Chávez from power in Venezuela. Most Latin American nations protested the coup, as did many Venezuelans. Conversely, during the days that Chávez was out of power, the Bush administration rapidly extended diplomatic recognition to his successor, interim president Pedro Carmona, who began to reverse several of Chávez's initiatives.[17]

Many in Latin America were confused by President Bush's actions and openly wondered if the coup had been orchestrated by the U.S. government as a means of exerting greater control over Venezuela's oil supplies, or as retaliation for Chávez's close relationship with Fidel Castro in Cuba.[18] However, less than forty-eight hours after the coup, a sympathetic group of military personnel called the Presidential Guard restored President Chávez to power in Venezuela in a counter-coup that met with the approbation of much of the Venezuelan population.

In 2004, Chávez was again targeted for removal from office when members of large businesses and oil corporations collected nearly two and a half million signatures calling for a national recall referendum against President Chávez. On August 15, 2004, for the first time in history, the leader of an entire country was subjected to a recall vote in which Venezuelans were asked to vote to either remove or maintain Chávez in office. When the votes were tallied, Chávez remained in office, achieving more than 59 percent of the votes cast. Former President Jimmy Carter oversaw the recall vote and certified that the result was free from significant error and representative of the people's wishes in Venezuela.[19]

HAITI REVISITED

As examined earlier, one of the significant junctures of the Clinton administration was the political chaos in Haiti. Following his first term as president of Haiti, Jean-Bertrand Aristide remained active in Haitian politics by forming a new political party designed to represent and appeal to the poorer sectors of Haitian society. In 2000 Aristide ran for another term as president of Haiti and won by a massive majority of the vote. Election observers from the OAS claimed that the election was rigged, and the U.S. government, which had fought in 1994 to return Aristide to power, now refused to support Aristide because of allegations of corruption.[20]

The economy of Haiti continued to stagnate, and the political situation deteriorated drastically after 2004 when the Haitian bicameral *Assemblee Nationale* ceased to function because elections had been cancelled in 2003 and no new representatives replaced those who reached the end of their elected terms. The results were disturbing; President Aristide began to rule Haiti by edict and proclamation without the democratic accountability of a legislative body to check his power.

As a result, popular support for Aristide dissolved both inside Haiti and throughout the international community. Violence and chaos spread throughout northern Haiti as most of the populace, led by the military, called for Aristide's capitulation. On February 29, 2004, Aristide signed a resignation letter and then boarded a U.S. aircraft that flew him to exile in the Central African Republic after he was denied permission to land in South Africa.

Since that time, Aristide has argued that he was forcibly abducted at gunpoint and in handcuffs from Haiti by the U.S. military, and then held against his will in the Central African Republic by the French military. French and American government spokespersons representing the administrations of both Jacques Chirac and George W. Bush have contended that these allegations are preposterous.

After nearly a month in the Central African Republic, Aristide returned to the Caribbean nation of Jamaica where many believed he was planning a return to Haiti. While in Jamaica, Aristide again publicly contended that he had been forcibly removed from power by U.S. Marines. The Bush administration continues to deny any involvement in abducting Aristide from Haiti. Later in 2004 Aristide departed Jamaica for South Africa, where he remained throughout 2005 and into 2006. In his absence, Haiti was governed by an interim president, Boniface Alexandre, who came to power on the day Aristide resigned.

BUSH'S LEGACY

By the early months of 2006, the Bush administration was still actively involved in the affairs of both Iraq and Afghanistan, and problems in Latin

American nations continued to receive less attention. In Colombia, the drug trade continued to flourish and terrorism proceeded unabated. In fact, during the early years of the twenty-first century, the country of Colombia had the unhappy distinction of being the kidnapping capital of not only the western hemisphere, but also the world.[21]

Argentina continued to struggle from the economic collapse it suffered in November and December of 2001 when the Argentine peso was so drastically devalued that it caused a run on Argentine banks. In Brazil, the largest country in Latin America, the people elected a socialist president, Luíz Inácio da Silva, in 2002. President da Silva struggled with fiscal and social reforms, and tried to keep Brazil active in regional and international affairs. The Altiplano nations of Peru, Bolivia, and Ecuador continued to struggle with democracy as drug traffic and production in their areas increased.

In Nicaragua, the Sandinista government of Daniel Ortega was replaced in 1990 by the election of Violeta Chamorro, the widow of a politically active newspaper editor who was assassinated in 1978. Originally a Sandinista herself, Chamorro left the Sandinistas in 1980 after it became clear that they refused to share power or enact all the social reforms promised to the people. Daniel Ortega ran for reelection twice after his first term as Nicaraguan president, and was defeated both times. But in 2006 Ortega continues to lead the Sandinista faction in Nicaragua, and will likely stand for reelection again in 2008.

In June of 2005, the United States approved the Central American Free Trade Agreement (or CAFTA) which would create a NAFTA-like trade arrangement between the United States and the countries of Central America—Guatemala, Honduras, El Salvador, Nicaragua, and Costa Rica—and the Dominican Republic in the Caribbean. If the Latin American nations belonging to the CAFTA proposal accept the conditions and ratify the treaty, it is very likely that other hemispheric trade proposals in South America will eventually follow. Furthermore, NAFTA and CAFTA are both important stepping stones leading to the implementation of the all-encompassing Free Trade Area of the Americas (or FTAA), which many in the U.S. and in Latin America anticipate with varying degrees of hope and hesitation.

Finally there is Cuba. Fidel Castro, who will turn eighty years old in 2006, has ruled the island since his successful rise to power in 1959. His control of Cuba has spanned nearly fifty years and corresponded with the presidencies of ten U.S. presidents including Eisenhower, Kennedy, Johnson, Nixon, Ford, Carter, Reagan, George H. W. Bush, Clinton, and George W. Bush. Many scholars and academics have pondered what will happen in Cuba when Fidel Castro dies. And even though Castro has named his brother Raúl Castro, who turned seventy-five years old in June of 2006, as his successor, many believe that Castro's death could very well spark a new Cuban revolution that could remove the communist government from power and propel Cuba into a new age of economic and social development. The role of the United States in post-Castro Cuba remains to be seen, but it is highly unlikely that the United States will simply take the role of a spectator and allow Cuba to move in any political or ideological direction following Fidel Castro's death. For the Cuban people, there is the bright hope that after more than 500 years of political, economic, and social slavery, they will finally have the opportunity to be truly free.

CENTURIAL PERSPECTIVES AND CONCLUSIONS

In 1992, Fredrick Pike concluded his challenging and thought-provoking monograph on civilization and nature in U.S.–Latin American relations with some interesting interpretations. Pike observes that despite the best efforts in the United States to control the peace, security, and prosperity of the hemisphere, America has lost control of Latin America. Increasingly, during the early years of the twenty-first century, some of Pikes predictions seem to be playing out. Many Latin American leaders seem to tow the U.S. line less frequently, and the United States has increasingly chosen to neglect Latin America, or turn a blind eye to the continuing poverty and violence that abounds in many areas of the hemisphere. Pike argues that U.S. policy regarding Latin America

> has resulted in a breakdown of constitutional order within the United States itself, leading to the circumvention of domestic and international laws, to the formation of a rogue state, monolithic, clandestine, and more powerful than the official state of constitutional checks and balances—a rogue state that violated national laws, [and] connived in and profited from drug trafficking. . . . Apparently the United States could no longer impose its will with impunity on recalcitrant . . . states. Instead, it could impose its will only by undermining the principles upon which western civilization presumably rests.[22]

Pike goes on to argue that the United States has lost control of the hemisphere not only politically, economically, and militarily, but morally as well. Pike labels this phenomenon the "Latin Americanization" of America, a situation where corruption resides in government and organized religion, where private and public debt soar out of control, and where addictions dominate the lives of angry citizens who desire restitution for wrongs that they do not fully comprehend.[23]

Some of Pike's interpretations are closely echoed by Carlos Alberto Montaner who has contended that Latin America in the twenty-first century can be divided into three different categories: the developing, capitalist-leaning countries of Mexico, Chile, Central America—especially Costa Rica—and possibly Colombia and the Dominican Republic; the indecisive countries of Peru, Bolivia, and Ecuador where reforms are desired but achieving them seems out of reach at the moment; and finally the populist, left-wing, and increasingly anti-American countries of Brazil, Argentina, Uruguay, Venezuela, Paraguay, and Cuba.[24] Montaner refers to the condition illustrated by Pike not as the "Latin Americanization" of America, but rather as the "uncivilization of Latin America." He states,

> in large parts of Latin America, something fearsome is taking place: The state is increasingly incapable of maintaining order and guaranteeing the security and property of its citizens.... This situation can be given the moniker *uncivilization*. Latin America, slowly, is "discivilizing." Governments are losing their ability to exert authority. Societies feel unprotected. Criminals are in charge, at times alone and at others with the complicity of corrupt police. Crimes go unpunished. Judges do not judge in fairness. Parliaments do not legislate with common sense. The rule of law and the delicate institutional fabric of the republics simply become diluted in the face of the generalized impotence of the society.[25]

A somewhat less mordant interpretation of the present state of U.S.–Latin American relations can be found in the recent writings of Joseph Tulchin who argues that the hemisphere is merely in a state of flux, caught between the demise of the Cold War and the onset of the War on Terror. According to Tulchin, the Americas are in a position of transition where the old models and paradigms are being reevaluated in light of our changing hemisphere and world. Tulchin posits,

> We are not in a unipolar world.... Latin American leaders appear ambivalent about the nature of U.S. hegemony and its effect on the national interests of their countries. Is the U.S. to be courted, to be opposed, to be shunned, to be neutralized? What lies behind some of the confusion with regard to U.S. hegemony is the real ambivalence, felt in many countries, as to how to insert themselves, in an active manner, into the new world community of nations. So long as the U.S. was an assertive hegemonic power, with clear imperialistic imperatives that overrode ideological loyalty to democracy or capitalism, as it was during the Cold War, the insertion of the Latin American nations was either passive or shaped by the United States. Now, however, the situation is different, and many countries are unsure how to proceed.[26]

Likewise, Coletta Youngers has insightfully argued that the most important problems facing the United States and Latin American nations are not issues of military power or ideological predilection, but rather are the social dilemmas of "persistent poverty and inequality" that plague every nation in Latin America.[27]

Nevertheless, as we cross the threshold of a new century there is always room for hope. The modern history of the western hemisphere has seen the advent of a new century only six times, and at each juncture, both positive and negative events spelled the potential for either hope or despair for the inhabitants of the New World.

In 1500 there was no United States of America nor were there any British colonies in North America. Christopher Columbus had made his first three voyages in the previous eight years, and in 1500 was arrested and returned to Spain in chains where he prepared for a fourth and final voyage in 1502. The Spanish Empire was making military and ecclesiastical preparations that would culminate in the conquest of both the Aztec and Inca empires in the New World. Vasco da Gama, sailing for Portugal, had rounded the Cape of Good Hope in Africa in 1498 and sailed on to India, thus paving the way for trade with the East Indies. Furthermore, Pedro Cabral claimed discovery of Brazil in 1500 for the Portuguese Crown, thus bringing the Portuguese into the western hemisphere. Finally, John Cabot, sailing for England in 1497, landed somewhere in Newfoundland, but political conditions in England prohibited much follow-up for the better part of the century.

In 1600 the British East India Company was incorporated by royal decree thus paving the way for the British to begin the settlement of North America. The colony of Jamestown was established in 1607 and it became the first permanent British colony in the hemisphere. Spain was quiet in 1600, having just suffered a massive defeat of their Spanish Armada at the hands of the British Navy. Spanish colonists in Mexico and Peru had established several cities, universities, and printing presses over the previous century. For Portuguese Brazil, most of the previous century had been spent cultivating sugarcane and deforesting the coast for the valuable brazilwood that was used in dye production.

In 1700 the Spanish Empire changed hands from the decrepit Hapsburg Dynasty to the French Bourbon Dynasty as Philip V—the grandson of Louis XIV of France—became the king of Spain. This dynastic change would eventually bring about massive reforms in the Spanish New World colonies over the next century. All thirteen British North American colonies were established by 1700 with the exception of Georgia which was founded in 1732. And following explorations in the Mississippi River Valley by French explorer La Salle, France established its Louisiana colony in 1699, which effectively separated the British colonies from the Spanish Empire in Mexico.

In 1800 the United States of America was a functioning independent government and nation that had won its independence from Britain almost twenty years earlier in 1783, and was under the presidency of John Adams. France briefly regained Louisiana in 1800—which it had ceded to Spain in 1762—and then lost it again when Napoleon sold it to the United States in 1803. In Latin America, the seeds of discontent were so well rooted among the Creole and peasant strata of society, that within the first two decades of the nineteenth century, almost every Latin American colony would win its freedom from Iberian control. Over the course of this century, U.S.–Latin

American relations would become grounded in the Monroe Doctrine, and troubled by American aspirations of dominion in Texas, California, and the Caribbean Basin.

By 1900 Cuba and Puerto Rico were finally liberated from Spanish control during the Spanish–American War. By 1903 Panama was removed from Colombia by Theodore Roosevelt and construction of the Canal began. The Roosevelt Corollary to the Monroe Doctrine quickly followed, paving the way for a half-century of aggressive military intervention in Latin America by the United States.

In 2000 the Panama Canal was, for the first time in history, governed by Panama following nearly a century of ownership by the United States. And although U.S.–Latin American relations have recently been much quieter as the United States wages its War on Terror in the Middle East, the ties that bind the nations of the western hemisphere together continue to hold.[28] NAFTA and other commercial and economic relationships continue to bridge the trade gaps that once plagued Latin American nations. And cultural borders continue to act as permeable membranes through which music, films, literature, languages, cultures, and perspectives pass daily.

As we move forward into the twenty-first century, it is painfully clear that the relationship between the United States and Latin America remains a work in progress. Some of the bridges of trust and cooperation that have existed in the past between the regions of the hemisphere have been compromised. But hope for peaceful relations remains. In 1927, in his fictional account entitled *The Bridge of San Luis Rey*, author, playwright, and Pulitzer Prize winner Thornton Wilder wrote, "The bridge seemed to be among the things that last forever; it was unthinkable that it should break."[29] However, the 100-year-old Inca bridge that Wilder describes did collapse and plummet five individuals to their deaths. Wilder concluded that when bridges fail, it is possible to rebuild them again through patience and love, just as the Bridge of San Luis Rey was rebuilt by replacing the old woven willow construction with much stronger stone.[30]

Likewise, the borders and brides that connect the United States and the nations of Latin America will continue to act as both avenues and barriers in the affairs of the western hemisphere. As we move forward into a new century, we can only hope that as our old cultural, social, economic, and political bridges collapse, either through excessive use or due to neglect and apathy, that we will have the courage, capacity, and perspective to rebuild stronger and better bridges that will lead us in the paths of hemispheric unity and peace.

A Chronology of U.S.–Latin American Relations[1]

1783   The United States of America wins its independence from Britain in the American Revolutionary War.

1803   The Louisiana Purchase between the U.S. government and Napoleon creates a common land border between the United States and Latin America.

1804   Haiti wins its independence from France.

1810   Chile and Colombia win their independence from Spain.

1811   Venezuela, Paraguay, and Uruguay win their independence from Spain.

1811   The No-Transfer Resolution is issued in the United States to prevent the transfer of the Florida territory from Spain to other European powers.

1816   Argentina wins its independence from Spain.

1819   The Adams-Onís Treaty between the United States and Spain cedes the Florida territory to the United States.

1821   Mexico and Central America win their independence from Spain.

1822   Brazil wins its independence from Portugal.

1822   Ecuador wins its independence from Spain.

1823   Central America declares its independence from Mexico; President James Monroe proclaims the Monroe Doctrine.

1824   Peru wins its independence from Spain.

1825   Bolivia wins its independence from Spain.

1836   The Mexican state of Texas rebels and becomes an independent nation.

1845   Texas admitted to the United States as a slave state.

1846   The Mexican War between Mexico and the United States begins; the United States and Colombia sign the Bidlack-Mallarino Treaty.

1848   The United States and Mexico end the Mexican War with the signing of the Treaty of Guadalupe Hidalgo.

1850   The United States and Britain sign the Clayton–Bulwer Treaty.

1853   Mexican President Santa Anna sells territory to the United States in the Gadsden Purchase.

1853   William Walker invades Baja California and Sonora Mexico.

1854   Three U.S. diplomats propose the Ostend Manifesto plan for purchasing or seizing Cuba from the Spanish Empire.

1855   American William Walker invades Nicaragua.

1860   William Walker shot by a Honduran firing squad.

1861   French conquest of Mexico by Napoleon III and Maximilian von Hapsburg; U.S. Civil War begins and lasts until 1865.

1867   Mexican President Benito Juarez executes Maximilian von Hapsburg following the French retreat from Mexico.

1879   The War of the Pacific between Chile, Bolivia, and Peru draws the attention of the United States.

1895   A border dispute between Venezuela and Britain results in the proclamation of the Olney Doctrine.

1898   The explosion of the *USS Maine* begins the Spanish American War, resulting in the independence of Cuba and Puerto Rico from Spain.

1901   The Platt Amendment is attached to the Cuban Constitution; the United States and Britain sign the Hay–Pauncefote Treaty.

1902   Venezuela's inability to pay its foreign debt results in a naval blockade by Britain, and as a result the Drago Doctrine is issued by Luis María Drago, foreign minister of Argentina.

1903   The United States and Colombia fail to conclude the Hay–Herrán Treaty; Panama wins its independence from Colombia (with help from the United States); The United States and Panama sign the Hay–Bunau-Varilla Treaty.

1904   President Theodore Roosevelt issues a series of statements, later known as the Roosevelt Corollary to the Monroe Doctrine, which greatly expands U.S. influence in the hemisphere.

1912   President William Howard Taft sends U.S. Marines to Nicaragua where they remain until 1933.

1914   Construction on the Panama Canal is finished.

1915   President Woodrow Wilson sends U.S. Marines to Haiti where they remain until 1934.

1916   Mexican General Pancho Villa rides into New Mexico, prompting General John Pershing to chase him unsuccessfully through northern Mexico; President Woodrow Wilson sends troops to the Dominican Republic where they remain until 1924.

1917   The Zimmermann Telegram is sent to Mexico from Germany during World War I.

1928   The Clark Memorandum on the Monroe Doctrine renounces the Roosevelt Corollary to the Monroe Doctrine.

1933   President Franklin D. Roosevelt announces the Good Neighbor Policy between the United States and Latin America.

1934   The Platt Amendment is abrogated as part of the Good Neighbor Policy.

1938   Mexican President Lázaro Cardenas nationalizes U.S. and British oil corporations in Mexico.

1941   Most Latin American nations support the United States by declaring war on the Axis Powers.

1948   Formation of the Organization of American States (OAS).

1954   Guatemalan President Jacobo Arbenz is ousted by the CIA.

1958   Vice President Richard Nixon's goodwill tour of Latin America is an embarrassing debacle.

1959   The Cuban Revolution of Fidel Castro succeeds in driving Fulgencio Batista from power.

1961   President John F. Kennedy institutes the Alliance for Progress; the Bay of Pigs invasion turns into a fiasco for the United States, and a victory for Cuba.

1962   The Cuban Missile Crisis begins in October.

1965   President Lyndon B. Johnson orders U.S. Marines to the Dominican Republic.

1973   Chilean President Salvador Allende is ousted by General Augusto Pinochet with CIA support.

1977   The United States and Panama sign the Panama Canal Treaties, which promise to return the Panama Canal to Panama by December 31, 1999.

1982   British Prime Minister Margaret Thatcher orders an invasion of the Falklands Islands to restore British control.

1983   President Ronald Reagan sends U.S. Marines to the Caribbean island of Grenada to prevent a communist takeover.

1986   The Iran-Contra Scandal forces the Reagan administration to back away from its Central American policy.

1989   President George H. W. Bush sends U.S. Marines to capture military dictator Manuel Noriega in Panama.

1994   The North American Free Trade Agreement (NAFTA) goes into effect; President Bill Clinton sends U.S. Marines to Haiti to restore Jean-Bertrand Aristide to power.

1999   Panama takes control of the Panama Canal on December 31.

2001   The 9-11 terrorist attack in the United States is condemned by the OAS.

2002   The Bush administration and the CIA are briefly suspected in a failed coup that temporarily removed Venezuelan President Hugo Chávez from power.

2004   American and French governments suspected in the removal of Jean-Bertrand Aristide from Haiti.

Notes

CHAPTER 1: FOUNDATIONS AND PERCEPTIONS

1. The Pan-American Highway is longer than the Trans-Siberian Highway which stretches a mere 6,200 miles and has a "gap" of over 1,000 miles between Chita and Khabarovsk, north of Mongolia and China.

2. Excerpt from "Mending Wall" from *The Poetry of Robert Frost*, edited by Edward Connery Lathem. Copyright 1930, 1939, 1969 by Henry Holt and Company. Copyright 1958 by Robert Frost, copyright 1967 by Lesley Frost Ballantine. Reprinted by permission of Henry Holt and Company, LLC.

3. Michael J. Kryzanek, *U.S.–Latin American Relations*, 4.

4. Fredrick B. Pike, *The United States and Latin America*, 44.

5. Fredrick B. Pike, *The United States and Latin America*, 43.

6. José Enrique Rodó, *Neighborly Adversaries*, 35.

7. Figures are based on information from *The CIA World Factbook*, July, 2005, http://www.cia.gov/cia/publications/factbook/ (July 2005).

CHAPTER 2: THE EUROPEAN ENLIGHTENMENT AND THE BIRTH OF U.S.–LATIN AMERICAN RELATIONS

1. Exceptional and highly recommended are Lester D. Langley's well-written books *The Americas in the Age of Revolution*, *The Americas in the Modern Age*, and *America and the Americas: The United States in the Western Hemisphere*.

2. For a very good interpretation of the political and economic development (and decline) of Western Europe during this time period, see Derek McKay and H. M. Scott, *The Rise of the Great Powers, 1648–1815*.

3. See Lester D. Langley, *The Americas in the Age of Revolution 1750–1850*, where the American Revolutionary War is treated in the greater context of the western hemisphere.

4. Bruce B. Solnick, *The West Indies and Central America to 1898*, 88–89. Since the early 1700s, the French and Spanish had intermittently relied on an agreement between the two monarchies loosely named the Family Compact; so-called because the first Spanish Bourbon king, Philip V (1683–1746), was the grandson of Louis XIV (1638–1715), the king of France.

5. For well-written treatments of the American Revolutionary War, see Robert Middlekauf, *The Glorious Cause: The American Revolution, 1763–1787*; and Edward Countryman, *The American Revolution*.

6. In 1793 King Louis XVI was sent to the guillotine by the French Convention. See, J. F. Bosher, *The French Revolution*.

7. See for example Isaiah 9:6: "For unto us a child is born, unto us a son is given: and the government shall be upon his shoulder: and his name shall be called Wonderful, Counselor, The mighty God, The everlasting Father, The Prince of Peace."

8. Charles IV, Maria Louisa, and Godoy all retired together to Rome where they lived on a French pension. Both Charles and Maria Louisa died in Rome in 1819. Godoy then returned to Paris where he died in 1851.

CHAPTER 3: THE INDEPENDENCE MOVEMENTS IN SPANISH LATIN AMERICA AND BRAZIL

1. Hubert Herring, *A History of Latin America from the Beginnings to the Present*, 241, emphasis added.

2. Lester D. Langley, *The Americas in the Age of Revolution 1750–1850*, 159–165.

3. Lester D. Langley, *The Americas in the Age of Revolution 1750–1850*, 115–130. Originally a Spanish colony, Haiti had been ceded to France in 1697 by the Spanish crown. Eventually, the eastern half of the island of Hispañola would become the Dominican Republic.

4. Brenda Gayle Plummer, *Haiti and the United States: The Psychological Moment*, 11. In 1808 the Dominican Republic threw off Haitian domination and was restored to colonial status under Spain.

5. Lester D. Langley, *The Americas in the Age of Revolution 1750–1850*, 135–144; Bruce B. Solnick, *The West Indies and Central America to 1898*, 171, 173.

6. See Robert Harvey, *Liberators: Latin America's Struggle for Independence*, 433; W. Dirk Raat, *Mexico and the United States: Ambivalent Vistas*, 38.

7. Lester D. Langley, *The Americas in the Age of Revolution 1750–1850*, 179–183.

8. Lester D. Langley, *The Americas in the Age of Revolution 1750–1850*, 183–185.

9. Lester D. Langley, *The Americas in the Age of Revolution 1750–1850*, 205–207.

10. See Robert Harvey, *Liberators: Latin America's Struggle for Independence*, 19.

11. Lester D. Langley, *The Americas in the Age of Revolution 1750–1850*, 195–200.

12. See Robert Harvey, *Liberators: Latin America's Struggle for Independence*, 281.

13. At that time the Viceroyalty of Peru was divided into Upper and Lower Peru. After independence was achieved in Peru, Peru was divided into two independent nations. Lower Peru became the modern country of Peru. Simón Bolívar created a new nation in Upper Peru which he named after himself, thus creating the modern nation of Bolivia. Lester D. Langley, *The Americas in the Age of Revolution 1750–1850*, 200–203.

14. Lester D. Langley, *The Americas in the Age of Revolution 1750–1850*, 203–205. Bernardo O'Higgins was the illegitimate son of Ambrosio O'Higgins, a native or Ireland who eventually became the viceroy of Peru. Bernardo O'Higgins took control of independent Chile in February of 1817 after José de San Martin turned down the offer. He ruled until 1823 when he was ousted from power and fled into exile in Peru.

15. Kenneth D. Lehman, *Bolivia and the United States: A Limited Partnership*, 11; Lawrence A. Clayton, *Peru and the United States: The Condor and the Eagle*, 23.

16. Lester D. Langley, *The Americas in the Age of Revolution 1750–1850*, 207–211.

17. See Robert Harvey, *Liberators: Latin America's Struggle for Independence*, 467.

18. E. Bradford Burns, *A History of Brazil*, 111–116.

19. E. Bradford Burns, *A History of Brazil*, 116–124.

20. Robert Harvey, *Liberators: Latin America's Struggle for Independence*, 475. In this way, both Brazil and Portugal remained under the control of the royal family of Portugal, the Braganças, even though politically and economically they became separate entities.

21. Between 1812 and 1815 the United States and Great Britain fought the War of 1812 in North America. The war began mostly over the issue of impressment wherein British ship captains forced U.S. citizens to fight for Britain against the French between 1803 and 1812. The war ended in 1815 with the ratification of the Treaty of Ghent, which enforced the stalemate condition referred to as *status quo ante bellum* wherein no territory changed hands at the end of the fighting.

22. Michael J. Kryzanek, *U.S.–Latin American Relations*, 23.

23. Lester D. Langley, *America and the Americas: The United States in the Western Hemisphere*, 34–37.

CHAPTER 4: THE MONROE DOCTRINE, MANIFEST DESTINY, AND THE MEXICAN WAR

1. Michael J. Kryzanek, *U.S.–Latin American Relations*, 22; Bruce B. Solnick, *The West Indies and Central America to 1898*, 174–175.

2. Although written years ago, the seminal work on the Monroe Doctrine has been and remains Dexter Perkins, *A History of the Monroe Doctrine*; cf. Gaddis Smith, *The Last Years of the Monroe Doctrine, 1945–1993*, 21.

3. Dexter Perkins, *A History of the Monroe Doctrine*, 27.

4. James Monroe, 7th Annual Message, December 2, 1823, Washington, D.C.

5. Michael J. Kryzanek, *U.S.–Latin American Relations*, 26; Dexter Perkins, *A History of the Monroe Doctrine*, 55–59, 129–131.

6. See U.S. Constitution, Article II, Section 3 which states, "[The president] shall from time to time give to the Congress Information of the State of the Union, and recommend to their Consideration such Measures as he shall judge necessary and expedient" [sic].

7. John L. O'Sullivan, "Annexation," *The United States Magazine and Democratic Review*, 17:85 (July–August, 1845), 5–10.

8. See Frederick B. Pike, *The United States and Latin America: Myths and Stereotypes of Civilization and Nature*, 40–43.

9. Frederick B. Pike, *The United States and Latin America: Myths and Stereotypes of Civilization and Nature*, 44.

10. Lester D. Langley, *The Americas in the Modern Age*, 18–19.

11. Michael C. Meyer, William L. Sherman, and Susan M. Deeds, *The Course of Mexican History*, 308.

12. W. Dirk Raat, *Mexico and the United States: Ambivalent Vistas*, 55.

13. David J. Weber, *The Mexican Frontier 1821–1846: The American Southwest under Mexico*, 158–165.

14. David J. Weber, *The Mexican Frontier 1821–1846: The American Southwest under Mexico*, 158–178.

15. David J. Weber, *The Mexican Frontier 1821–1846: The American Southwest under Mexico*, 242–246.

16. David J. Weber, *The Mexican Frontier 1821–1846: The American Southwest under Mexico*, 22–24.

17. Stephen L. Hardin, *Texian Iliad: A Military History of the Texas Revolution*, 5–11.

18. One of the very best sources on the Texas Revolution and the Battle of the Alamo can be found in the extremely readable book by Stephen L. Hardin, *Texian Iliad: A Military History of the Texas Revolution*. One of the highlights of this remarkable book is the wonderful illustrations created by Gary S. Zaboly.

19. Michael J. Kryzanek, *U.S.–Latin American Relations*, 27.

20. John H. Jenkins, ed., *Papers of the Texas Revolution*, 13, The Alamo.Org, http://www.thealamo.org/asked.html#twentyfive (June 2005).

21. The brief period of Texan nationhood has had lasting effects in the modern state of Texas which are reflected in some modern Texan products and services such as Lonestar, the National Beer of Texas, and *Texas Monthly*, the National Magazine of Texas, to name only two.

22. Dexter Perkins, *A History of the Monroe Doctrine*, 65.

23. Michael C. Meyer, William L. Sherman, and Susan M. Deeds, *The Course of Mexican History*, 326–328.

24. Michael C. Meyer, William L. Sherman, and Susan M. Deeds, *The Course of Mexican History*, 328–329.

25. Josefina Zoraida Vázquez, "War and Peace with the United States," in *The Oxford History of Mexico*, edited by Michael C. Meyer and William H. Beezley, 360–363.

26. Josefina Zoraida Vázquez, "War and Peace with the United States," in *The Oxford History of Mexico*, edited by Michael C. Meyer and William H. Beezley, 363–364.

27. Josefina Zoraida Vázquez, "War and Peace with the United States," in *The Oxford History of Mexico*, edited by Michael C. Meyer and William H. Beezley, 365–367.

28. The area of the states of New Mexico, Arizona, Nevada, Utah, Colorado, Wyoming, California, and Texas comes to roughly 1,065,296 square miles. By contrast, the 1803 Louisiana Purchase granted to the United States around 828,000 square miles.

29. Josefina Zoraida Vázquez, "War and Peace with the United States," in *The Oxford History of Mexico*, edited by Michael C. Meyer and William H. Beezley, 368–369.

30. See Lester D. Langley, *America and the Americas: The United States in the Western Hemisphere*, 32–40.

CHAPTER 5: NINETEENTH-CENTURY U.S. IMPERIALISM AND THE SPANISH AMERICAN WAR

1. Reliable sources on William Walker are somewhat sparse. Two of the most obvious places to start are Walker's own memoirs entitled *The War in Nicaragua* and a biography by Albert Z. Carr, *The World and William Walker*; cf. Thomas M. Leonard, *Central America and the United States: The Search for Stability*, 22–30.

2. Bruce B. Solnick, *The West Indies and Central America to 1898*, 177–178.

3. Eventually British Honduras won its freedom from Britain in 1981 and became the nation of Belize, but Guatemala refused to even recognize Belizean independence until the very end of the twentieth century.

4. One of the contradictions surrounding William Walker is the fact early on in New Orleans: he had gone into print as an advocate of abolition and had been a whistle blower against a group of American filibusters headed for Cuba and intent on blatant violation of international neutrality laws. By the time Walker had taken up residence in Nicaragua, he had switched to a proslavery position in Nicaragua, and had violated international neutrality laws himself on three separate occasions.

5. Bruce B. Solnick, *The West Indies and Central America to 1898*, 134–135.

6. W. Dirk Raat, *Mexico and the United States: Ambivalent Vistas*, 75; Dexter Perkins, *A History of the Monroe Doctrine*, 107.

7. Dexter Perkins, *A History of the Monroe Doctrine*, 149.

8. Lars Schoultz, *Beneath the United States: A History of U.S. Policy Toward Latin America*, 41–43.

9. William Seward (1801–1872) served as the U.S. Secretary of State for both Presidents Abraham Lincoln and Andrew Johnson. He was responsible for encouraging much of the territorial expansion of the United States during the later years of the nineteenth century.

10. Lars Schoultz, *Beneath the United States: A History of U.S. Policy Toward Latin America*, 79.

11. G. Pope Atkins and Larman C. Wilson, *The Dominican Republic and the United States: From Imperialism to Transnationalism*, 9–20.

12. Bruce B. Solnick, *The West Indies and Central America to 1898*, 179–181.

13. G. Pope Atkins and Larman C. Wilson, *The Dominican Republic and the United States: From Imperialism to Transnationalism*, 20–27; Lester D. Langley, *America and the Americas: The United States in the Western Hemisphere*, 92. The only exception of significance has been the island of Puerto Rico, which is technically part of the United States but has never been fully enfranchised.

14. William F. Sater, *Chile and the United States: Empires in Conflict*, 31; Kenneth D. Lehman, *Bolivia and the United States: A Limited Partnership*, 38; Lawrence A. Clayton, *Peru and the United States: The Condor and the Eagle*, 51.

15. Lars Schoultz, *Beneath the United States: A History of U.S. Policy Toward Latin America*, 91–95.

16. In 1884, Chile and Bolivia could only agree on a truce, not an actual treaty. The actual treaty that officially ended the hostilities between the two nations was not ratified until 1904.

17. Lars Schoultz, *Beneath the United States: A History of U.S. Policy Toward Latin America*, 95.

18. Lars Schoultz, *Beneath the United States: A History of U.S. Policy Toward Latin America*, 95–106.

19. Lars Schoultz, *Beneath the United States: A History of U.S. Policy Toward Latin America*, 101.

20. Lars Schoultz, *Beneath the United States: A History of U.S. Policy Toward Latin America*, 107–109.

21. Judith Ewell, *Venezuela and the United States: From Monroe's Hemisphere to Petroleum's Empire*, 75.

22. Lars Schoultz, *Beneath the United States: A History of U.S. Policy Toward Latin America*, 108, citing an 1876 communiqué between the Venezuelan foreign minister in Washington, D.C., and U.S. Secretary of State Hamilton Fish.

23. Mohammed A. O. Ishmael, *Guyana News and Information*, "Guyana's Western Border, 1893–1905; 696. Secretary of State of the United States, Mr. Richard Olney to Mr. Thomas Bayard, Ambassador of the United States to Great Britain," June 1995, http://www.guyana.org/Western/1893%20to%201905.htm (June 2005).

24. See Michael J. Kryzanek, *U.S.–Latin American Relations*, 33–34, citing *Foreign Relations* (1895) 1:558 (Olney to Bayard, July 20, 1895).

25. See Michael J. Kryzanek, *U.S.–Latin American Relations*, 34, citing *Foreign Relations* (1895) 1:564–565 (Salisbury to Paunceforte, November 24, 1895).

26. Louis A. Pérez Jr., *Cuba and the United States: Ties of Singular Intimacy*, 55.

27. Lester D. Langley, *The Americas in the Modern Age*, 55–60.

28. Frederick Jackson Turner proposed his Frontier Thesis in 1893 in a speech entitled, "The Significance of the Frontier in American History." Although others had thought along these lines for a few years, it was Turner's delineation of the idea of the vanishing frontier that had such an enormous effect on historical theory in the United States for the next century.

29. Lester D. Langley, *The Americas in the Modern Age*, 60–65.

30. See John T. Bethell, "A Splendid Little War," *Harvard Magazine*, November–December, 1998.

31. Lester D. Langley, *America and the Americas: The United States in the Western Hemisphere*, 99.

32. See Teddy Roosevelt's personal memoirs of the campaigns associated with the battles of Santiago and San Juan Hill in *The Rough Riders*, edited by Caleb Carr.

33. Alaska was purchased from Russia in 1867 for more than $7 million and became a U.S. state in 1959. In 1893 the Hawaiian Islands became a U.S. protectorate but the islands did not become an official state until 1959.

34. Michael J. Kryzanek, *U.S.–Latin American Relations*, 36–38; Lester D. Langley, *The Americas in the Modern Age*, 86–87.

CHAPTER 6: GUNBOAT DIPLOMACY, PANAMA, AND THE NEW WORLD POLICEMAN

1. Dexter Perkins, *A History of the Monroe Doctrine*, 228.

2. See John T. Bethell, "A Splendid Little War," *Harvard Magazine*, November–December, 1998.

3. See for example David McCullough, *The Path between the Seas: The Creation of the Panama Canal 1870–1914*, 247.

4. Judith Ewell, *Venezuela and the United States: From Monroe's Hemisphere to Petroleum's Empire*, 100.

5. Lester D. Langley, *The Americas in the Modern Age*, 78.

6. The Drago Doctrine; Letter from Luis María Drago to Martín García Mérou, December 29, 1902, Buenos Aires.

7. Lester D. Langley, *The Americas in the Modern Age*, 79–81.

8. For a complete treatment of the events leading up to the construction of the Panama Canal, please see the thoroughly researched and well-written book by David McCullough, *The Path between the Seas: The Creation of the Panama Canal 1870–1914*.

9. Michael L. Conniff, *Panama and the United States: The Forced Alliance*, 24.

10. Thomas L. Pearcy, *We Answer Only to God: Politics and the Military in Panama, 1903–1947*, 16, 19.

11. Michael L. Conniff, *Panama and the United States: The Forced Alliance*, 45; Thomas L. Pearcy, *We Answer Only to God: Politics and the Military in Panama, 1903–1947*, 26.

12. Stephen J. Randall, *Colombia and the United States: Hegemony and Interdependence*, 72; Michael L. Conniff, *Panama and the United States: The Forced Alliance*, 63; Thomas L. Pearcy, *We Answer Only to God: Politics and the Military in Panama, 1903–1947*, 36.

13. Some years later in 1916 the United States and Nicaragua ratified the Bryan–Chamorro Treaty. Under the provisions of this treaty, Nicaragua agreed to lease to the United States various territory and islands on the Pacific Ocean coast of the country in return for a U.S. payment of $3 million. The idea was that in the future, the United States might decide to construct another Central American Canal, and the Bryan–Chamorro Treaty was the guarantor that the United States could proceed if it desired to do so.

14. Michael L. Conniff, *Panama and the United States: The Forced Alliance*, 68.

15. Michael L. Conniff, "Panama Since 1903," in *The Cambridge History of Latin America, Vol. VII, Latin America since 1930: Mexico, Central America and the Caribbean*, edited by Leslie Bethell, 606–607.

16. Stephen J. Randall, *Colombia and the United States: Hegemony and Interdependence*, 76.

17. Michael J. Kryzanek, *U.S.–Latin American Relations*, 41–42.

18. The shelling caused the only casualties of the entire revolution; they apparently hit and killed a Chinese shopkeeper and his donkey. See Algis Ratnikas, *Timelines of History*, "Timeline Panama," August 2001, http://timelines.ws/countries/PANAMA.HTML, (June 2005).

19. This *USS Maine* (BB-10) was built between 1899 and 1901 in memory of the previous *USS Maine* (ACR-1) that was sunk in the Havana Harbor immediately prior to the outbreak of the Spanish-American War.

20. Thomas L. Pearcy, *We Answer Only to God: Politics and the Military in Panama, 1903–1947*, 36–37.

21. Stephen J. Randall, *Colombia and the United States: Hegemony and Interdependence*, 96. It was not until the Thomson–Urrutia Treaty of 1921 between the United States and Colombia that the United States came close to an official apology and paid Colombia a remuneration of $25 million.

22. G. Pope Atkins and Larman C. Wilson, *The Dominican Republic and the United States: From Imperialism to Transnationalism*, 37–41; Lester D. Langley, *The Americas in the Modern Age*, 79–80.

23. Unlike the Monroe Doctrine, or most of the other documents that shaped and defined U.S.–Latin American relations, the Roosevelt Corollary was not a single document. It was in fact a series of speeches, many of which were State of the Union addresses, delivered by Theodore Roosevelt between 1901 and 1906.

24. Theodore Roosevelt, 1st Annual Message, December 3, 1901, Washington, D.C.

25. Theodore Roosevelt, 2nd Annual Message, December 2, 1902, Washington, D.C.

26. Theodore Roosevelt, 4th Annual Message, December 6, 1904, Washington, D.C.

27. Speech made by Theodore Roosevelt on February 15, 1905, in the U.S. Senate. See Samuel Flagg Bemis, *The Latin American Policy of the United States*, 157, citing *Foreign Relations*, 1905, 334–335, emphasis added.

28. Theodore Roosevelt, 5th Annual Message, December 5, 1905, Washington, D.C.

29. Theodore Roosevelt, 6th Annual Message, December 3, 1906, Washington, D.C.

30. Several sources outline many of the occurrences of American intervention and imperialism in the countries of Latin America. See, for example, Marc Becker, *History of U.S. Interventions in Latin America*, March, 1999, http://www2.truman.edu/%7Emarc/resources/interventions.html (August 4, 2004); see also *The Simonides Site: Military History and Archaeology*, "The War Zone 1800–1899," and "The War Zone 1900–1999," May 18, 2003, http://www.simonides.org/users/bibliotheca/links/wars/wars-1900/1900.html (August 4, 2004). Dr. Becker also cites several printed sources including William Blum, *Killing Hope: U.S. Military and CIA Interventionism since World War II* (Common Courage Press, 1995).

31. Bryce Wood, "The Making of the Good Neighbor Policy," in *Neighborly Adversaries: Readings in U.S.–Latin American Relations*, edited by Michael LaRosa and Frank Mora, 105; Lester D. Langley, *The Americas in the Modern Age*, 98–100.

32. W. Dirk Raat, *Mexico and the United States: Ambivalent Vistas*, 69–70.

33. W. Dirk Raat, *Mexico and the United States: Ambivalent Vistas*, 102–117. Interestingly, General Pershing's official rank was General of the Armies of the United States, a rank higher than that of a five-star general. General Pershing is one of only two men to ever hold this military rank. The other is George Washington, and Washington was awarded the rank of General of the Armies posthumously in 1976.

34. W. Dirk Raat, *Mexico and the United States: Ambivalent Vistas*, 115.

35. For a complete treatment of the U.S. intervention in Nicaragua and the events surrounding Sandino's revolution, see Neill Macaulay, *The Sandino Affair*, which is the seminal work on Sandino and his insurrection. See also Thomas M. Leonard, *Central America and the United States: The Search for Stability*, 88–101.

36. Lester D. Langley, *The Americas in the Modern Age*, 114–115.

37. Neill Macaulay, *The Sandino Affair*, 9–10.

38. Lester D. Langley, *The Americas in the Modern Age*, 115–117.

39. Michael J. Kryzanek, *U.S.–Latin American Relations*, 45–50.

CHAPTER 7: THE GREAT DEPRESSION, THE GOOD NEIGHBOR POLICY, AND WORLD WAR II

1. J. Reuben Clark Jr., U.S. Undersecretary of State, to Henry L. Stimson, U.S. Secretary of State, Washington, D.C., December 17, 1928, *Memorandum on the Monroe Doctrine*, Department of State Publication #37 (Washington, D.C.: Government Printing Office, 1930).

2. J. Reuben Clark Jr., U.S. Undersecretary of State, to Henry L. Stimson, U.S. Secretary of State, Washington, D.C., December 17, 1928, *Memorandum on the Monroe Doctrine*, Department of State Publication #37 (Washington, D.C.: Government Printing Office, 1930).

3. E. Bradford Burns, *A History of Brazil*, 346, 349–350.

4. Paul J. Dosal, *Doing Business with the Dictators: A Political History of United Fruit in Guatemala, 1899–1944*, 17–33; Thomas L. Karnes, *Tropical Enterprise: The Standard Fruit and Steamship Company in Latin America*, 1–18.; Lester D. Langley, *The Americas in the Modern Age*, 76.

5. Thomas L. Karnes, *Tropical Enterprise: The Standard Fruit and Steamship Company in Latin America*, 37–52.

6. Thomas M. Leonard, *Central America and the United States: The Search for Stability*, 141.

7. Thomas M. Leonard, *Central America and the United States: The Search for Stability*, 65, 72–74, 93–94.

8. Robert MacCameron, *Bananas, Labor, and Politics in Honduras, 1954–1963*, 13.

9. John Kobler, "Sam the Banana Man," *Life Magazine*, 30:8, 1951.

10. Dexter Perkins, *A History of the Monroe Doctrine*, 314.

11. Franklin Delano Roosevelt, First Inaugural Address, March 4, 1933, Washington, D.C.

12. "Treaty between the United States of America and Cuba; May 29, 1934," *The Avalon Project at Yale Law School*, June 2005, http://www.yale.edu/lawweb/avalon/diplomacy/cuba/cuba001.htm (June 2005).

13. Thomas L. Pearcy, *We Answer Only to God: Politics and the Military in Panama, 1903–1947*, 76.

14. W. Dirk Raat, *Mexico and the United States: Ambivalent Vistas*, 126.

15. Lester D. Langley, *The Americas in the Modern Age*, 125–126.

16. Lester D. Langley, *The Americas in the Modern Age*, 127–128.

17. Lester D. Langley, *America and the Americas: The United States in the Western Hemisphere*, 134–140.

18. Lester D. Langley, *The Americas in the Modern Age*, 130–136.

19. See, for example, Richard Doody, "Chronology of World War II Diplomacy 1939–1945," *The World at War*, http://worldatwar.net/timeline/other/diplomacy39-45.html (June 2005), and "The Americas", *World War-2.net*, http://www.worldwar-2.net/timelines/the-americas/the-americas-index.htm (June 2005).

20. Lester D. Langley, *The Americas in the Modern Age*, 136–138.

21. For a complete treatment of Latin American involvement in World War II, see the excellent books by R. A. Humphreys, *Latin American and the Second World War*, Vol. 1 1939–1942, and Vol. 2 1942–1945.

22. Frank D. McCann, "Brazil and World War II: The Forgotten Ally," *Estudios Interdisciplinarios de America Latina y el Caribe*, 6:2 (July–December 1995), http://www.tau.ac.il/eial/VI_2/mccann.htm (June 2005).

23. See Friedrich E. Schuler, "Mexico and the Outside World," in *The Oxford History of Mexico*, edited by Michael Meyer and William Beezley, 534–541; and Michael Meyer, William L. Sherman, and Susan M. Deeds., *The Course of Mexican History*, 606–607.

24. Alan Knight, "The Rise and Fall of Cardenismo, c. 1930–c. 1946," in *Mexico since Independence*, edited by Leslie Bethell, 303.

CHAPTER 8: THE COLD WAR, THE CUBAN REVOLUTION, AND THE CUBAN MISSILE CRISIS

1. Harry S. Truman, "Truman Doctrine," Address before a Joint Session of Congress, March 12, 1947, Washington, D.C., *The Avalon Project*, July 2005, http://www.yale.edu/lawweb/avalon/trudoc.htm (July 2005).

2. Lawrence A. Clayton, *Peru and the United States: The Condor and the Eagle*, 150.

3. Thomas M. Leonard, *Central America and the United States: The Search for Stability*, 136–143; Lester D. Langley, *The Americas in the Modern Age*, 167.

4. Piero Gleijeses, *Shattered Hope: The Guatemalan Revolution and the United States, 1944–1954*, 98–107; Richard H. Immerman, *The CIA in Guatemala: The Foreign Policy of Intervention*, 48–57.

5. Lester D. Langley, *The Americas in the Modern Age*, 168.

6. See Lars Schoultz, *Beneath the United States: A History of U.S. Policy Toward Latin America*, 337–338; Richard H. Immerman, *The CIA in Guatemala: The Foreign Policy of Intervention*, 117–118.

7. Piero Gleijeses, *Shattered Hope: The Guatemalan Revolution and the United States, 1944–1954*, 380–381.

8. See Sebastian Balfour, *Castro*, 21–34.

9. Ministerio de Educación Superior 1983, p. 244, cited in Sebastian Balfour, *Castro*, 41.

10. Thomas G. Paterson, *Contesting Castro: The United States and the Triumph of the Cuban Revolution*, 76.

11. Louis A. Pérez Jr., *Cuba and the United States: Ties of Singular Intimacy*, 238, 242.

12. Louis A. Pérez Jr., *Cuba and the United States: Ties of Singular Intimacy*, 243.

13. Michael J. Kryzanek, *U.S.–Latin American Relations*, 62; James G. Blight and Peter Kornbluh, eds., *Politics of Illusion: The Bay of Pigs Invasion Reexamined*, 50, 87–88; Clara Nieto, *Masters of War: Latin America and U.S. Aggression from the Cuban Revolution through the Clinton Years*, 74–78.

14. Mark J. White, *Missiles in Cuba: Kennedy, Khrushchev, Castro and the 1962 Crisis*, 21–22.

15. See *Alleged Assassination Plots Involving Foreign Leaders: An Interim Report of the Select Committee to Study Governmental Operations with Respect to Intelligence Activities*, United States Senate, 94th Congress, 1st Session, Report No. 94-465, November 20, 1975 (Washington D.C.: U.S. Government Printing Office, 1975).

16. New York Times, April 24, 1959, cited in Aleksandr Fursenko and Timothy Naftali, *"One Hell of a Gamble": Khrushchev, Castro, and Kennedy 1958–1964, The Secret History of the Cuban Missile Crisis*, 10. Castro made other confusing references to his political ideology with such quotes as "I am not a communist and neither is the revolutionary movement," and "I am a Marxist Leninist and I will be one until the last day of my life."

17. Aleksandr Fursenko and Timothy Naftali, *"One Hell of a Gamble": Khrushchev, Castro, and Kennedy 1958–1964, The Secret History of the Cuban Missile Crisis*, 70. Here the authors are citing a secret KGB document entitled "Memoirs not for Publication," written in the 1970s by Aleksandr Alekseev, Soviet Ambassador to Cuba. The authors are clear to state that they were not permitted to read the document, but they were informed that this story about Che Guevara was contained in the text of the document.

18. Mark J. White, *Missiles in Cuba: Kennedy, Khrushchev, Castro and the 1962 Crisis*, 50; Aleksandr Fursenko and Timothy Naftali, *"One Hell of a Gamble": Khrushchev, Castro, and Kennedy 1958–1964, The Secret History of the Cuban Missile Crisis*, 188–189.

19. Office of the White House Press Secretary, "Radio-TV Address of the President to the Nation from the White House, October 22, 1962," in Laurence Chang and Peter Kornbluh, eds., *The Cuban Missile Crisis, 1962: A National Security Archive Documents Reader*, 160.

20. Office of the White House Press Secretary, "Radio-TV Address of the President to the Nation from the White House, October 22, 1962," in Laurence Chang and Peter Kornbluh, eds., *The Cuban Missile Crisis, 1962: A National Security Archive Documents Reader*, 163.

21. See C. G. Fenwick, "The Quarantine against Cuba: Legal or Illegal?" *The American Journal of International Law*, 57:3 (July 1963), 588–592.

22. "Khrushchev Letter to Kennedy, October 26, 1962," in Laurence Chang and Peter Kornbluh, eds., *The Cuban Missile Crisis, 1962: A National Security Archive Documents Reader*, 198.

23. "Prime Minister Fidel Castro's letter to Premier Khrushchev, October 26, 1962," in Laurence Chang and Peter Kornbluh, eds., *The Cuban Missile Crisis, 1962: A National Security Archive Documents Reader*, 199.

24. "Premier Khrushchev's communiqué to President Kennedy, accepting an end to the missile crisis, October 28, 1962," in Laurence Chang and Peter Kornbluh, eds., *The Cuban Missile Crisis, 1962: A National Security Archive Documents Reader*, 236.

25. Ernest R. May and Philip D. Zelikow, *The Kennedy Tapes: Inside the White House during the Cuban Missile Crisis*, 358.

26. See John Charles Chasteen, *Born in Blood and Fire: A Concise History of Latin America*, 275–301.

CHAPTER 9: THE END OF NONINTERVENTION AND THE END OF THE COLD WAR

1. See Michael J. Kryzanek, *U.S.–Latin American Relations*, 63–65, 69–71; cf. Lester D. Langley, *The Americas in the Modern Age*, 190–202.

2. Gaddis Smith, *The Last Years of the Monroe Doctrine, 1945–1993*, 115. See also Clara Nieto, *Masters of War: Latin America and U.S. Aggression from the Cuban Revolution through the Clinton Years*.

3. Gaddis Smith, *The Last Years of the Monroe Doctrine, 1945–1993*, 121.

4. Lester D. Langley, *The Americas in the Modern Age*, 205.

5. Lester D. Langley, *The Americas in the Modern Age*, 206.

6. G. Pope Atkins and Larman C. Wilson, *The Dominican Republic and the United States: From Imperialism to Transnationalism*, 142–144.

7. Lars Schoultz, *Beneath the United States: A History of U.S. Policy Toward Latin America*, 351.

8. Lars Schoultz, *Beneath the United States: A History of U.S. Policy Toward Latin America*, 351; cf. Gaddis Smith, *The Last Years of the Monroe Doctrine, 1945–1993*, 88–89.

9. Lars Schoultz, *Beneath the United States: A History of U.S. Policy Toward Latin America*, 352.

10. William F. Sater, *Chile and the United States: Empires in Conflict*, 148, 154–155.

11. William F. Sater, *Chile and the United States: Empires in Conflict*, 160–161; cf. Gaddis Smith, *The Last Years of the Monroe Doctrine, 1945–1993*, 134.

12. Lester D. Langley, *America and the Americas: The United States in the Western Hemisphere*, 222–223; Lars Schoultz, *Beneath the United States: A History of U.S. Policy Toward Latin America*, 349; Gaddis Smith, *The Last Years of the Monroe Doctrine, 1945–1993*, 133.

13. William F. Sater, *Chile and the United States: Empires in Conflict*, 162.

14. William F. Sater, *Chile and the United States: Empires in Conflict*, 160–161.

15. William F. Sater, *Chile and the United States: Empires in Conflict*, 182–184.

16. Lester D. Langley, *The Americas in the Modern Age*, 226–231.

17. Lars Schoultz, *Beneath the United States: A History of U.S. Policy Toward Latin America*, 360–361.

18. Lars Schoultz, *Beneath the United States: A History of U.S. Policy Toward Latin America*, 361; Lester D. Langley, *America and the Americas: The United States in the Western Hemisphere*, 227; William F. Sater, *Chile and the United States: Empires in Conflict*, 186–187.

19. Lester D. Langley, *The Americas in the Modern Age*, 235; Michael J. Kryzanek, *U.S.–Latin American Relations*, 75–79.

20. See Gaddis Smith, *The Last Years of the Monroe Doctrine, 1945–1993*, 139.

21. Thomas M. Leonard, *Central America and the United States: The Search for Stability*, 170–174.

22. Lars Schoultz, *Beneath the United States: A History of U.S. Policy Toward Latin America*, 363.

23. Panamanians had recently carried out a revolution in the Canal Zone in 1964 in which U.S. troops killed Panamanian student protesters who wanted to raise a Panamanian flag in the Canal Zone. As a result, in 1965 the United States and Panama attempted to renegotiate the Panama Canal Treaty, but ultimately failed to accomplish anything. Michael L. Conniff, *Panama and the United States: The Forced Alliance*, 125–128.

24. Michael L. Conniff, *Panama and the United States: The Forced Alliance*, 135; Gaddis Smith, *The Last Years of the Monroe Doctrine, 1945–1993*, 134–136.

25. Michael L. Conniff, *Panama and the United States: The Forced Alliance*, 135; Gaddis Smith, *The Last Years of the Monroe Doctrine, 1945–1993*, 134–136, 149.

26. Gaddis Smith, *The Last Years of the Monroe Doctrine, 1945–1993*, 148–149.

27. Lester D. Langley, *America and the Americas: The United States in the Western Hemisphere*, 235–236.

28. Ronald Reagan, "Remarks at the Quadrennial Convention of the International Longshoremen's Association in Hollywood, Florida," July 18, 1983, *The American Presidency Project*, http://www.presidency.ucsb.edu/ws/index.php?pid=41596&st=&st1= (July 2005).

29. Ronald Reagan, "Remarks at the Quadrennial Convention of the International Longshoremen's Association in Hollywood, Florida," July 18, 1983, *The American Presidency Project*, http://www.presidency.ucsb.edu/ws/index.php?pid=41596&st=&st1= (July 2005).

30. Lester D. Langley, *America and the Americas: The United States in the Western Hemisphere*, 247; Thomas M. Leonard, *Central America and the United States: The Search for Stability*, 187.

31. David Rock, *Argentina 1516–1987: From Spanish Colonization to Alfonsín*, 374–375. The British had actually had a presence in the islands since the late 1700s, sharing the territory sporadically with Spain. After the wars for independence in the 1820s, Argentina claimed the islands and tried to govern them until 1833 when the British drove them out and retook the islands as part of the British overseas empire.

32. David Rock, *Argentina 1516–1987: From Spanish Colonization to Alfonsín*, 377–378.

33. David Rock, *Argentina 1516–1987: From Spanish Colonization to Alfonsín*, 378.

34. David Rock, *Argentina 1516–1987: From Spanish Colonization to Alfonsín*, 379, 380.

35. Gaddis Smith, *The Last Years of the Monroe Doctrine, 1945–1993*, 169–171.

36. David Rock, *Argentina 1516–1987: From Spanish Colonization to Alfonsín*, 382.

37. David Rock, *Argentina 1516–1987: From Spanish Colonization to Alfonsín*, 381.

38. Gaddis Smith, *The Last Years of the Monroe Doctrine, 1945–1993*, 183.

39. Gaddis Smith, *The Last Years of the Monroe Doctrine, 1945–1993*, 184.

40. Two sources on the events of the scandal include Donald T. Regan, *For The Record: From Wall Street to Washington* and Oliver North, *Taking the Stand: The Testimony of Lieutenant Colonel Oliver L. North. The Complete Transcripts of His Testimony before the Select Committee of the House and Senate.*

41. Lars Schoultz, *Beneath the United States: A History of U.S. Policy Toward Latin America*, 365; Thomas M. Leonard, *Central America and the United States: The Search for Stability*, 189; Gaddis Smith, *The Last Years of the Monroe Doctrine, 1945–1993*, 203. Later in 1985, Smith reports that the Congress approved $100 million more for Nicaragua, but this was the last money officially approved by the U.S. government.

42. Gaddis Smith, *The Last Years of the Monroe Doctrine, 1945–1993*, 201.

43. Lars Schoultz, *Beneath the United States: A History of U.S. Policy Toward Latin America*, 365. In December of 1992, President George H. W. Bush pardoned several of the individuals involved in the Iran-Contra Scandal.

44. For accounts of the U.S. invasion of Panama, see Christina Jacqueline Johns and P. Ward Johnson, *State Crime, the Media, and the Invasion of Panama*; and Luis E. Murillo, *The Noriega Mess: The Drugs, the Canal, and Why America Invaded*. For Noriega's own description of the events surrounding his removal from power, see Manuel Noriega and Peter Eisner, *America's Prisoner: The Memoirs of Manuel Noriega.*

45. Gaddis Smith, *The Last Years of the Monroe Doctrine, 1945–1993*, 219.

46. Michael L. Conniff, *Panama and the United States: The Forced Alliance*, 157–159.

47. Michael L. Conniff, *Panama and the United States: The Forced Alliance*, 160.

48. Gaddis Smith, *The Last Years of the Monroe Doctrine, 1945–1993*, 219.

49. Michael L. Conniff, *Panama and the United States: The Forced Alliance*, 165; Gaddis Smith, *The Last Years of the Monroe Doctrine, 1945–1993*, 219–220. Noriega will be eligible for parole in 2006 but it is expected that if paroled, Noriega will be extradited back to Panama to be tried for murder.

50. Michael J. Kryzanek, *U.S.–Latin American Relations*, 91–94.

51. William Pfaff, *Los Angeles Times Syndicate*, January 7, 1990, cited by Michael L. Conniff, *Panama and the United States: The Forced Alliance*, 166.

CHAPTER 10: CROSSING THE THRESHOLD OF A NEW CENTURY

1. Robert A. Pastor, "The Clinton Administration and the Americas: The Postwar Rhythm and Blues," *Journal of Interamerican Studies and World Affairs*, 38:4 (Winter 1996), 99–128.

2. John Herd Thompson and Stephen J. Randall, *Canada and the United States: Ambivalent Allies*, 293. See also Anthony T. Bryan, "The New Clinton Administration and the Caribbean: Trade, Security, and Regional Politics," *Journal of Interamerican Studies and World Affairs*, 39:1 (Spring 1997), 101–120.

3. Lester D. Langley, *The Americas in the Modern Age*, 265–266.

4. John Sweeney, "Clinton's Latin America Policy: A Legacy of Missed Opportunities," *Backgrounder*, The Heritage Foundation, No. 1201, July 6, 1998, http://www.heritage.org/Research/LatinAmerica/BG1201.cfm (July 2005).

5. Robert A. Pastor, "The Clinton Administration and the Americas: The Postwar Rhythm and Blues," *Journal of Interamerican Studies and World Affairs*, 38:4 (Winter 1996), 102.

6. Robert A. Pastor, "The Clinton Administration and the Americas: The Postwar Rhythm and Blues," *Journal of Interamerican Studies and World Affairs*, 38:4 (Winter 1996), 103.

7. John Sweeney, "Clinton's Latin America Policy: A Legacy of Missed Opportunities," *Backgrounder*, The Heritage Foundation, No. 1201, July 6, 1998, http://www.heritage.org/Research/LatinAmerica/BG1201.cfm (July 2005); c.f. Robert A. Pastor, "The Clinton Administration and the Americas: The Postwar Rhythm and Blues," *Journal of Interamerican Studies and World Affairs*, 38:4 (Winter 1996), 106–107.

8. Robert A. Pastor, "The Clinton Administration and the Americas: The Postwar Rhythm and Blues," *Journal of Interamerican Studies and World Affairs*, 38:4 (Winter 1996), 110–112.

9. John Sweeney, "Clinton's Latin America Policy: A Legacy of Missed Opportunities," *Backgrounder*, The Heritage Foundation, No. 1201, July 6, 1998, http://www.heritage.org/Research/LatinAmerica/BG1201.cfm (July 2005).

10. George W. Bush, "George W. Bush's Speech on Latin America," *Newsmax.com*, August 25, 2000, http://www.newsmax.com/articles/?a=2000/8/26/195405 (August 2005).

11. George W. Bush, "George W. Bush's Speech on Latin America," *Newsmax.com*, August 25, 2000, http://www.newsmax.com/articles/?a=2000/8/26/195405 (August 2005).

12. Otto J. Reich, "U.S. Interests in Latin America," *The Heritage Foundation*, October 31, 2002, http://www.heritage.org/Research/LatinAmerica/WM173.cfm, Web Memo #173 (August 2005).

13. Coletta Youngers, "The U.S. and Latin America After 9-11 and Iraq," *Foreign Policy in Focus*, June 2003, http://www.fpif.org/pdf/reports/PRlatam2003.pdf, *fpif.org* (August 2005).

14. Coletta Youngers, "The U.S. and Latin America After 9-11 and Iraq," *Foreign Policy in Focus*, June 2003, http://www.fpif.org/pdf/reports/PRlatam2003.pdf, *fpif.org* (August 2005).

15. Coletta Youngers, "The U.S. and Latin America After 9-11 and Iraq," *Foreign Policy in Focus,* June 2003, http://www.fpif.org/pdf/reports/PRlatam2003.pdf, *fpif.org* (August 2005).

16. Otto J. Reich, "U.S. Interests in Latin America," *The Heritage Foundation,* October 31, 2002, http://www.heritage.org/Research/LatinAmerica/WM173.cfm, Web Memo #173 (August 2005).

17. Lester D. Langley, *The Americas in the Modern Age,* 263.

18. Coletta Youngers, "The U.S. and Latin America After 9-11 and Iraq," *Foreign Policy in Focus,* June 2003, http://www.fpif.org/pdf/reports/PRlatam2003.pdf, *fpif.org* (August 2005); Otto J. Reich, "U.S. Interests in Latin America," *The Heritage Foundation,* October 31, 2002, http://www.heritage.org/Research/LatinAmerica/WM173.cfm, Web Memo #173 (August 2005).

19. Stephen Johnson, "The Road to Hemispheric Security," *The Heritage Foundation,* December 14, 2004, Heritage Lecture No. 859 http://www.heritage.org/Research/LatinAmerica/hl859.cfm (August 2005).

20. Otto J. Reich, "U.S. Interests in Latin America," *The Heritage Foundation,* October 31, 2002, http://www.heritage.org/Research/LatinAmerica/WM173.cfm, Web Memo #173 (August 2005).

21. Carlos Alberto Montaner, "Latin America: Fragmentation and Forecasts," *The Heritage Foundation,* June 2, 2005, http://www.heritage.org/Research/LatinAmerica/hl883.cfm (August 2005); Otto J. Reich, "U.S. Interests in Latin America," October 31, 2002, http://www.heritage.org/Research/LatinAmerica/WM173.cfm, *Web Memo #173, The Heritage Foundation* (August 2005).

22. Fredrick B. Pike, *The United States and Latin America: Myths and Stereotypes of Civilization and Nature,* 339.

23. Fredrick B. Pike, *The United States and Latin America: Myths and Stereotypes of Civilization and Nature,* 352–358.

24. Carlos Alberto Montaner, "Latin America: Fragmentation and Forecasts," *The Heritage Foundation,* June 2, 2005, http://www.heritage.org/Research/LatinAmerica/hl883.cfm (August 2005). Montaner subsequently clarifies the current situation in Central America by pointing out that Honduras, El Salvador, and Guatemala are among the most unstable in the hemisphere, with Nicaragua and Panama likely to follow.

25. Carlos Alberto Montaner, "Latin America: Fragmentation and Forecasts," *The Heritage Foundation,* June 2, 2005, http://www.heritage.org/Research/LatinAmerica/hl883.cfm (August 2005).

26. Joseph S. Tulchin, "Hemispheric Relations in the 21st Century," *Journal of Interamerican Studies and World Affairs,* 39:1 (Spring 1997), 33–43.

27. Coletta Youngers, "The U.S. and Latin America after 9-11 and Iraq," *Foreign Policy in Focus,* June 2003, http://www.fpif.org/pdf/reports/PRlatam2003.pdf, *fpif.org* (August 2005).

28. Lester D. Langley, *The Americas in the Modern Age,* 266–272.

29. From *The Bridge of San Luis Rey* by Thornton Wilder, Copyright © 1928 The Wilder Family LLC and the Barbara Hogenson Agency, Inc. All rights reserved.

30. From *The Bridge of San Luis Rey* by Thornton Wilder, Copyright © 1928 The Wilder Family LLC and the Barbara Hogenson Agency, Inc. All rights reserved.

A CHRONOLOGY OF U.S.–LATIN AMERICAN RELATIONS

1. The information in this chronology of U.S.–Latin American relations was based on information in other similar documents such as Marc Becker, "Latin American Chronology," http://www.ilstu.edu/class/hist127/chron.html; Mark Rosenfelder, "U.S. Interventions in Latin America," http://www.zompist.com/latam.html; and Richard W. Slatta's two chronologies, "Ancient and Colonial Latin American History Time Line," http://legacy.ncsu.edu/classes/hi300001/hi215time.htm, and "Time Line of U.S. Latin American Relations," http://legacy.ncsu.edu/classes/hi300001/hi453time.htm, October 2005.

Bibliography

Atkins, G. Pope, and Larman C. Wilson. *The Dominican Republic and the United States: From Imperialism to Transnationalism*. Athens: University of Georgia Press, 1998.

Balfour, Sebastian. *Castro*. New York: Longman, 1995.

Bemis, Samuel Flagg. *The Latin American Policy of the United States: A Historical Interpretation*. New York: W.W. Norton and Company, 1967.

Bethell, John T. "A Splendid Little War." *Harvard Magazine*, November–December, 1998.

Blight, James G., and Peter Kornbluh. *Politics of Illusion: The Bay of Pigs Invasion Reexamined*. Boulder: Lynne Rienner Publishers, 1998.

Bosher, J. F. *The French Revolution*. New York: W.W. Norton and Company, 1988.

Bryan, Anthony T. "The New Clinton Administration and the Caribbean: Trade, Security, and Regional Politics." *Journal of Interamerican Studies and World Affairs*, 39:1 (Spring 1997), 101–120.

Burns, E. Bradford. *A History of Brazil*. New York: Colombia University Press, 1993.

Bush, George W. "George W. Bush's Speech on Latin America." *Newsmax.com* (August 25, 2000). http://www.newsmax.com/articles/?a=2000/8/26/195405 (August 2005).

Carr, Albert Z. *The World and William Walker*. Westport, CT: Greenwood Press, 1975.

Chang, Laurence, and Peter Kornbluh. *The Cuban Missile Crisis, 1962: A National Security Archive Documents Reader*. New York: The New Press, 1998.

Chasteen, John Charles. *Born in Blood and Fire: A Concise History of Latin America*. New York: W.W. Norton and Company, 2001.

Clayton, Lawrence A. *Peru and the United States: The Condor and the Eagle.* Athens: University of Georgia Press, 1999.

Conniff, Michael L. "Panama since 1903." In *The Cambridge History of Latin America, Vol. VII, Latin America since 1930: Mexico, Central America and the Caribbean.* Edited by Leslie Bethell. Cambridge: Cambridge University Press, 1990.

Conniff, Michael L. *Panama and the United States: The Forced Alliance.* Athens: University of Georgia Press, 2001.

Countryman, Edward. *The American Revolution.* New York: Hill and Wang, 2003.

Dosal, Paul J. *Doing Business with the Dictators: A Political History of United Fruit Company in Guatemala, 1899–1944.* Wilmington, DE: Scholarly Resources, 1993.

Ewell, Judith. *Venezuela and the United States: From Monroe's Hemisphere to Petroleum's Empire.* Athens: University of Georgia Press, 1996.

Fenwick, C. G. "The Quarantine Against Cuba: Legal or Illegal?" *The American Journal of International Law,* 57:3 (July 1963), 588–592.

Frost, Robert. *The Poetry of Robert Frost.* New York: Owl Books, 2002.

Fursenko, Aleksandr, and Timothy Naftali. *One Hell of a Gamble: Khrushchev, Castro, and Kennedy 1958–1964, The Secret History of the Cuban Missile Crisis.* New York: W.W. Norton and Company, 1997.

Gleijeses, Piero. *Shattered Hope: The Guatemalan Revolution and the United States, 1944–1954.* Princeton: Princeton University Press, 1991.

Hardin, Stephen L. *Texian Iliad: A Military History of the Texas Revolution.* Austin: University of Texas Press, 1994.

Harvey, Robert. *Liberators: Latin America's Struggle for Independence.* New York: Overlook Press, 2000.

Herring, Hubert. *A History of Latin America from the Beginnings to the Present.* New York: Alfred A. Knopf, 1962.

Humphreys, R.A. *Latin America and the Second World War.* 2 vols. London: University of London Press, 1981–1982.

Immerman, Richard H. *The CIA in Guatemala: The Foreign Policy of Intervention.* Austin: University of Texas Press, 1982.

Jenkins, John H., ed. *Papers of the Texas Revolution.* Austin: Presidial Press, 1973.

Johns, Christina Jacqueline, and P. Ward Johnson. *State Crime, the Media, and the Invasion of Panama.* New York: Praeger, 1993.

Johnson, Stephen. "The Road to Hemispheric Security." *The Heritage Foundation* (December 14, 2004), Heritage Lecture No. 859, http://www.heritage.org/Research/LatinAmerica/hl859.cfm (August 2005).

Karnes, Thomas L. *Tropical Enterprise: The Standard Fruit and Steamship Company in Latin America.* Baton Rouge: Louisiana State University, 1978.

Knight, Alan. "The Rise and Fall of Cardenismo, c. 1930—c. 1946." In *Mexico since Independence.* Edited by Leslie Bethell. New York: Cambridge University Press, 1991.

Kobler, John. "Sam the Banana Man." *Life Magazine,* 30:8, 1951.

Kryzanek, Michael J. *U.S.–Latin American Relations.* New York: Praeger, 1990.

Langley, Lester D. *America and the Americas: The United States in the Western Hemisphere.* Athens: University of Georgia Press, 1989.

Langley, Lester D. *The Americas in the Age of Revolution 1750–1850*. New Haven: Yale University Press, 1996.

Langley, Lester D. *The Americas in the Modern Age*. New Haven, CT: Yale University Press, 2003.

LaRosa, Michael, and Frank O. Mora. *Neighborly Adversaries: Readings in U.S.–Latin American Relations*. Lanham, MD: Rowman & Littlefield Publishers, 1999.

Lehman, Kenneth D. *Bolivia and the United States: A Limited Partnership*. Athens: University of Georgia Press, 1999.

Leonard, Thomas M. *Central America and the United States: The Search for Stability*. Athens: University of Georgia Press, 1991.

Macaulay, Neill. *The Sandino Affair*. Chicago: Quadrangle Books, 1967.

MacCameron, Robert. *Bananas, Labor, and Politics in Honduras, 1954–1963*. Syracuse: Syracuse University Press, 1983.

May, Ernest R., and Philip D. Zelikow. *The Kennedy Tapes: Inside the White House during the Cuban Missile Crisis*. Cambridge: Harvard University Press, 1997.

McCann, Frank D. "Brazil and World War II: The Forgotten Ally." *Estudios Interdisciplinarios de America Latina y el Caribe*, 6:2 (July–December 1995).

McCullough, David. *The Path between the Seas: The Creation of the Panama Canal 1870–1914*. New York: Simon and Schuster, 1977.

McKay, Derek, and H. M. Scott. *The Rise of the Great Powers, 1648–1815*. New York: Longman, 1983.

Meyer, Michael C., William L. Sherman, and Susan M. Deeds. *The Course of Mexican History*. New York: Oxford University Press, 2003.

Middlekauf, Robert. *The Glorious Cause: The American Revolution, 1763–1787*. Oxford: Oxford University Press, 1985.

Montaner, Carlos Alberto. "Latin America: Fragmentation and Forecasts." *The Heritage Foundation* (June 2, 2005). http://www.heritage.org/Research/LatinAmerica/hl883.cfm (August 2005).

Murillo, Luis E. *The Noriega Mess: The Drugs, The Canal, and Why America Invaded*. Berkeley, CA: Video Books, 1995.

Nieto, Clara. *Masters of War: Latin America and U.S. Aggression from the Cuban Revolution through the Clinton Years*. New York: Seven Stories, 2003.

Noriega, Manuel, and Peter Eisner. *America's Prisoner: The Memoirs of Manuel Noriega*. New York: Random House, 1997.

North, Oliver. *Taking the Stand: The Testimony of Lieutenant Colonel Oliver L. North. The Complete Transcripts of His Testimony before the Select Committee of the House and Senate*. New York: Pocket Books, 1987.

O'Sullivan, John L. "Annexation." *The United States Magazine and Democratic Review*, 17:85 (July–August 1845), 5–10.

Pastor, Robert A. "The Clinton Administration and the Americas: The Postwar Rhythm and Blues." *Journal of Interamerican Studies and World Affairs*, 38:4 (Winter 1996), 99–128.

Paterson, Thomas G. *Contesting Castro: The United States and the Triumph of the Cuban Revolution*. New York: Oxford University Press, 1994.

Pearcy, Thomas L. *We Answer Only to God: Politics and the Military in Panama, 1903–1947*. Albuquerque: University of New Mexico Press, 1998.

Pérez, Louis A., Jr. *Cuba and the United States: Ties of Singular Intimacy*. Athens: University of Georgia Press, 2003.

Perkins, Dexter. *A History of the Monroe Doctrine*. Boston: Little, Brown and Company, 1963.

Pike, Fredrick B. *The United States and Latin America: Myths and Stereotypes of Civilization and Nature*. Austin: University of Texas Press, 1992.

Plummer, Brenda Gayle. *Haiti and the United States: The Psychological Moment*. Athens: University of Georgia Press, 1992.

Raat, W. Dirk. *Mexico and the United States: Ambivalent Vistas*. Athens: University of Georgia Press, 1996.

Randall, Stephen J. *Colombia and the United States: Hegemony and Interdependence*. Athens: University of Georgia Press, 1992.

Regan, Donald T. *For the Record: From Wall Street to Washington*. New York: Harcourt Brace Jovanovich, 1988.

Reich, Otto J. "U.S. Interests in Latin America." *The Heritage Foundation* (October 31, 2002). http://www.heritage.org/Research/LatinAmerica/WM173.cfm, Web Memo #173 (August 2005).

Rock, David. *Argentina 1516–1987: From Spanish Colonization to Alfonsín*. Berkeley: University of California Press, 1987.

Rodó, José Enrique. "Ariel." In *Neighborly Adversaries: Readings in U.S.–Latin American Relations*. Edited by Michael LaRosa and Frank Mora. New York: Roman & Littlefield, 1999.

Roosevelt, Theodore. *The Rough Riders*. New York: Modern Library, 1996, Reprint.

Sater, William F. *Chile and the United States: Empires in Conflict*. Athens: University of Georgia Press, 1990.

Schoultz, Lars. *Beneath the United States: A History of U.S. Policy Toward Latin America*. Cambridge, MA: Harvard University Press, 1998.

Schuler, Friedrich E. "Mexico and the Outside World." In *The Oxford History of Mexico*. Edited by Michael C. Meyer and William H. Beezley. New York: Oxford University Press, 2000.

Smith, Gaddis. *The Last Years of the Monroe Doctrine: 1945–1993*. New York: Hill and Wang, 1994.

Solnick, Bruce B. *The West Indies and Central America to 1898*. New York: Alfred A. Knopf, 1970.

Sweeney, John. "Clinton's Latin America Policy: A Legacy of Missed Opportunities." *Backgrounder, The Heritage Foundation*, No. 1201 (July 6, 1998). http://www.heritage.org/Research/LatinAmerica/BG1201.cfm (July 2005).

Thompson, John Herd, and Stephen J. Randall. *Canada and the United States: Ambivalent Allies*. Athens: University of Georgia Press, 2002.

Tulchin, Joseph S. "Hemispheric Relations in the 21st Century." *Journal of Interamerican Studies and World Affairs*, 39:1 (Spring 1997), 33–43.

Vázquez, Josefina Zoraida. "War and Peace with the United States." In *The Oxford History of Mexico*. Edited by Michael C. Meyer and William H. Beezley. New York: Oxford University Press, 2000.

Walker, William. *The War in Nicaragua*. Tucson: University of Arizona Press, 1985.

Weber, David J. *The Mexican Frontier 1821–1846: The American Southwest under Mexico*. Albuquerque: University of New Mexico Press, 1982.

White, Mark J. *Missiles in Cuba: Kennedy, Khrushchev, Castro and the 1962 Crisis.* Chicago: Ivan R. Dee, 1997.

Wilder, Thornton. *The Bridge of San Luis Rey.* New York: HarperCollins Publishers, 1998.

Wood, Bryce. "The Making of the Good Neighbor Policy." In *Neighborly Adversaries: Readings in U.S.–Latin American Relations.* Edited by Michael LaRosa and Frank Mora. Lanham: Rowman & Littlefield Publishers, 1999.

Youngers, Coletta. "The U.S. and Latin America After 9-11 and Iraq." *Foreign Policy in Focus* (June 2003). http://www.fpif.org/pdf/reports/PRlatam2003.pdf (August 2005).

Index

About the Author

STEWART BREWER is Assistant Professor of History at Dana College.